Eavesdropping: Loretta Young Talks about her Movie Years

Edward J Funk

Part One: Introduction

Loretta: This isn't doing much for my humility; here I am fascinated with what I'm talking about because it is me that I'm talking about. And the time just flies by....

Ed: You.... You...... that's how you look at it. The way I look at it is that you are able to concentrate, hour after hour, on all these questions I ask you.....I never sense your impatience. I mean there must be times you're .....

Loretta: Well, if there is, I certainly don't feel it. I'm just fascinated with me. That's all I can tell you.

This little snippet of conversation between Loretta Young and me transpired during more than one hundred hours of taped interviews conducted in 1990 while sitting in Loretta's exquisitely decorated Beverly Hills living room. In addition, Loretta and I forged a close friendship during the remaining ten years of her life, and our discussions continued throughout.

Recently, I culled through all of this material to write a fresh biography, *Behind the Door: the Real Life of Loretta Young.* I realized that I had so much information regarding her personal life, information no one else had or has, and I made the strategic decision to focus the book in that direction.

Behind the Door: the Real Life of Loretta Young, delves into a select few of her ninety-eight films; enough to know she was a major movie star and her battles to get there and remain for the next twenty-five years. Loretta and I discussed at least ninety of them. Some merited only a few sentences, but others involved several pages of the written transcripts. The films discussed in the previous book are also discussed here but with expanded comments.

Today, voices able to recall a career from the silent era, through the golden years of film have been extinguished. And Loretta's isn't just any voice; she tells us from a star's perspective, an Academy Award-winning actress, and an exquisite beauty. She discusses the actors, the directors, the producers, the clothes (and more clothes!), what she learned about acting, her innumerable "crushes" on her leading men, her reputation as being "difficult," the roles she wanted, the roles she didn't. It's eighty thousand words of memories, a discussion on which, hopefully, classic film buffs will enjoy eavesdropping.

I did not have the availability of the Internet and Wikipedia in 1990. I did have access to the Margaret Herrick Library of Motion Picture Arts and Sciences where I researched the films as best I could, and I viewed approximately seventy of her films which she had in her own library. I watched a few of them with her, but only a few, because she didn't particularly like watching her films. She preferred watching films of the current day, or if we did view any of her past work, it was episodes of her television shows.

I quote many movie reviews in my discussions with Loretta. Unfortunately, over the past quarter of a century, with moves from various attics and garages, the sources of those reviews have been lost. However, I do remember bound copies of reviews from *The New York Times* and *The Hollywood Reporter* on the shelves of the Herrick library, and I think they were the main sources. Also, in those days, when you approached the desk and mentioned a particular movie, you were presented with a packet of various clippings related to that project. Like the reviews, I have the essence of those clippings but no longer the sources.

I'm not a film historian. My questions were those of a writer and, I must admit, a fan. However, I was always open to where Loretta wanted to take the conversation. This could mean a discussion could jump from her career, to her love life, to her family life, to her spiritual life. The tape would keep running, and it did, until I had twenty-five-hundred pages of typed transcripts.

What follows are the portions of those transcripts that focused on Loretta's film career. If the conversation seems disjointed at times, it's because Loretta's comments regarding a particular film could arrive days, weeks, or even months apart. Basically, it is a conversation between Loretta and me, but it also includes, in a very limited way, the voices of her older sisters, Pol, short for Polly Ann, and Bet, short for Betty Jane (AKA Sally Blane). The voices of Josie Wayne, Loretta's best friend and first wife of John Wayne, and Peter Lewis, Loretta's son, are also heard.

The films appear in the order of the years they were released. Loretta's personal interest in them increased as the years passed. This was partly due to fresher memories but probably due to her having more control, thus being more invested. I intended to use still photographs relevant to her films .... until I realized the exorbitant cost (permission from copyright holders) of such an effort. Fortunately, they are available on-line for you to enjoy. The films are indexed by the year they were released for those who want to skip around.

Part Two: Child Extra

Ed: Do you think you went to movies before you were in movies?

Loretta: I don't think so. Because I was in them at 4 years old.

Ed: Do you remember how that all came about?

Loretta: We were playing in the backyard one day and Uncle Trax (who was a production assistant for director, George Milford, at Lasky Studios) said, "Who wants to go to the studio and work today and make $5?" We all said, "We do! We do!" I just copied Pol and Bet and all the older kids, whoever was there. Anyway, he picked the littlest ones and we went over to the studio, and he said, "Now, we're going to the costume department and you're going to get all dressed up." So all these ladies came in and they put little tulle, not even pants, just a piece of tulle around our middle with a big bow, and they put funny little wings........Lasky Studios was on Vine Street when I was four years old and we lived practically across the street. Well, we lived on Selma which was a couple of blocks away next door to Sessue Hayakawa.

1917

THE PRIMROSE RING

Loretta: THE PRIMROSE RING was my very first movie….. Mae Murray was the star. I flew around in the air like a fairy. Robert Leonard who was married to Mae Murray directed it … Colleen (cousin) and I went to live with them for six months as a result of having met on that film.

We worked a lot when we were kids.

SIRENS OF THE SEA

Ed: Was Mae Murray in SIRENS OF THE SEA?

Loretta: No, Louise Lovely and Jack Mulhall were the leads in that picture…… You saw (Loretta had shown me a picture the first day I met her) Ben Alexander in that line-up and us…….Sally, my brother Jack and me. Jack was the littlest one. He got taken out to sea and he could have been lost but Jack Mulhall was doing a scene and he saw this……something bobbing out there and he said, "I think there's a kid out there." He just jumped in and went out and grabbed him and brought him back in. He was going out. Well, I was four, so he was two.

Ed: What do you remember about doing this?

Loretta: Not much.

Ed: Did you work for several days?

Loretta: We were there two or three weeks. We were little nymphs in this one as well.

1919

THE ONLY WAY

Loretta: It was with Fanny Ward and Theodore Roberts, and what I remember about it was the operating table. I also remember the director asking me, "Can you cry?" I said, "Oh, yes. I can cry." I didn't know he meant could I "act" crying. So, anyway, he said, "Now you come in and look at that lady and you just cry. Your heart is broken; you think your favorite doll is all dead and broken, and you'll never see that beautiful doll again, and then you cry."

I thought to myself, "That's a silly thing to say. I don't have any favorite doll." I didn't know what he was doing. I didn't know that he was trying to ....

He said, "Roll the camera. She's ready now," and he said, "Now, cry," and I just looked at him. I thought, "Here goes my whole career. I couldn't have been more than five or six, but I knew that if I didn't do what the director told me, I couldn't go to the studio anymore." Finally, he said, "Cut!"

Uncle Trax said, "Just a minute," and he said, "C'mon Gretchen (Loretta's birth name)", and he took me by the hand. I was little and he ran me around the lot, my feet were just barely touching, I remember I was just flying in the air, but he had a good hold of me. And he brought me back, and he stood me in front of the camera and then he said, "Cry!" He didn't hit me but he slapped his hands in front of my face, and it scared me. I was out of breath anyway and excited, and I started to cry and started to cry real tears. Well, of course, I was in from then on, you know. I could do anything. That was probably the beginning of my acting career. I knew that if I cried, then I would be doing what the director wanted.

Ed: And you were very eager to please the director ....

Loretta: Oh, yes, that's what acting was in those days. You didn't have a script. You didn't know anything. He'd say, "Now, walk into the room and stand over there by that chair and that man will come in the door and you look at him like you like him a lot, and then he'll come over to you and put his arm around you, and you'll be shy and pull away from him. Now you think you can do that?" "Oh, yes," and, of course, you exaggerate everything because they'd cut right in the middle of what you're doing and put a title, "She loves him," ....

Ed: Would they say exaggerate this.....

Loretta: No, they'd just say, "More and more, that's good!" If you were crying, he'd say, "Cry harder, cry harder...." And if you were smiling and it wasn't enough, they'd talk you through it. They talked the whole time the camera was grinding...they didn't just let you do what you were doing.

Ed: I had never stopped to think.....of course, there would be no reason why they'd stop talking....

Loretta: Sure, they talked all the way through it. And there was background music; they usually had a little organ and a violin and maybe a guitar, and they played music all day long.

Ed: This was standard in silent movies...?

Loretta: Yes, and the song I used to cry to all the time in LAUGH, CLOWN, LAUGH, was "Estella". It went like (hums).....and I'd cry. I don't know why....

1921

THE SHEIK

Loretta: On THE SHEIK, Uncle Trax was then a production manager. They needed a lot of children. All four of us and my two cousins, all went along (to location shooting near Oxnard CA). It got cold at night......I guess it was in the summertime though ....it must have been....because they wouldn't have taken a chance of taking all those people up to Oxnard.....They had dunes up there, and I must say it was beautiful. It looked just like the Sahara desert they tell me.....although I've never been to the Sahara Desert.

Ed: Where did you sleep?

Loretta: It was a huge tent, and I remember them putting make-up on us every day. They would show us the rushes at the end of each week. This was out in the desert.

Ed: Tell me more about the tent. What was going on? You were there for a few weeks?"

Loretta: Oh, we were there for four or five weeks. Polly Ann's coming over tonight; she can tell you more. See, I was four and she was eight.

(Polly Ann's memories of THE SHEIK)

Polly Ann: We lived in a big tent; all the families lived in this tent. They put a screen around each family for a little bit of privacy, but the tent itself was like a big circus tent.

In the morning, they'd put us, two or three kids at a time, in a big washing tub and they'd pour a bowl of henna over you. It was a dark brown. We'd try getting it off at night but we couldn't. We probably didn't get it all off until six months later.

Ed: Was your mother with you on location?

Polly Ann: No, Aunt Collie and Uncle Trax were. Mama avoided anything related to the studio as often as she could.

Ed: What do you remember about Valentino?

Polly Ann: Most of the adults went into town at night, but he didn't because he had boils all over his body and mainly on his buttocks, and he had to ride that horse every day in the desert. But he was so nice. In silent movies they used to have musicians off to the side while the camera rolled to set a mood, and sometimes they would come over in the evening to the tent and play for us kids. Valentino would come and would play a guitar for us along with a cowboy who used to be around the studios all the time. He played beautifully, too....... the two of them played for us.

Ed: Any other memories about THE SHEIK?

Polly Ann: I remember one night we were playing......we heard an awful racket ......it was coming from the camels, and a couple of cowboys got up and came to our tent and told us that we needn't be afraid, that the camels were afraid of the horses, and when they got close to them, they'd start screaming........

Another time, I remember everyone was so excited at breakfast.....they had meals in a huge tent....just huge. There were two sisters who were actresses, Jane and Eva Novak, who were playing extras .....a snake had gotten under one of their cots......

Part Three: Under Contract to First National

<u>1927</u>

NAUGHTY BUT NICE

(Polly Ann discusses how Loretta got this role that lead to Loretta's contract with First National.)

Polly Ann: Metro was doing a picture in which they hadn't decided who the leading lady was going to be, either Joan Crawford or Dolores Del Rio. The casting director knew me and I had done a long shot for Joan Crawford when she couldn't work. He told me, "You have to come on location to Denver, Colorado." A friend of mine, Bobby Agnew, knew Mervyn LeRoy personally. Mervyn LeRoy was Colleen Moore's gag man. Bobby knew that this picture was coming up, and they were going to hire five young girls to work with Colleen Moore. They were supposed to be at a boarding school. So I had two offers at the same time, and Bobby had helped me find so much work in the past that I didn't want to let him down, but I already had the commitment to Metro. I asked Mom, "What should I do?" She said, "Call Mervyn and ask him if he could use Gretchen instead." So I did, and he said, "Have her come up." She got it. And I went to Metro. (End of discussion with Polly Ann at this point).

Ed: Wasn't it after that film that your name was changed to Loretta. Where did that come from?

Loretta: Colleen Moore had a doll, I guess.

Ed: Okay, That part of the story is true, then.

Loretta: I don't know. Mama read it in the paper that my name was changed from Gretchen to Loretta. I learned to accept it now, but I never *liked* it for me.

Ed: The story I read was that Colleen Moore somehow noticed a little girl that stood out.

Loretta: Maybe she did, I don't know.....

Ed: But you don't remember her talking to you and discussing your name change and.....

Loretta: No. I think that was publicity, between you and me. And it only became publicity after I became ......

Ed: a star or at least a leading lady.........

Loretta: A leading lady, I think....

Ed: I think the director of NAUGHTY BUT NICE was Millard Webb....

Loretta: Never heard of him.

Ed: How about the actors....Donald Reed?

Loretta: I don't remember him....

Ed: Claude Gillin?

Loretta: These are all silent actors. I wouldn't remember them. I was twelve years old.

Ed: Do you remember your role at all?

Loretta: No

Ed: My guess is that you were some kind of school girl because that was what the movie was about....

Ed: What about seeing the rushes? I've read in interviews with you that you started doing that early.....

Loretta: I wasn't supposed to. But, I made friends with the projectionist and when the company went in and sat down, I would sneak in the projection room, and he'd move over and I'd look at it through the hole in the projection room.

Ed: Did you see the rushes on all your films?

Loretta: Almost always. I'm glad I did because it allowed me to try this ...... that's good or that's bad......

You see, a director can tell you ten times to listen to what the other person is saying ......listen. But if you're conscious of the new hat or what you have on ......you can pretend like you're listening but you're not listening ....You can see it on the screen, however. A director would never be able to explain that but I saw it.

HER WILD OAT

Ed: .....with Colleen Moore......you did this right after NAUGHTY BUT NICE.

Sally told me the director placed a camera at each end of the hall and that you ran fast so that you would be sure to be at the front to get your face on the screen......and then you'd slow down and let the others pass you so that, as you all ran back the other way, you'd be out front again..... She thought that was very clever of you.....

Loretta: I don't know whether I did or not...

ROSE OF THE GOLDEN WEST (aka ROSE OF MONTEREY)

Ed: I can't find anything on this film. What do you remember?

Loretta: Gilbert Roland and Mary Astor. I remember going to San Juan Capistrano and it was a costume picture. I don't remember my costume, but I remember Mary Astor....she looked so beautiful. I can see her, but I can't see me.

1928

Part Four: Leading Lady Status

LAUGH, CLOWN, LAUGH.

Loretta: I remember we went to some formal gardens in Pasadena. We were there for about a week. We were lucky if we got one shot a day, that's all he cared about, Brenon, the director. They had a fence that I was supposed to climb over, and it had barbed wire on it. Of course, you couldn't see it, but I did. I kept saying, "This barb wire hurts...."He said, "No, no, no......just go up."

He threw a chair at me one day.......

They tested about 50 girls for this thing, and he picked me because I think I was scared of him, and I should have been.......Herbert Brenon.......he had a nervous breakdown. He had been in a sanitarium, and he had just come out. He had done PETER PAN with Betty Bronson, so he was a hotshot whether he was crazy or not.

He made my life so miserable; he really did. I don't know why I didn't get an ulcer, particularly at that age (14). I'd come back from lunch, and he'd stand me in front of the entire company, and he'd say, "Everyone, sit down. Now Gretchen,"...... and he'd sit there and bawl me out. "Now, I don't know why you ever thought you could be an actress. You can't even walk, you can't do anything." Every day after lunch, I'd get this bawling out for no reason at all. Never when (Lon) Cheney was on the set. Never.

His assistant director had said to me ..."Now, he doesn't like crybabies, so don't cry." So no matter what he said to me ....I wouldn't cry ....I'd just gulp it down. We were doing a scene one day where I was supposed to cry, and he said to me, "Now you come here and you see this man and you're living with him. Do you know what I mean? You're in love and you're living with this man and he's going to leave you, now cry......come into the room and cry......." So, I would....... He said, "No! I mean real tears."

Apparently, Lon Chaney had slipped back onto the set because he wasn't in the scene and he said, "Herbert, let me talk to her for a minute." Anyway, he said, "Honey, I think he wants you to cry"....... He said, "Roll em! Roll em!

From then on, Lon Cheney would not leave the set when I was working, and Brennon just pulled back......

Ed: He was watching over you.

Loretta: He was. Yes.

Ed: What a nice man.

Loretta: Oh, yes. He was wonderful.......and if I couldn't get it in the first take or second take, he'd come up behind me ......"Try this, try that." Oh yes, he was marvelous.

One day there was a scene (laugh) ….. we were in a theater at Metro, the back lot….. they had a whole theater…… and it held 1000 people, I guess, and they had all these extras (sitting in the seats). And the camera was in the back of the theater, and we're on the stage. They had a tightrope which was about eight feet off the floor, and I had been doing close-ups on a rope that was just barely off the floor. But, apparently, the thing with the tightrope ……the thing everybody is scared to death of is, when the thing rolls . If you don't have the roll, it will go the other way and cut you because it's wire.

Ed: I never appreciated the danger.

Loretta: So, anyway, Brennon says, "Now, Gretchen, all you have to do is walk on the stage, take a bow and go up and stand with the parasol, and I will cut to the double going across the line"…… Finally, I get up there, and I stop, and he said, "You're spoiling my shot….Walk across the wire." I was doing fine until I looked down on the first rows and there were a couple of extras that I used to work with all the time and was crazy about, one named Florence, and she was just horrified. That scared me, and I looked at her and jumped off. I just slid across the stage on my legs, all the splinters went in. The whole audience was scared to death.

His whole attitude then was……"Oh, my little ……my little star……oh, what have I done……oh, I have injured my little star." I remember thinking, "Oh, shut up!" I was so mad at him. Lon Chaney was on the set that day and said, "Get her over to the doctor's office." I don't know how many splinters they took out.

Fortunately, they gave me gas or something because I don't remember the pain of it.

Ed: I didn't realize you did a love scene in LAUGH, CLOWN, LAUGH.

Loretta: Oh, I'm sure. There must have been kisses or something. Count.....what's his name? Very attractive. Nils Asher. Very attractive man.

Ed: How old was Nils Asher?

Loretta: Oh, twenty-four, I guess. I'm just making that up. But if I was 14/15, he was older than I was. He was very kind to me, very kind. Wonderful looking. Dark hair, Very ......tall, very attractive.

I remember one day Herbert Brenon said to me, "Now, I want you to feel in LOVE with this man. He walked into this room and you're madly in love with him. You're living with him. You're sleeping with him. I want to see that on your face when he walks in the door. You know what 'm talking about?" "Oh, yes, yes. I know." I didn't know what he was (laugh, laugh) talking about.

Anyway, three or four times ....."Ah, terrible, terrible.....cut! cut!" and he bawled me out some more. Ranted at me. Finally, Nils said to me, "Would you like a banana split tonight?" I said, "Yes." "When you walk into the room, think of a banana split and how you'd like that and don't think of anything else." That's what I did and the director printed it.

I realized that whatever someone wanted me to do, I'd just try to do it. That's the way silent pictures were, see. I don't know. For a long time, I didn't know they had a script. I thought the director made it up on the set as he went along. Silent pictures, they could have been very easily........there would be an idea...........There's a man and a woman and a runaway train.....they had that much.....people did what they wanted to do, and there was very little supervision. *Nobody* knew what they were going to do, and it got on film unless it was grotesque, and sometimes even that was good. In silent pictures when I started....they made them up as they went along.

Ed: Let's go back to where you said Herbert Brenon threw a chair at you? Just once....?

Loretta: ....yes, just once.......but if it hit me, it would have killed me. Apparently, I wasn't moving quickly enough. It was one of those canvas chairs; he wasn't strong enough to throw anything heavier. Everyone else was horrified, but they were scared to death of him because I think he was merciless, and he'd pick on one person.....God forbid that he'd switch from that person to you.

(Both Loretta's older sisters, Sally and Polly Ann, visited Loretta on the set of LAUGH, CLOWN, LAUGH. Here are their memories.)

Sally: I was on the set. And he said, in front of her, "We should have gotten Sally to do this part."

Polly Ann: He said the same thing about me when I'd visit her, too. He was trying to push.......

Sally: .... Get her angry.......He was soooo wrong. She just hated going to work.

Polly Ann: I don't know how she took it.

Sally: She used to cry and tell Mom she wasn't going to work.

Polly Ann: I know. But that movie is what made her career.

Sally: Oh, Mom was so relaxed. Mom didn't ever go to the studio with any of us.

(Back to Loretta)

Ed: Why was he calling you Gretchen rather than Loretta?

Loretta: I don't think he called me anything. Most of the time it was, "Hey you." He wouldn't even dignify me with a name. I remember at the preview of this picture, it was down on Wilshire, I keep thinking that it was the Wiltern.....but maybe I'm wrong. I don't think that theater was there at that time. I can see the lobby, and we were coming out as the preview and the press was there. So was Jesse Lasky. Why, I don't know. He didn't have anything to do with it because it was a Metro picture. He came up to me and said, "Loretta, you were really wonderful in this picture. You're going to be a big star" .... All of a sudden, I see Herbert Brenon walking toward me. He said, "Well, I wanted to get a performance out of you, and it may have been difficult at times, but I got it," and he turned and walked away. He meant it as a compliment, but he couldn't even do that with any grace.

Ed: Who accompanied you to the preview, your mother?

Loretta: On no. She wouldn't bother. I don't know. Maybe someone from the studio. Or maybe Pol or Bet.

Ed: Here's what *Variety* said about LAUGH, CLOWN, LAUGH. "Loretta Young is rather a pale personality for the principal female role....."

Loretta: I looked pretty. I looked like a scared fawn, that's all............

LAUGH, CLOWN, LAUGH, was really my first lead ....from then on, I stayed in leads. It wasn't because I was a better actress than some of the other girls I worked with at that time, but I LOOKED like a leading lady. I was delicate looking, and that's what they thought women should look like in those days, slender, soft and vulnerable.

The cameraman was James Wong Howe......he was absolutely marvelous.........
I saw him one day, probably while I was over at Metro doing CAUSE FOR ALARM (1951). I thought he had been long gone......but he had been a young fellow on LAUGH, CLOWN, LAUGH. He said, "Loretta?" I turned around and this charming little man....He said, "You look marvelous." I said, "Thank you."

"I'm James Wong Howe......I photographed you in your first starring movie." I said, "Oh, I can't believe it." He went on to do marvelous things.

THE MAGNIFICENT FLIRT

Loretta: I was sent over to play the daughter of Florence Vidor....who was a big star at that time. She had been married to King Vidor and she was gorgeous......

We came to a scene where I had to cry. Harry d'Arrast (director)came to me and said-----Okay, now we're going to cry ....(weak cry......) ......never dawned on me to use some menthol .... they just blow it into your eyes, and then you start to cry, and then you keep going. He said, "Well, is there anything I can do to help you?" I said, "Mr. Cline used to put his arm around me and just say, 'Oh, dear, oh dear.'"

He said, "What!" he thought I was crazy ....and he didn't attempt to do it, so the assistant director came over to me and said, ..."Listen, Gretchen or Loretta"........whatever he called me ...... "do you think if we can get Eddie Cline over here......?" I said, "I always cry for him. I just finished a picture and I cried all the time."

So they called Eddie Cline who was at another studio and asked him........would he come right over ......Yes, he'd be right over. He came over to the studio and walked me around the block about five minutes, and I came back crying big tears.

But I could never cry for Harry d'Arrast because I was too crazy about him…….. too embarrassed. Darling man…… I was in love with Harry d'Arrast.

Part Five: Warner Brothers absorbs First National

Loretta: (1928) First National was kind of limping along, and Warner Brothers came in with sound and just took the whole industry by storm.....they were on Sunset, I think......and they bought First National and just moved in, lock, stock, and barrel. They bought their stars and took on everybody that was First National and turned it into Warner Brothers........

SCARLETT SEAS

Loretta: That was with Richard Barthlemess. I remember I was doing my studies on the set, and Mrs. Holliday the teacher was there with me. John Dillion, the producer, came in and said to Richard Barthlemess, "Dick, you better watch yourself. This Young girl almost took a scene away from you yesterday." I heard it and started to blush; I was so embarrassed. All I had tried to do was what the director told me. Richard Barthlemess said, "Well, if she can, fine." Then he came over to me. He said, "Gretchen, I want to tell you something. When you get to be a big star.....and you will.......I think one of these days. Remember the better the people are around you, the better you look. Always fight for the best actors you can. They make you work better, and it makes the whole show better. When the show's good, you're all good in it."

There was kind of a hierarchy in our business at that time ....kind of royalty: he and Ronald Colman and William Powell.

Ed: Reading a review: "Loretta, the captain's daughter, has a small role, but is as angelic as ever…" it says, "It's a sound picture but no dialogue."

(SCARLETT SEAS was Loretta's first film that used Warner Brother's Vitaphone sound system; it featured music but not the actors' voices.)

Loretta: I'll tell what I was really thrilled with: the first time I saw my name in lights on the marquee. It wasn't LAUGH, CLOWN, LAUGH because they just had Lon Chaney's name. I don't know what the picture was, but I just stood there and looked at it for quite a while, and I couldn't have been more than sixteen."

Ed: How about SCARLETT SEAS?

Loretta: I don't remember. Could have been. You can say it was………

Ed: This was a year when you became a Baby Wampas Star. What was that all about?

Loretta: I don't know. They picked four or five girls each year and called them Baby Wampus Stars. I think it was just publicity. In some of these scrapbooks that you'll find in the garage, they're in that……because I remember I ran across it. Carole Lombard and Sally and …..I think I was in the group the last year they did that….

1929

THE SQUALL (Loretta's first talking picture)

Ed: Review: "Loretta Young as the innocent Irma is a beautiful screen subject. Her voice, however, is identical with commencement exercises in a grammar school."

Loretta: (laugh), (laugh), That's cute. Well, I was probably how old?

Ed: Sixteen. What about Alexander Korda?

Loretta: Oh, I was crazy about him. He was a good director. He was nice…….. foreigner of course ……He was married to Merle Oberon later on.

He did some wonderful movies. THE SQUALL was not one of his best.

I played a sweetheart role but Myrna Loy had the bigger part (as the gypsy). I remember in the preview, there's a scene at the end where the gypsy's gone through every man in the house, including the father and sons and the servants, and all the women in the house are FURIOUS with her. They hear the gypsy band coming to pick her up. She goes out of the compound for some reason, and the women close the gate and lock it. Put a bolt over it so she can't come in……..She's banging on the gate and saying, "Please, please, let me in. It's Nubi! It's Nubi!" Someone in the back of the theater yelled, "Come on girls! For God's sake, let her in!" Destroyed the movie, of course. So they cut the scene down.

Sometimes these things are good ideas, but they string them out too long until someone gets annoyed and talks back to the screen......you can't have that because it destroys the picture.

Ed: What was it like, your first talking role?

Loretta: They had a little room attached to each stage which was a sound room. You went in there, and they had this machine with a disc, and that was what your voice was on..... You'd listen to it after each scene. So if you weren't self-conscious to begin with, you sure were after that little disc began playing. And my voice! They said, "You can't tell the difference between Loretta and Carroll Nye (who played Loretta's sweetheart)....... Her voice is too low."

Women's voices were supposed to be pretty.......up little things, (Loretta demonstrates), like that. May McEvoy's voice was way up like that ....she was the first talking actress, I guess, in THE JAZZ SINGER.

Anyway, I thought my voice was fine, but they didn't think so. So I kept trying to talk higher and higher. Of course, it didn't do any good at all. They were going to let me go but decided not to. Al Rockett (First National Studio head) had said, "If you do let her go, I'm going to put her under personal contract because I think she's got talent."

They decided I didn't have a "good voice", but that they'd promote me as having a "fine voice" and that people would get used to it.

Ed: Explain it to me again….. the actual process. Did you speak your lines simultaneous to acting a scene?

Loretta: Yes. They did the scene on the set. The camera was in a box, too, and the microphone was the God on the set ………You'd hear, "I'm sorry, I didn't get it on the microphone; she turned away for a second." Without that, you're dead. It was in its infancy, and it was very stupid, of course……….Never mind the acting, just say the words.
'

Ed: That must have been a distracting experience to have to act and not turn your head from the microphone.

Loretta: It was an experience in discipline. I don't think it was a very good acting experience because it lost sight of the fact that you were acting. It was what they called, "speaking into the microphone," that's all.

Ed: Did it take longer?

Loretta: Oh, yes. We shot it all at night because there were no sound stages. The camera was in a booth and that click-click-click you didn't hear, but you could hear outside noises. If a truck went by, you heard that. Many a time we stopped in the middle of a scene and the director said, "Sorry, we got a truck. All right.

Start all over again." We did it all at night so it must have taken five times as long to shoot it.

Ed: So you were working late into the night as a young girl ......

Loretta: Oh yes, I'd get tired and then get a cold and then maybe get the flu or something and then off I'd go to the hospital.

Ed: The studio hospital?

Loretta: No, regular hospital. Queen of Angels, usually. And the minute I did, they'd take me off salary. I was making.......I don't know........$150 a week, but that was a lot of what we lived on.......

Ed: That had to be a lot of money

Loretta: It was a lot of money. I started at $50 or $60 a week. And then each six months it went up $25 or $50, whatever it did, if they picked up your option. When I finished all those years later, I was still making $1500 at Twentieth Century-Fox.........That's right.

Ed: Back to talking pictures. Did you have ambivalence about them?

Loretta: In fear of them? Heaven's no. Again, if you have a good healthy respect for yourself and, so help me, I have all my life, nothing in that way daunts you.

(About Mrs. Holliday the studio teacher)

Loretta: I don't know what her first name was. Roddy McDowell told me he also had Mrs. Holliday as teacher.

Ed: She was with you from age 12.

Loretta: She was fat and she was soft and just darling. When we'd go on location, we'd go out to make still pictures at Griffith Park or do something...... she used to drive the car. It was gear shift in those days, and she put the thing into second and never put it in third, and we'd go along in second, and it used to drive me crazy. Never shifted! And, I didn't have the guts to say, "Mrs. Holliday, why don't you shift into third?" Isn't it funny how you can remember things like that. Why I never got up the nerve to ask her to go into third.

Ed: Says a lot about this woman. So oblivious.

Loretta: She would talk a lot.

One time I was doing three pictures at once. There was one in the morning, one in the afternoon, and one at night. Mrs. Holliday never knew about the one at night. Some guy would say to me, "We're going to dismiss you, and you go to your dressing room but don't take your makeup off. After Mrs. Holliday goes home, come back on the set and we'll work tonight." I'd say, "All right, fine." It never bothered me. You know, when you're taught to take direction from the director, you think everyone's God.

Mrs. Holliday was a very easy teacher. Not very demanding. I don't think she taught me much academically, but she was very good about teaching me manners and respect for older people and being on the set on time.

Ed: Didn't you learn that kind of thing from your mother?

Loretta: Automatically, but not in the studio. Mama didn't like the studio. She didn't come near it if she could help it.

Ed: So you didn't spend four hours studying?

Loretta: Oh, no. That's what we were supposed to be doing. Oh, she'd say, "Let's have the geography lesson," and she'd tell me about Italy, and what people were like, and where it was, and how interesting it was, and that the Vatican was there.

THE GIRL IN THE GLASS CAGE

Ed: a silent picture released after FAST LIFE

Loretta: It was supposed to be dialogue, but they released it dumb (still a silent film). Ralph Dawson directed that. I don't remember. I know it was a terrible one. The girl in the glass cage was a ticket seller at a movie theater. That's all she was.

FAST LIFE

Ed: That was your first picture with Douglas Fairbanks, Jr. ......

Loretta: That was a very good picture, supposedly. Chester Morris was a stage actor, and he had just made a smash success in it on stage. He ended up playing the second lead in the movie. I don't know why he did that. I guess he wanted another movie.

Ed: What did you think of Chester Morris?

Loretta: I thought he was a good actor and a very nice man. He looked strange to me. His nose was kind of (Loretta gesturing)....like that...kind of sharp and flat. I don't know. And very slick hair, a lot of brilliantine on it, very tight on his head.

Ed: Was that the first time you met Douglas Fairbanks, Jr.?

Loretta: That I'm conscious of. I really don't remember.

Ed: You made six movies with this man.

Loretta: (laugh), (laugh). I wasn't very impressed with him ever and never had a crush on him. And I think the reason I didn't was, as I told you before, I never seem to fall in love with men who did not fall in love with me. I think, well, who wants to throw a ball against a piece of putty...... Doug wasn't one bit interested in me and never has been except as a friend.

The studio must have liked us together.

Ed: FAST LIFE. What was the story?

Loretta: I don't know. Just fast life. There were two men in love with the same girl, I guess.

Ed: reading a review: "Loretta Young, who plays the maiden over whom the shooting occurs and whose husband is condemned to the death house...........shows more promise with each production.....one of Hollywood's prettiest ingénues, she is also gifted with an excellent speaking voice." This is just a few months after THE SQUALL ....

Loretta: Well, they decided, I think, (laugh) that I had a good speaking voice.

FORWARD PASS

Loretta: Eddie Cline directed it. Allan Lane (co-star). I vaguely remember him, not fat, but good-looking......... a football story.

Ed: Review: "backed with a quartet of tunes, one of which Loretta Young warbles...."

Loretta: Warbles.....(laughs) (laughs) (laughs). I would like to see it if we have it.

Ed: "a contralto", meaning you ----- "she's not hard on the ear...."

Loretta: Really. I can't imagine.

Ed: It goes on to say, "Miss Young's debut as a songstress of the intimate type is okay....."

(Following is a conversation between Ed, Loretta, and Josie Wayne, the first Mrs. John Wayne, and close friend to Polly Ann, Sally, and Loretta since their adolescent years.)

Ed: (addressing this question to Josie) By the time Loretta was at Warner Brothers, she was an established star and leading lady. How did Polly Ann and Sally respond to Loretta's rising career?

Josie: I was never aware of any jealousy, but they used to kid her. They'd say, "Oh here comes the star"........ something like that...

Loretta: Oh, yes. If I'd come home and cry about something too much, then they'd cut a star out of a newspaper and pin it on my door.....but it wasn't a running thing. Because Mama wouldn't have put up with that.

I remember one night at the dining room table, I was crying about some part I was scheduled to do, and I didn't think it was good enough. Maybe it was THE STORY OF ALEXANDER GRAHAM BELL......Bet was there. Anyway.....talk about me-me-me (Loretta referring to herself)... Bet said, "Oh, you just make me sick. I'd give my eye-tooth for that part, and here you are crabbing about it." It never dawned on me.

Now, I don't think Polly Ann.......

Josie: I don't think so either.....

Ed: I asked Polly Ann about the time she was doing the leading lady roles in westerns; was she envisioning for herself a major film career? She really stopped and thought about it for a minute, and she said no, she really didn't think she did. She just saw it as a way to make some money.

Loretta: That's right. Bet did.....wanted it....

Josie: I think Bet wanted more of a career....certainly more than Polly Ann, and I don't think that Georgi (Georgiana, the youngest sister) was ever really interested.

Loretta: Oh, no. She was too shy. She still is.

THE SHOW OF SHOWS

Ed: SHOW OF SHOWS....86% in color in 1929. Your first color movie.....

Loretta: ....not very good if it is....

Ed: Warner Brothers: Frank Fay, Beatrice Lilly, and again, no mention of Loretta...

Loretta: (laugh) (laugh) ..... I'm not surprised. We were part of the Sister's Number...Molly O'Day and Sally O'Neil, they were sisters. And Sally Blane and Loretta Young ..... we were sisters. There were four or five sets of sisters...some of them really weren't sisters as it turned out. That's how honest they were. We were playing different nationalities...We were the French ones.....and it was the same little ditty, and the same little waltz down the stage, and the same little kicks off the stage.

Ed: Did you sing in French?

Loretta: (laugh) (laugh) Oh, no. I hardly sang at all. It was silly. Really silly. None of us could sing....

1930

TRUTH ABOUT YOUTH

Loretta: (laugh) (laugh)

Ed: Directed by William Seiter

Review: "Featuring Loretta Young, David Manners and Conway Tearle. This film will do fairly well as hit and run..."

Loretta: See how stupid a review is? How could they possibly know what's going to go and what isn't going to go? They do know what they see. If they see very little, and they don't like what they see, they can say that. But to say that this film will do very well as a hit and run. What the hell does that mean?

Ed: They predict the box office all the time....

Loretta: They have no right to do that (laugh) (laugh)

LOOSE ANKLES

Loretta: Oh, I was a rich girl...

Ed: also has Ethel Wales....

Ed: Any exciting memories of LOOSE ANKLES?

Loretta: (laugh) (laugh) No. You're not going to get anyplace
with this stuff today.....this whole period of my life....it's just too
far gone...

THE MAN FROM BLANKLEYS

Loretta: That's John Barrymore and was the last picture where
he played the romantic lead. I had an enormous crush on him. On
the set he looked absolutely marvelous. The story was a dinner
party someplace, and they needed an extra man at the last
minute, and they couldn't find him, so they hired a man from
Blankley's to come. I really don't remember the story, but I was
the daughter of the house and had on dinner clothes.

He looked marvelous, and we shot it at Warner Brothers on
Sunset Boulevard. The dressing rooms there...... you had to go up
a flight of stairs ....the men's were that way ......and the
womens' were this way. I was just leaving for the set one
morning, and this apparition came flying up the steps ....
pajamas on and what hair there was flying in the wind ...... and
flew by me and said, "Good morning, Loretta......", and I didn't
know who it was. And it was John Barrymore before he got all
his make-up on and everything on him that he was wearing at

the time -----corsets and everything. I didn't realize who it was until he walked onto the set. He said, "Now, I wasn't very long, was I." The crush was crushed.

Ed: Alfred Green directed MAN FROM BLANKLEYS

Loretta: Did he? Alfred Green and his goosing stick. Studio people are not like any other people in the world. It's very informal. Alfred Green had a little stick that he used to carry around....."goosing" ....those little things that you never mentioned .... it was just offensive, unattractive, you just didn't do it. Initially, I didn't know what they meant by it until I saw him hit someone on the behind with it, or touch them ......and the man jumped and I thought...... "I wonder if it has electricity in it." I remember thinking, "If he ever does that to me, I'm simply going to look at him and walk off the set. I won't laugh, and I won't be part of it." He never did. He never came near me. Ever. I guess he was sensitive enough to know I'd either burst out crying or walk off the set.

Ed: What did you think of John Barrymore to work with him?

Loretta: I thought he was wonderful. And he was. Very professional.

Ed: Was John Barrymore a scene stealer?

Loretta: Well, if he was, I wouldn't have known it. It wouldn't have made any difference anyway; I wouldn't have known how to handle that. This business of backing up or turning around.....I don't remember any of that nonsense at all with him. I think that's all made up stuff.

I remember one thing about that studio and about that time: they had a wardrobe department full of beautiful clothes. I think they had been made for May McAvoy, and every couple of years they would sell these clothes to the actors or anybody in the business.......not to the public, but to director's wives, or actresses or writers. I bought the most beautiful caramel-colored velvet dress that had a fur collar and cuffs on it. I guess it was mink. It had a little hat out of the same color, but it was felt. I just loved that thing and wore it and wore it. My sisters and I bought an awful lot. And they'd sell them for little to nothing.

Ed. Did May McAvoy wear that dress in THE JAZZ SINGER?

Loretta: I don't know whether it was made for her or not, but it was in her wardrobe. See, in those days, they had a Carole Lombard Wardrobe, a Loretta Young Wardrobe, a Sylvia Sidney Wardrobe .... So whenever you did a picture, they never sold your clothes right away ....they just hung them in your wardrobe and kept them very well. Then, eventually, they would use them on the second leads. So they built up the star's wardrobes. Mine were always very good. Travis Barton did some of mine. Eventually, they'd sell them off.

SECOND FLOOR MYSTERY

Ed: Grant Withers....... the next picture is SECOND FLOOR MYSTERY ....

Loretta: That was Grant?

Ed: Right. You were making this picture when you married Grant. "Grant Withers..... Loretta Young...."

Loretta: Grant got first billing?.... that's interesting. All I have to say about those Warner's people is they are chauvinist pigs because they........(laugh) if they get a chance to ......they put the man first.

Ed: reading a review: "Grant Withers and Loretta Young are able to fringe another one of those upstairs murder mysteries with the much needed help of travesty......."

Loretta: Travesty....what does that mean?

Ed: ....travesty is usually a disaster...

Loretta: ....absurdity...

Ed: What do you remember?

Loretta: Nothing. I don't remember her (Loretta's character) at all. And I don't remember him. You know, you're so self-oriented at that age. If you had asked me who was in that picture with me and didn't tell me Grant Withers, I wouldn't have remembered it was him. I did BROKEN DISHES with Grant. Mervyn LeRoy directed it. It was a terrible picture, just terrible, and I knew it then.

Ed: Back to SECOND FLOOR MYSTERY........ H. B. Warner...

Loretta: He was a big star. He played the Christ in the original KING OF KINGS, and he was a brilliant actor. Was he in it?

Ed: Yes

Do you remember being very much in love with your leading man at this time?

Loretta: No.

Ed: You ran off and married him....

Loretta: As I told you. I didn't really want to get married to him; I just didn't know how to say no. And Bet remembers my telling Mama weeks before...."No matter what Grant (Withers) says to you, don't give me permission to marry him..."

Ed: Where does Betty Compton come into this?

Loretta: She was an actress. Grant Withers was going with her steadily when we met. She was quite important to the motion picture industry......not Mary Pickford....but a star...

Ed: Pretty?

Loretta: Yes, I thought so. Blonde and not unlike Glenda Farrell.

Ed: Let's check the book, here .... BROKEN DISHES, 1930. Boy, you did a lot of movies in 1930.

Loretta: Yep....

Ed: One-two-three-four-five-six-seven, eight movies.

Loretta: That's right. In one year, I did eight movies.

Loretta: So what do you remember about working in these? Were you the leading lady in all these movies?

Loretta: I was the leading lady, always. From the time I did LAUGH, CLOWN, LAUGH with the exception of THE MAGNIFICENT FLIRT. That's a funny little thing about me, but it pleases me *not* to play the second lead. I know that some of the second leads are better parts.....certainly Myrna Loy's part in THE SQUALL, which was the second lead, was much better than mine because she had some character to her. I was just a little Hungarian dumb leading lady. But we have our little foibles.....your own little kinks in your brain....

ROAD TO PARADISE

Loretta: It's a very good one. I saw it not long ago.

Ed: So have I. It is good.

Loretta: I played a dual role in that.

Ed: You were very young. At the end, you can see the copyright, and it was 1929. So you would have been sixteen-years-old and a leading lady playing a double role......

Loretta: That was the role that Polly Ann played my double. It was after I marred Grant, and we had just consummated this marriage in our apartment (Loretta's mother had persuaded her to come home right after they eloped with the hope of an annulment, but that didn't last). Polly Ann wouldn't speak to me, and she didn't speak to me for the whole picture. She didn't care what anyone else said, she wouldn't speak to me. She played the other part when they had to shoot over her shoulder.

Ed: Oh.....

Loretta: There's one shot where she turns around and it's her profile. It looks enough like mine that the people didn't question it, but really it was Pol. Not too long ago, she sat here and looked at it, and I said, "Pol, that's you!" She said, "No, it isn't." (Loretta) "It was when I was trying to get back into Mama's good graces, and she wouldn't have me, and you wouldn't talk to me," and it took me ten minutes to persuade her.....she said, "Oh, yes, I remember that."

Review: "Miss Young as a society girl and crook's protégé looks attractive. Beyond that, there is something in the fact that her precise enunciation, action, manners, are the same throughout, inferring that she may not be suited for character work.

Loretta: (laugh), (laugh), That's kindly put, "I don't think she's much for character roles....."

Ed: I thought you were very different as the society girl than you were as the ....

Loretta: Well, there was a very slight....... I didn't play it with a blonde wig or an accent.....

KISMET

Ed: "Starring Otis Skinner, directed by John Dillon, featuring Loretta Young, David Manners, Mary Duncan and Sidney Blackmer."

Loretta: What did I do about David Manners? (A few weeks earlier, Loretta had received a letter from a clergyman asking if she would write a note to David Manners who was living in a nursing home in Santa Barbara.)

Ed: You wrote him.....

Loretta: Good.

Sidney Blackmer. He always played the villain. He was kind of portly and older. Who was the girl?

Ed: Mary Duncan....

Loretta: She was attractive. That would have been the Marlene Dietrich part (referring to the 1944 remake.)

Ed: Review: "Both Loretta Young and Mary Duncan have little to do....."

Loretta: We look pretty....that's it. Look pretty and do what you're told. That reminds me......they had distributors out twice a year, and they gave big parties for them, and, of course, they invited all the contract players. I remember going, and I was very surprised when an old man, he was probably 40, came and asked me to dance. I said, "Oh, no thank you." I didn't know him, I hadn't met him. So I'm not going to dance with some old goat I didn't know.

One of the publicity men came over and said, "Loretta, do you have any objections to dancing with this man?" I said, "Well, I don't know him." He said, "You don't know any of the distributors here." I said, "You mean I'm here to dance with the distributors? No thank you," and I went home. Took a taxi.......they had picked me up in a limo (laugh) (laugh).

DEVIL TO PAY

Loretta: In THE DEVIL TO PAY I replaced Constance Cummings, a wonderful English actress, and I didn't know why. I was told to go over and see Sam Goldwyn and be the leading lady. I sneaked into the projection room to see some of the film that they were running .... wanting to see, really, what they didn't like. When I saw her she was so wonderful in the part, and she was English, and her accent was beautiful, and everything about her was lovely. My stomach just dropped. I thought, "Oh, Lord, if they don't like this, what am I going to do?"

I didn't dare tell anybody I had seen it because I wasn't supposed to, so I just tried to forget about it. Sam Goldwyn used to replace people all the time: the director, the leading lady, the leading man, on almost every picture he did.

I do think the answer as to why Constance Cummings was replaced was that she looked solid. I didn't. I looked fragile. I looked insecure which I was. And this long neck adds kind of a gazelle look to everything.

I just did what I was told to do and tried dropping my r's. Some of the expressions looked like a seventeen-year-old girl. The pouty kind of thing. But just one or two slipped in for that performance. Otherwise, she looked like a one-dimensional English society girl, but just one dimensional. When she was mad she was mad. When she was happy, she laughed too much. When you're in doubt, laugh.....

Ed: ....you were good going down the slide....

Loretta: Anything like that was natural and easy.....I think the reason that some of the scenes are so self-conscious is because of the accent...

Ed: Review: "Ronald Colman and Loretta Young featured......with Florence Britton .....Myrna Loy. No one has a chance to catch up to Colman on performance, but balance of support, including second lead Loretta Young, is continually helpful and sufficiently smart in smart surroundings."

You told me that you had a big crush on him.

Loretta: Oh, heavens, yes.

Ed: You would have still been married to Grant.

Loretta: In my mind I was divorced two weeks after I was married. I have no memories of Grant at the time I was making that picture.

Ed: Grant is gone as far as......

Loretta: Long gone.

When the picture started, I was so madly in love with Ronald Colman, I couldn't get near him or say anything to him. I had a coach for my English accent, and the director, George Fitzmaurice, asked him, "What's the matter with her? Is she all right when you're in the dressing room rehearsing her....?" He said, "Yes." Anyway, he finally said, "She's just terrible in the shot", and he asked me, "What's the matter?" I said, "I have got such a crush on Ronald Colman; I just can't do anything around him." George Fitzmaurice must have said something to Ronnie because from then on, he was just warm enough to me that I buttered up and opened up but not enough to cause any problems for him or me.

1931

BEAU IDEAL

Ed: How did you end up working for Herbert Brenon again after the way he treated you on LAUGH, CLOWN, LAUGH?

Loretta: It was a small part, but a good part, and he wanted me very much to do it, and I guess I didn't know how to say no. I don't know why because I was under contract to another studio and didn't have to. He was all right to me on that one. I wasn't his patsy this time; he had picked someone else. I got to stand by and watch which was no fun either. There's something about a bully that is so distasteful. It's so.........it reveals so much about them. .....

THE RIGHT OF WAY

Ed: Fred Kohler...

Loretta: oh yes...

Ed: William Janney...

Loretta: I don't remember him....

Ed: Review: "Loses his memory in the back woods and falls for a post office girl...."

Loretta: That's convenient....The only thing I remember about that......I'm afraid of horses, and there was a scene when I was talking to Conrad Nagel, and I had some sort of peasant costume, I think, and there was a horse. I'm standing next to it. I don't know if I was supposed to be riding it or he was, but anyway, we're standing talking, and this horse would just lift up his hooves and plant them right next to my feet. I'd move like this and he'd move over further. He stepped on them one time, and I thought he crushed my foot.

Ed: Was that part of the story?

Loretta: No, no. The horseman explained to me that if you're really afraid of horses, there's an acid which exudes from two little things under your tongue, and they can smell it. You can't ride them; they won't have you around. They just step all over you.

I kept moving away. The man said, "She's out of camera." I said, "The horse is stepping all over me." They finally had a man down there hold his feet outside the camera, and the horse would look around like this (Loretta demonstrates a dirty look) and scare me to death......(laugh) (laugh) (laugh)

We got the scene but it was just terrible..... It must have been on location; I don't remember where. Well, most of the time, location would be on the back lot or the biggest location shoot would be to go out to the San Fernando Valley to some ranch.............

Ed: I'm confused. Was THE RIGHT OF WAY a First National Picture or a Warner Brothers film?

Loretta: They were like sister studios, but Warner Brothers owned everything.

Ed: What did you do on the days you weren't filming?

Loretta: I spent an awfully lot of time in the gallery to shoot portraits. They'd call me in at 9:00. They always had a make-up person, a hairdresser, and a wardrobe woman, and Elmer Fryer ..... he had a couple of assistants, and you just worked. Elmer was one of my good friends at the studio because when you work with a photographer, it's a very close relationship.....

Ed: Different techniques? Music?

Loretta: I used to have music all the time because I asked for it.

Ed: ....off in your own dream world....

Loretta: No. You had to be more disciplined than that. You didn't move because if you did, you lost the picture. In those days ......they'd say, "One, two, three, four"....you'd hold it that long.

Ed: I'm curious. Did you ever estimate how many photos you have posed for over the years?

Loretta: Helen Furguson (one of Loretta's publicists) came up with a figure of 50,000. I don't know how she reached that number, but it seems credible to me.

Ed: Wow!

THREE GIRLS LOST

Loretta: That's with John Wayne

Ed: Made for Fox, director was Sidney Lanfield......Al Rockett was associate producer.

Loretta: He used to be at First National.....maybe that's why I was in it.

Ed: Starring Loretta Young, John Wayne, Lew Cody, Joyce Compton

Loretta: Joyce Compton. She's a beautiful girl, blonde and very pretty. The director picked on her, I thought. He'd tell her, "Just watch Loretta, for heaven's sake. You're just terrible. You're stiff"....... and you're this and that. She got so nervous she couldn't even remember her dialogue. He said, "Oh, forget it. I'll take a close-up." Well, he took so many close-ups, and then he spent hours on making her say exactly the right thing. The picture ended with a lot of long shots of the rest of us and all these close-ups of this beautiful girl. I remember thinking at the time, "Maybe that's not such a bad idea. I shouldn't be so glib with the dialogue, and I'd get a lot more close-ups."

Ed: I don't get it. Why the close-ups?

Loretta: He had to get the lines. If she couldn't remember them in the scene, then he'd do a close-up so at least he got the dialogue, see?

But, really, close-ups should be used sparingly, and then they count. You should only use close-ups to make a point. But every department thinks it's the most important, and the cutting department, I'm sure, after it's shot on the set, feels it has to cut a lot. So long-shot, medium shot, close-up, ¾ shot.....they want to chop up all this stuff because they've got it. But it seems to me if two of us are sitting here talking (in a scene), it should be played in the two-shot, tight if you can, and over the shoulders, more than individual close-ups because it is as important what the other person is doing while you're talking as it is that you're talking....

Ed: But...I'm curious...... what does it feel like to sit and look at the screen and see your own face, you know, three stories tall?

Loretta: Well, if it's a beautiful close-up, you just sit there and lick your lips, it's so gorgeous....it's a wonderful feeling. "Oh, isn't it marvelous!" Then it's gone in a second. And it really isn't you. See, I'm not looking at me....I'm looking at that girl.

There are some close-ups in *The Portrait* (an episode of *The Loretta Young Show*) which are some of my favorites....but it isn't me; it was that girl whose father was so mean to her and she had a scar on her face....

Ed: ....it's not you.....

Loretta: It's her life ....not mine that I'm watching. And the combination of my age at that time...46 or 47...because it was toward the end of .....(the series)....Apparently, it was at the peak of my looks and I had enough practice at acting, all those pictures and all those weeks on TV over a lot of years, that I was perfectly at ease and not afraid ... *to take my time.* Most actors rush through things....

Ed: ....take your time?

Loretta: ...with the whole process of thought and speech and reaction and whatever you're doing. If you rush....there must be a reason for the character to rush. If you're trying to talk to somebody, make your points.....just like we're doing here. With experience, the ability to create another character, another person, matches the peak of what your looks are going to be...

(Back to THREE GIRLS LOST)

Ed: John Wayne?

Loretta: I knew him personally, and I loved him. I thought he was darling. He did what he was supposed to do and that was all. I mean, he wasn't good or bad; he was just John Wayne. I was just Loretta Young.

Ed: Why didn't you have a crush on him?

Loretta: Because I knew Josie.

Ed: They were dating already?

Loretta: They had been dating since he was in college. Also, you see, he wasn't thrilled with me. There has to be that spark, at least with me there has to be that spark. And there still has to be.

TOO YOUNG TO MARRY

Ed: Starring Loretta Young and Grant Withers…….you get top billing this time around…..with O.P. Heggie and Emma Dunn……

Loretta: She was a stage actress, and so was he. There was a mother and a father and a house…..I don't know……it was a dull little thing.

Ed: It was about a domineering woman who browbeats her family. You played the daughter who wants to marry the grocery boy. Review: "Miss Young is the usual sweet thing …….that strikes against her domineering mother." It had originally been titled BROKEN DISHES. Any memories?

Loretta: Yes, Mervyn LeRoy directed it. They probably changed the name from BROKEN DISHES to TOO YOUNG TO MARRY because I was considered too young to marry.

Ed: ......and you had married Grant Withers....

Loretta: That's why they put him in it.

BIG BUSINESS GIRL

Ed: Ricardo Cortez, Frank Albertson

Loretta: William Seiter directed. He also started THE BISHOP'S WIFE and Sam Goldwyn replaced him with Koster. William Seiter was married to Marian Nixon who was also a big actress....

Ed: Must have been in the silents......

Loretta: I don't know. She wasn't that big but a leading lady like I was. She didn't go on. The reason you heard of me was because I went on.

Ed: Joan Blondell was also in this movie .... Review: "The director, William Seiter, took a chance allowing Miss Young to lose sympathy when he permitted her to brazenly cross her legs before the new boss."

Loretta: (laugh) (laugh) Brazenly cross and show her legs? (laugh) (laugh) (laugh) The reviews are hysterical.......

Ed: No romance with Ricardo Cortez?

Loretta: He was in MIDNIGHT MARY

Ed: No sparks?

Loretta: No sparks with Ricardo Cortez

Ed: Frank Albertson?

Loretta: No sparks. Frankie was just a friend.

Ed: Memories of Joan Blondell?

Loretta: Not really, except she was from New York and she came out the same time Jimmy Cagney did. She was a good actress I thought.

(About Lucile the hairdresser)

Loretta: She was a lovely woman, big woman, and I was just beginning. Perc Westmore was head of make-up and hairdressing at First National and then Warner Brothers........ he put her with me. My hair was long at the time, and she had long hair herself so she knew how to handle it. She was an alcoholic. She'd come to the studio, and I could smell it in the dressing room. She'd always be there before I was, but she was only half there; once or twice I'd let her start to do my hair and she'd get too close to me with the curling iron. I'd say, "I'll do it, Lucille. I'll do it." I learned to do my own hair because that woman was an alcoholic, and I didn't want anyone to know it.

Ed: .....get her in trouble

Loretta: and she was with me until I was married. I was 27.

Ed: ......that's a sweet story....

Loretta.....Well......(laugh) anyway. Poor Lucille, I just felt sorry for her. Finally I'd say, "I don't want to see you on the set until after lunch." She knew that meant sleep it off, see. I'll always be grateful to her because, with her problem, I learned how to do my own hair.

THE RULING VOICE

Ed: Director: Edward H. Griffith

Loretta: Oh, yes. Ed Griffith. Yes, that's right. Wally Houston was the big star from New York, and he was wonderful.

Ed: ......he was wonderful

He played my father, and he was wonderful to work with because he knew his craft. He was very sure of himself. No nonsense went on, and he treated me just like a father would a daughter. I just fell right in step with it.

Ed: ....sympathetic gangster......

Loretta: She didn't know it. When she did find out, he didn't say, "Oh, how terrible." He said, "That's what I am. How do you think you got all this money......" It took him a long time to come around to seeing her point of view.

She didn't know because she had been away in Europe at school. I'm trying to think, my one line in French ....(Loretta says something in French) .....I don't know, I've forgotten. But there was one line in French I had to learn to say to him ......(laugh) (laugh). I don't think I did it very well. But I was proud of it. I thought I'd never forget it, but I have.

Ed: ....also David Manners

Loretta: David Manners, yes. He was a stock leading man.....the juvenile lead. That's what I was afraid they'd turn me into, and that is why I fought so much. (Loretta projected this thought to the years she worked for 20th Century-Fox) Zanuck.........I think it took me two years to finish my contract because he kept adding time when I'd refuse to do a picture. I'd walk out and he'd say, "Fine, walk out," and he'd add three more months....

PLATINUM BLONDE

Loretta: The best director I liked to work with was Frank Capra. I was all right in the picture, but Jean Harlow was much better in it. They even changed the title from GALLAGHER, which is the part I played, to THE PLATINUM BLONDE which is the part she played. Somehow or other, I don't know how I managed this, but I did not resent it, because I liked Jean first of all. She was kind of overpowering, overwhelmingly sexy. She undulated onto the set. She didn't even walk. And she didn't know she was doing it. I think that's just the way her body moved. She could laugh quicker than anybody else could, and you'd have to take yourself *very* seriously to pull that off and not be natural.

She was not in any way, shape, or form, anything like the books that are written about her. I never saw any of that, but, of course, I didn't take her out at night, either. But I saw her at enough parties, and I watched her behave, and she behaved just like the rest of us did. She looked, however, so voluptuous and ripe and ready to pluck that, she walked on the set and all the guys would go "UHHHHHHHHHH" when she walked by. Frank Capra and Bob Riskin would sit right there and rewrite scenes for her just because she was so ....she was really the first "Sex Goddess" that I'm conscious of.

Ed: They were more concerned about a collaborative.....

Loretta: They were more interested in what finally got on the screen....

Ed: Even if it became more of a Jean Harlow picture than Loretta Young's?

Loretta: They couldn't help but do it. If she and I walked into a room together, you're not going to look at me. That was not my .... If I was an Ava Gardner, and I was competing with Jean Harlow, I probably wouldn't have felt as easy as I did about it.

Ed: What about Robert Williams?

Loretta: Well, now, I was wild about him. He was an actor from New York.

Everybody from the stage lorded it all over us movie folk, because they had training, and we didn't. And they usually had good voices, and we were lucky if you could hear us. There was no schooling for us. There hadn't been for them either, except that they'd been on the stage, and we considered that rehearsal for motion pictures, which indeed, it was. Although the art form may be even more difficult for the stage than it is for motion pictures because it takes the whole of you, not just your thoughts when the camera comes in for a close-up. Really, stage actors were "actors." Motion picture stars started out being personalities more than great actors.

(Back to Robert Williams)

Loretta: He had great charm. Unfortunately, he was married, and I found this out about three weeks into the picture. I don't know why I wasn't smart enough to ask right away. His wife wasn't here. She was in New York.

Ed: Did you have an entourage at this point?

Loretta: Everything....

Ed: .....but not a secretary?

Loretta: No, I never had a secretary.

Ed: If you had a secretary you could say, "Find out the story on this man......."

Loretta: We were never that obvious. That wasn't cool.

Ed: ......you wouldn't be that revealing.......

Loretta: No. Nor that conniving, nor that cold-blooded.....calculating ......we weren't. Things just happened as they happened ....He was little. Not tall. Dark hair and charming eyes.

When I said I was a little bit in love with every leading man, that isn't true. I've been trying to think that's true. I had an automatic crush on every leading man, before I ever met him, because I wanted to have.

Ed......part of the fun....

Loretta: Part of the fun and part of the ambiance and a part of the excitement. It makes you work better. You're the girl in the show and he.........there's an intrigue about it. It was very easy to do because they very seldom cast an ugly, mean man in a role.

Bobby Williams had done one thing (film) with Ina Claire; really, most of it was just his back......he was doing things that leading men in motion pictures wouldn't do. Frank Capra, who could certainly pick his stars, picked him for the lead.

One day we were rehearsing a scene, and he (Williams) said, "I don't think I like that idea. Where did that come from?" He was used to doing this kind of back and forth on the stage. He and Frank Capra were talking......finally in the middle of it, Frank said, "What do you think, Loretta?" I said, "It doesn't make any difference what I think. You just tell me what you want me to do; I'll try to do it." Very gently he said, "Oh no, Loretta ....that's all acting is ......thinking". Very gently. And, of course, that's the method acting. That's studio acting. Because they're working all the time, not just when they're on camera.....

I think the reason Frank was such a good director was that he *never* pinned you in any way. You were always able to leave all the valves open so that you could just kind of take in everything that came along ....any little idea from him or the wind or your own idea or somebody else's. But, if you're scared, if you're closed up, if you're not at ease with the director or the people you're working with, nothing gets through. You're so busy protecting yourself or your feelings or your creativity or whatever it is, that's all you can do.

(After Watching PLATINUM BLONDE with Ed, Loretta has a change of opinion about Robert Williams)

Loretta: You know something I did notice about him this time......he never listened to either one of those women (the roles Loretta and Jean Harlow played).....and he didn't look at them. Because there were expressions on both of our faces that he should have said, "What's the matter?" It was a purely....self-

oriented.....self-indulgent chauvinistic pig
performance.......(laugh)

1932

TAXI

Loretta: I had forgotten all about that picture ......Someone sent
me a print three years ago. When I put it on.......I thought ....I'm
going to be a leading lady again in this picture ....Jimmy Cagney
was a big star at the studio so he's going to have all the part and
I'll probably be in a fourth of the picture.

So I had already decided this.......I was looking at it all alone, and
I just wanted to see what I looked like. I was delighted because,
apparently, he wasn't the big star yet. Maybe he hadn't done THE
PUBLIC ENEMY, I don't know. They, his and mine, were equal
parts. They were very good parts and we were well cast, really. I
looked very sensitive and very pretty and very lady-like, and he
looked like a tough street kid, very masculine, and it worked. The
chemistry worked because we did like each other.

I was excellent in it, and of course, he was .... in anything he
was. I was surprised at my performance, and I think, probably,
because I was trying to keep up with him. I did notice in long
speeches, a very bad habit. A good director should have caught
this. When I had a long speech, I was inclined to just rush it. To
say the words. Just to get them out. Just to prove I knew the
speech. Well, that isn't what we do in life. You have to stop and
think ......what you're going to say next.

But Jimmy was able to talk fast but still make every point; it was like a machine gun firing. I noticed in this picture I just talked fast, all mushed together. At the time, I thought I was acting.......

Ed: Off screen, did he talk fast?

Loretta: No, not particularly. His manners off screen were those of a perfect gentleman.

Ed: You were eighteen. You were still learning. Review: "Loretta Young does better than usual as the orphaned miss. At least there is more solidarity to her portrayal than there generally is in her case, but more depth is still to be desired behind a beautiful face."

Loretta: I think that's right. I would say that's a good review of the picture ..... Well, what do you expect from an 18-year-old?

Ed: You said that you and Cagney liked each other. Crush?

Loretta: Big crush on him, but the sweetest and nicest and purest kind of crush. He never knew it. All that tough stuff of his used to roll right off because I knew he didn't mean me. He treated me with kid gloves.

There was one scene where we were sitting in a restaurant, and I think it's in a nightclub. He's got his arm around me, and I've got my head on his shoulder, perfectly relaxed. I think they had just been married, and that's the way she felt about him. "He'll take care of me. This little tiny fellow."

When the camera rolled, he was in character; there was no getting around it. And I think for a woman to have a man who is violent that way, but she's the only one he's sensitive with and sweet and soft with, it's doubly important to her then. Even playing a character in a picture, you felt a part of that.

I found him ……. most appealing, most attractive. He was very happily married, but I guess he must have liked me enough to…..to put a little extra effort forth…..

Ed: Was he tough with the director?

Loretta: Oh no. He'd listen very carefully. "Well, I'll try but….that, no" Of course, what he would do would be right anyway. You really can't direct a personality like Cagney too much. It's like trying to direct Marlon Brando in his heyday or Cary Grant, or even Clark Gable. Because they are so much themselves. Or Spencer Tracy…….

Ed: Why not Loretta Young? Why don't you throw yourself in that category?

Loretta: Because in my mind I was not that strong of a personality. I need direction. I like direction. I don't like coaching…..there's a difference. When you tell someone how to do something, that drives me crazy because then I say, "You do it then. It will only be second-hand if I do it the way you want me to do it." I didn't know in my silent days. They'd say, "Walk in and do this." I didn't know that it depended on how you walked in and what your attitude is.

Direction, I think, is seeing an over-all scene, and if you can pull it out of each one what you see in that over-all scene, provided that you've got the right concept of that scene. Now, if somebody comes along and they've got a little different concept, you have to be loose enough to accept this, because that's what you're paying for, the talent.

Ed: What about Roy Del Ruth as a director?

Loretta: He must have been good, because it's a good picture, but he said to me one day…….we were near a staircase, and I guess it was up to an L (elevated train.) Jimmy and his two pals were there, and I'm at the foot of the staircase, and Roy Del Ruth came over to me and said, "Don't do it in the rehearsal, but in the take, just before you leave, whatever he says, slap him in the face and run up the stairs as quick as you can. Because he will be right after you.

I've already told the other actors to grab him and not let him get you" ……….and it was really unnecessary to behave that way with an actor like Jimmy Cagney. He was too professional, and I don't know what Roy Del Ruth thought he was going to get out of it that he didn't get out of every scene Jimmy did.

Anyway, he talked me into it, and I thought, "If I'm going to do it, I'd better do it well and do it once only." So I hit him and ran up the stairs quickly, and he was right after me........instinct, I guess. The other actors grabbed him, and I came down the stairs. I said, "Jimmy, oh, I'm so sorry"..... He said to the director, "That really wasn't necessary...."

To be honest, Roy was very sweet, but not a very good director....but I did a lot with him though........

I had a dream about Jimmy while we were working on the picture. I was in a lot of water so there must have been a pool. There was dirt in the pool but water too. I tried to get at the sides and I'd slip down. And my family, oh a lot of them, my brother, my mother, sisters, everybody all standing around and saying .... "Well, hurry up Gretch, C'mon, c'mon, hurry up." But nobody did anything to help me. And, all of a sudden, he comes in and says, "Well, give the kid a hand....." and just sort of looked at everybody. "Help her, she's going to drown." And finally, he says, ..."Oh, well," he takes his coat off and dives into the filthy water and saves my life. I don't know what happened after that.

When I woke up the next morning, I must have memorized that dream. Otherwise, it would have faded away. But, I probably thought about it and went over it again so much so that all these years later I can still see where the people were in that dream.

THE HATCHET MAN

Ed: Edward G. Robinson is the most unlikely looking Chinese man, but what I wonder about you in this film is, you were beautiful, but you looked less like Loretta Young than any other thing I've seen you in.

Loretta: Oh, yes. Because my whole face was distorted. Here's what they did to me. They put some spirit gum on tape and let it dry. Then they had a little hole with some string on it and then pull your face back like this and tie it to the back of your head and put a wig on top of it.

Ed: Didn't that hurt?

Loretta: Yes! The second day when they took it off, chunks of flesh fell out....

Ed: ooooooh...

Loretta: And then they put new skin on it and it burns like mad. It finally got so I could only work one day and had to be off two days. And then work one day and be off three days.

Ed: This is an unlikely role because you were kind of like a Chinese, well, not a tart exactly.....

Loretta: She was from a good family. Chinese, you know, or the Orientals, they don't have the same kind of moral standards that we do. I mean, they don't even think that way. The women for so long, they were just.....

The immorality of playing a role of that kind never bothers me because it did not condone it; it proved it wrong.

Ed: she paid....

Loretta: What I object to is saying, "This is it, Baby, and it's okay .....Everybody does it and it's okay." That's what I object to.

Ed: You were very good in that......I noticed it was directed by William Wellman.

Loretta: Bill was an honest director, and he liked me also. We did a lot of pictures together. MIDNIGHT MARY, CALL OF THE WILD....... HEROES FOR SALE with Richard Barthlemess. Bill thought I was good. See, anytime anyone thought I was good, then I got better.... a little bit better. But all you have to do is have someone tell you, "Well, you didn't win any Academy Awards you know......"and I'd shrivel up like a prune....

PLAY GIRL

Ed: Directed by Ray Enright

Loretta: Ray Enright. Oh, yes. He had gray hair and he was kind of portly and he had blue eyes and I think he wore a cap a lot.....

Ed: Cinematographer..........

Loretta: Gregg Toland.......Oh, the best. He turned out to be Sam's (Goldwyn) top cameraman.

Ed: Review: "Starring Loretta Young and Norman Foster with Winnie Lightner. As a department store slave, Loretta Young squeezes out her assignment, more than it would afford the average actress."

Loretta: Well, it was a good one......There was a scene in a booth of some kind, and I was pregnant, and they had a hard time getting it into the picture......Norman thought I was good and told me so, and he was from the stage, and therefore, I thought he knew what he was talking about......which he did.

Ed: Was that the first time you met him?

Loretta: Yes, we did two or three pictures together.

Ed: Was he fun?

Loretta: Back in those days.....yes, a lot of fun.

WEEKEND MARRIAGE

Loretta: That was with Norman Foster, wasn't it?

Ed: Yes.....and directed by Thornton Freeland

Loretta: I don't remember him.

I remember playing a joke on Norman. He was with Claudette Colbert at the time. Someone had given me a little vial of *vile* perfume. Terrible. Something like the stuff you buy in

Honolulu......Anyway, it never leaves you. We had just finished the picture, and he was going to meet Claudette's train. I said, "Goodbye and give Miss Colbert my best," and with that I poured this perfume all over him. He was furious. He didn't think it was a bit funny, and she didn't either, apparently.

I didn't hear about it until years afterwards. He finally said to me, "Oh, she was furious. All the cheap perfume......He couldn't convince her that I had just poured it on him. She thought he had been carrying on with different people. Maybe he had, I don't know, but he hadn't been tearing around with me........

Ed: How long were Norman and Claudette Colbert married?

Loretta: For a long time.....until he married Sally. They (Norman and Claudette) weren't really married....they were just together .....but no one has come out and said they weren't married........they never had a marriage license.

Ed: Review: ....."Loretta Young and Norman Foster do a brave and interesting job with the answer to the old: 'Should the wife work and be independent?' question.'"

Loretta: ......a big interesting question (laugh) (laugh)...My God, if she doesn't work, she doesn't eat......

LIFE BEGINS

Loretta: Eric Linden was on that. Darling boy. Aline MacMahon was wonderful in it. Glenda Farrell was in it. These were all stage people, and I was thrilled to death because I had to romp to keep up with them. Ruth Gordon was a big star in New York at that time, and they had given me her part. I was playing a girl who had been in prison and was having a baby, and they were letting her out just long enough to have the baby. The whole story is that the husband realizes that she's having trouble, and he says, "Save my wife; I don't care about the baby....." and they don't; they save the baby..... At the end, the doctor tells him, "If I had saved her, she'd have gone right back to prison. At least you have something to remember her...... a little girl."

Ed: Review: "Miss Young is convincing throughout in a none-too-easy role...."

Loretta: I was in bed most of the time. That doesn't have anything to do with it.....the fools. Well, it was dramatic. And she dies in the picture. Ordinarily, the leading lady doesn't die.

Ed: I saw in my notes that you were doing research by visiting a maternity ward in October, 1932, so you must have made this movie subsequent to that......

It appears there were two directors: James Flood and Elliott Nugent.

Loretta: I was crazy about Jimmy Flood. Elliott was a little too distant for me, but Jimmy Flood was right out there in the open. They did a good job together. I don't know how they both directed that because ordinarily, you're looking at ....of course, I'd pick Jimmy, finally, to look at every time because he was more sympathetic with me. And probably Elliott, who was from the stage, was more sympathetic with the stage actresses.

I don' know why they co-directed because each of them was good enough by himself. It's the only time it has ever happened to me.

THEY CALL IT SIN

Loretta: It's good. I saw it not long ago. I've got it. George Brent. David Manners......Louis Calhern.....he plays the bad guy, and my character was his kept woman for a while.

The movie had very little to do with sin......yes it does. But it is more or less about a good girl who under certain circumstances has to sleep with someone to get ahead, and then she's still in love with the good guy.

Ed: In one review they say, "David Manners is a Warner Brothers reject now....."

Loretta: Oh, that's nasty, isn't it. Why would they say a thing like that?

Ed: It is nasty. Is this the time you were interested in George Brent? You would have been nineteen.

Loretta: Probably. (silence.....) (laugh) (laugh). Well, I guess so. I couldn't wait to get to the set because he'd say, "Oh, here I am," and I'd come running. Of course, anybody put up with anything in those days ..... you could be as free as you wanted to be. We did a personal appearance tour after that.

Ed: What did you do on these personal appearance tours?

Loretta: We did a little skit about a honeymoon couple. This would be part of the entertainment when people went to the movies .... oh.......the most embarrassing thing happened in St. Louis. We were rehearsing the skit. I was supposed to be changing from my travelling suit into a hostess gown while George and I were having a conversation. There was a screen around me while I changed. The theater manager came up and said that they couldn't see my head. He brought the screen to my dressing room where he measured it so that the audience would be able to see my head. In those days we didn't wear brassieres, just little step-ins, and garter belts, and stockings, and that was it. Then we'd put on a full slip and the dress.

I remember it was a hot day, and my mother had on a big white hat with the dark blue ribbon around it. George and I were going along with our little eight-minute skit. We were talking as I was backing up while I was undressing so as not to knock over the screen .... this was later .... there was a real audience out there. All of a sudden, I saw this white hat sail down the side aisle and tear out the side door. The people were applauding like mad and I was bowing, and George was making some kind of gesture, but I didn't understand what he was trying to communicate to me. I continued to undress, saying the dialogue all the time, and I was down to my panties and stockings, and then I slipped into my negligee as rehearsed, and came out from behind the screen and continued the show.

When we finished our skit, we took our bows, and, as I went off the stage. The manager was there, and he was saying, "Oh, I'm so sorry." Just then I see my mother shaking her head to tell the manager to stop talking; I look around and see George, and he was doing the same thing. Finally, Mama explained what happened. "When you went behind the screen to change, you backed away from it; the further you backed away, the more the audience saw. You ended up stark naked from the waist up." I said, "Oh, no! I can't believe it!" I just flew up to my dressing room burning with embarrassment. I don't know how I ever got onto the stage again.

Ed: Wow! Was there any notoriety related to this?

Loretta: The marvelous thing was that not one reviewer even mentioned it. Those were gentler days.

Ed: I'm curious .... was it your movie they were showing?

Loretta: I don't think it was ours....... I would have remembered that, don't you think?

Ed: Yes (laugh) (laugh)

Loretta: I don't know....I'm such a nut anyway....(laugh) (laugh) (laugh) (laugh)

Ed: How often would you perform this skit?

Loretta: Five times a day, I'm sure. Seven days a week. We were out for, I think, two weeks. I remember we finished in St. Louis.

Ed: Was this your first personal appearance tour?

Loretta: I think that was the only one I did. I think.

1933

EMPLOYEE'S ENTRANCE

Ed: First National production, Roy Del Ruth.....Warner Brother's release.....Warren William, Loretta Young, Wallace Ford, Alice White.....Great overall reviews....

Loretta: Why? Was it any good? Did you see it?

Ed: I saw it. I think I know why it was good then......because it represented a new attitude.....timely politically. But, I was in shock! Shock! (laugh) (laugh)

Loretta: (laugh) (laugh) I was sleeping with a man.

Ed: the big boss. That Warren William ......

Loretta: Sleazy-looking guy, wasn't he?

Ed: .....mean looking guy. I wasn't quite sure at first what went on, but you find out at the big company party, you go to his hotel room.......and make him happy .....you realize that at the beginning of the story.... You felt so guilty......

Loretta: Oh, I wasn't guilty then.....

Ed: she takes poison....

Loretta: Oh, she does?

Ed: She was able to be resuscitated and her husband starts paying more attention to their marriage......was there enough of a lesson there (to meet Loretta's stated criteria that if bad behavior wasn't rewarded, then she didn't mind playing the character)?

Loretta: I don't think I thought it clearly through in those days. Okay, I don't think it was.
You see, in those days, I don't even think I thought of the morality or immorality of it. I was aware of the example I was giving in my personal life, not in the parts that I played. That I grew into later.

The only time I'm conscious of really making an effort not to play an immoral part or something that was against my own personal beliefs was a picture I was supposed to do for Metro. I don't remember the name of it. Jack somebody was the director... I didn't want to play the bad girl.....

Ed: Was the picture ever made?

Loretta: Carole Lombard did it.

(Back to EMPLOYEE'S ENTRANCE)

Ed: Review: "Loretta Young does well as the model to the store who is secretly married to the manager's protégé."

Loretta: Loretta Young DOES WELL..... I don't think that's a very good review, do you? I think it's kind of BOR-RING! (laugh) (laugh)

Ed: You got married in that movie in a beautiful church. I was curious where that was supposed to be....

Loretta: Most of the time we just went into a real church......Blessed Sacrament church is beautiful.

GRAND SLAM

Ed: Warner Brothers.....William Dieterle

Loretta: Wonderful director, Bill Dieterle was. He did THE ACCUSED and THE DEVIL'S IN LOVE.....with the man I didn't like particularly, the actor (Victor Jory)........

Paul Lucas........he was the male lead in GRAND SLAM. In my day, screen kisses were always just lips on lips, never open-mouthed. One day, Paul dived down my throat in a kiss, and I was horrified. I backed up. Sidney Hickox was the cameraman and saw what happened. He said to Paul, "You son-of-a-bitch, if you ever do that again, I'll blast you!" He didn't do it again.

Paul must have been at least twice as old as I was and........ I thought he looked older in that film than he did later on. I don't know what the story was. He was never a very attractive man. I think, the poor man,....this can happen I'm sure. He was married and happily married, and if you're used to kissing someone that way and you kiss ....I mean it didn't have to be a premeditated, "Oh, boy, I'll show her!"

Ed: It seemed strange to me that they made a movie about bridge (card game)....It must have been a mania back then.

Loretta: It must have been. It never was with me.

ZOO IN BUDAPEST

Ed: Paul Fix was the villain in ZOO IN BUDAPEST.

Loretta: He's villainous looking.....his mouth went down and his mouth was thin. An awfully nice fellah. He wasn't this kind of fellah at all, but yes, he always played villains.

Ed: You were blonde....

Loretta: It's a wig.

Ed: You kissed a monkey.....

Loretta: I didn't like kissing the monkey. Would you like kissing a little smelly monkey? No.

Ed: Was there location shooting?

Loretta: ZOO IN BUDAPEST we did on a soundstage. The whole zoo.

Ed: How long did you spend making this movie?

Loretta: Ten weeks. This is one of my freelance pictures before I signed with 20th Century....

Ed: Your First National contract was up?

Loretta: I don't think I signed with .....something's going on in my mind.....ask me about it later....

THE LIFE OF JIMMY DOLAN

Loretta: Directed by Archie Mayo. A big fat man. Very pleasant.

Ed: with Douglas Fairbanks, Jr., Loretta Young, Aline MacMahon, Guy Kibbee......he gets the best review....

Loretta: I'm sure. He was a character actor and he played my father in lots of things .....he played my father in TAXI.

Ed: ....like him?

Loretta: Yes, he was a darling and charming man....

Ed: This is the movie where you played with a young Mickey Rooney.

Loretta: Have we got it here........

Ed: Yeah..... and John Wayne is also in this movie but you didn't have any scenes with him...he had a small role as a boxer......

Loretta: This might have been the picture when I was celebrating my eighteenth birthday...... All along I had been convinced that I wouldn't get parts unless I was eighteen .....I did four or five films with Douglas Fairbanks, Jr. and he asked me on my birthday how old I was. I said, "Eighteen". He said, "Gretch, you've got to get on with this thing. We've worked together two or three years....and you've been eighteen since the day I met you."

HEROES FOR SALE

Loretta: Another Bill Wellman. All I remember about that is the horse's hooves....

Ed: That was an interesting movie.....strange political messages....

Loretta: Well, I believe that there were so many communists, card holding members, in the motion picture industry ......but if I were a communist and a good communist and I wanted to influence the world with my ideologies, I would certainly go to the motion picture industry, and where they made the most movieswhich was in in the U.S. and the most important ones at that time. They were bright and well-read on everything to do with their beliefs. And I know our business was just riddled with them. So they would give you a situation that would appeal to the pure and honorable and loyal American, but they would leave you with a doubt.

Ed: There appeared to be a false premise to the story......

Loretta: What was the false premise you found in it?

Ed: Well, you worked as a laundry girl......Thomas had already been an unheralded World War I veteran ......He, in conjunction with another guy, comes up with this invention that was going to make everything go so much quicker in the laundry business. But they said, "Okay, but we'll only sell you this patent if you agree that you'll never use this to reduce any jobs." It could easily be construed as a labor-saving device..... so to what end would someone buy it if you couldn't run your business more efficiently with less labor? ....But the movie used that (don't cut jobs) as an assumption and then built from there. Riots in the street, etc. I guess you could do laundry in a quicker way without firing anybody if the amount of business increased accordingly........ but that's a variable factor. It was confusing.....

Review: "Loretta does get some sympathy ..... she marries the hero and gets trampled by the mob...."

MIDNIGHT MARY

I was loaned to MGM to do that as kind of a punishment. I had
pestered the studio to do BERKELEY SQUARE with Leslie
Howard. I had a big crush on him. It was kind of an ethereal,
mysterious kind of costume piece.

Ed: ....a period piece......

Loretta: Yes. And I was dying to do it. I didn't get to. Heather
Angel got that. It didn't do too well because it was either ahead
of its time or it wasn't done.......it was ethereal; it was all to do
with the next world and with going back and coming.......

Warner Brothers sent me and Bill Wellman.....he was under
contract to Warner Brothers, too......I guess we were both being
punished. It was a little, not important picture. It was what they
called a programmer, not a B picture; MGM didn't deign to make
B pictures. Anyway, Bill Wellman was a very clever director and
....

Ed: You can see it in that movie...

Loretta: Wonderful things.....of course, that could have been the
cutter, or the producer, of just sliding over to the next scene. No
fade out or fade in, none of that. A lot of the scenes that Wellman
directed.....for instance, just seeing the child's eyes (referring to
her character) on the judge's desk and then the poor little thing
faints. You never see her faint, you just see her...... He was very,

very talented, I thought. Also in the scene where we were supposed to be nine years old, Una Merkel and myself. We looked nine and we acted like nine year olds, arms and legs going all different directions .....he had to hire giants for extras and a policeman and the other.....and all great big truck tires ......

Ed: ....oversized....

Loretta: everything was oversized. Anyway, BERKELEY SQUARE was neither a financial success nor an artistic one. And MIDNIGHT MARY played the Roxy Theater in New York for three weeks; that was unheard of; it broke all the records for three weeks . It was just #1 Box Office for a couple of months, one of the ones they call a sneaker. I've seen it now, and I certainly don't have to be ashamed of it. It was very good.

Of the three players who were in it, my name was above the other two, so the studio must have considered me the star of MIDNIGHT MARY.

Years later, Jean Louis told that he was absolutely delighted with this picture. (Jean Louis would have been still living in Paris when MIDNIGHT MARY was released. Eventually, he came to the United States and became Columbia Pictures' top couturier. He and Loretta were friends for forty years before they married in 1993). Well, Adrian made the clothes, you see, and the clothes were beautiful. They were in the time of that period but the clothes of that period were beautiful. They were soft, and the shoulders weren't too large, and they used a lot of satin. There was a gorgeous little tiny fringe evening hat I wore ......

(Years later) 20th Century-Fox had dubbed me the most perfect back in the world. I think they said a bunch of chiropractors got together and decided this, but it was just a publicity stunt, I'm sure. But Adrian emphasized this idea with the no-back gowns he designed for me...

Ed: Ricardo Cortez...........

Loretta: Ricardo Cortez was perfectly cast. He's tough. He was mean. He didn't have to act mean. He was!

Ed: Right......

Loretta: You know, there are some actors, when they're relaxed, they're mean. He was!

Ed: Did you date him?

Loretta: Oh, no!

Ed: Well, that's on my list of people you dated....

Loretta: Oh, no. No way.

Ed: Okay.

Loretta: If you were sitting at the same table at a party or something....that happened quite often .... the photographers would get a picture of you sitting next to that person, and they'd say they were "dating." Of course, you weren't dating at all. You came with your date, and he came with his own date.

Ed: What about Franchot Tone?

Loretta: Franchot Tone was very cool and aloof. I think he was going with Joan Crawford at that time and her glamour rubbed off on him. I thought it was marvelous …….. it rubbed off on me as well. Joan was a *big* …..star at Metro.

Ed: In some scene you see a marque in that movie that said….

Loretta: Joan Crawford…..This is how clever they were. When they had a star, they just starred you down the line.

Ed: How old was William Wellman?

Loretta: Bill was in the Lafayette Esquadrills in the First World War. They called him Wild Bill Wellman. And he was wild. He had a plate in his head. Wonderful-looking man, I thought. Very kind of Montgomery Flagish looking….chiseled……not very tall.

Ed: For some reason, I thought he didn't get along with women, but he did with you…..

Loretta: Yes he did. He was a rough guy, but he had a very sweet/soft side in him. He *liked* me, and I knew that. You can tell ….you can smell whether people like you or don't…..and sometimes they can't help it…..it's just chemistry.

Ed: Back to the scene when you played the nine-year-old. Was that difficult?

Loretta: Oh, very easy. Just giggle......all girls do that.

Ed: I think I'd be self-conscious.

Loretta: An actor cannot be self-conscious. You have to be willing to make a fool of yourself in front of people and in the movies, in front of millions of people.

Ed: What you did so well in that movie ..... knowing what I know about your growing-up years now .....there was a lot of innocence in your growing-up years, yet this was a girl who had none of that, your character.....

Loretta: She was misused, abused in a way....

Ed: You had this look on your face so often in that movie, kind of fatalism, distant ... how did he (William Wellman) do that?

Loretta: He didn't. I did. Any woman with imagination ..... Acting, I think, is a wonderful bit of therapy for anyone because you can do, really, anything that you might be tempted to, and you really aren't doing it, because you're only acting. Because there's a lot of attraction, I find, in evil. Usually, it's so covered up with beauty that you don't see the evil.

The only real school I went to was being around people, and you study people, all kinds of people. You don't cash out anyone because each of us, we all have the same drives, the same desire for happiness, the same desire for wealth and security, and we want people to like us. Everybody is the same only more or less.....

SHE HAD TO SAY YES

Loretta: Who was in it?

Ed: Lyle Talbot .....

Loretta: I couldn't stand Lyle Talbot. I went out with him a couple of times but .....Yuk! I didn't like anything about him.

Ed......and Regis Toomey. You were a "customer girl".....

Loretta: Oh, yes, she was a secretary who went on to be a ....well, when I was doing those things (laugh) (laugh), it never dawned on me that I was supposed to be sleeping with him....

Ed: It really didn't?

Loretta: No, no.

Ed: Because I was surprised how frank that was back in a movie 60 years ago.....

Loretta: Ah ha. I mean, I don't suppose it would have made any difference to me at the time, but we just never thought that way. I didn't. I just thought I was his girlfriend, as opposed to his lover, until we got married, see. But.....(laugh) that's what I thought.

I notice that as we go over these titles, they were what they call "sexy" hooker titles: THE TRUTH ABOUT YOUTH, SHE HAD TO SAY YES, THE DEVIL'S IN LOVE, MIDNIGHT MARY. With MIDNIGHT MARY, there was some connection because she was living with a gangster, but in these others......

In THEY CALL IT SIN, yes, I certainly think she was supposed to be living with that man, but you'd never know it the way I was playing it.

THE DEVIL'S IN LOVE

With your not-so-favorite co-star, Victor Jory. Directed by William Dieterle....

Loretta: I did a couple with him. I did THE ACCUSED with him. He was a wonderful director .....both times. I don't remember much about THE DEVIL'S IN LOVE. Something about the desert...

Ed: Review: "....both Jory and Young had an-even balanced performance...."

Loretta: are we lousy or are we great...?

Ed: Why didn't you like Victor Jory?

Loretta: I don't know. Chemical, I'm sure. We were doing a scene.......I guess my hair was down, and he leaned over .....it was supposed to be a love scene .....we were standing up because he just leaned over to kiss me, and he was talking like this, and I don't know, his breath kept blowing my hair, and it annoyed me to no end; I can't tell you. And, also, it was very warm on the set. Anyway, he just leaned over to kiss me, and I just shivered. I didn't mean to, but I did and Dieterle said..... *"Cut!"*

He came to me and asked, "What's the matter?" I said, "I'm not going to kiss him." He said, "You have to. It's a love scene." I said, "I don't care. He blows on my hair." Well, he can't tell the man not blow on my hair ..... It was just one of those.....no reason....

Ed: How did things go from then on?

Loretta: I don't remember. I don't remember whether I kissed him or didn't. Anyway, I was glad when the scene was over. I don't think I had any crush on him....I usually manage a crush on most every leading man ..... some would be very little crushes, and some would be bigger crushes, and some developed into much more serious crushes; but this man....I didn't feel anything about, and I think this just turned it into the other direction.

Ed: Here's a quote from Victor Jory, "This gloriously beautiful and capable creature was not happy to be loaned to Fox to work with someone of inferior stature to her. As a result, the picture has a peculiar love scene in which we didn't actually kiss. It may look as if we did, but if you study it closely, you'll see that she didn't allow such intimacy....."

Loretta: ....that's not true...

Ed: (continuing with the Jory quote) "and on the set she seldom bothered to speak to me...."

Loretta: Ahhh.....poor man. I didn't like him....(laugh) (laugh) I didn't dislike him. I just didn't like him. Nothing to do whatever......Afterwards, I always feel terrible if I make someone feel uncomfortable. I wish I could know that at the time. I think I have learned that in the last 10, 15, or 20 years of my life, to try NOT to make people uncomfortable. But sometimes you can walk in a room, and just by being there people are uncomfortable. I don't know what it is..."

Ed: He (Victor Jory) did go on to say that most people that he knew that worked with you had the highest regard for you.....

Loretta: He was right. He was the one man.....but there is a kiss, and he kissed me on the mouth, but that's the way we always kissed in those days......

Poor Victor Jory...to remember someone that way. What about the end of the story? Did she marry him or David Manners?

Ed: She gets Victor Jory....

Loretta: She's a nut. Why did she pick him?

Ed: He's the lead....

Loretta: Oh, all right….

Ed: Wasn't Dieterle a German actor?

Loretta: Yes, he was an actor in Germany, a very attractive, good-looking man, a big man….and turned director when he came over here…..

Ed: Harsh German or gentle German…..

Loretta: An enormous gentleman…very quiet and very subtle and very….I thought a wonderful director.

MAN'S CASTLE

Loretta: Just a pleasure for me to go to work every day because not only was I working in a script that I was crazy about and knew I was right for it, but the whole situation, the best of everything….the best director…, the best cameraman, the best cast, and I was falling in love with the leading man (Spencer Tracy), and I thought, "Oh, boy, this is it!"…..see…Then I found out he was married….separated but married. That he was a Catholic, and that he had been married in the church.

Before MAN'S CASTLE, even in the terrible ones, I always got good reviews. I was up and coming and they were all kind. In our business, when we were getting started, they
gave everyone a boost along the way, and then when we'd get there or even near it, they started the pot-shooting. With MAN'S

CASTLE, I saw the rushes and I knew it was good. You can't go wrong with this story and that cast and that director and that writer. It was all there. The reviews came out on this thing, and most of them were marvelous for everyone. I remember one review. It gave Spencer a rave and Borzage a rave, and it got down to me and their critique of my whole performance in this thing was, "Miss Young is pretty as usual." Period. And I nearly died. I was working on another picture at the time and I thought, "Oh, everybody knows I'm terrible".......it just pulled the rug out from under me.

Bet (Loretta's sister): The people doing the review aren't the people doing the job. That's the point.

Loretta: And they really don't know anything about acting. Otherwise they'd be actors. When they give a long reason why the actor is no good, that always puzzles me.......... who are they to say if they're not even actors?

Ed: I'll give my review of this movie....I was living in Florida when I saw this on TV.....I just remember a scene when you're standing there.....just the expression on your face, that combination of being so in love and so afraid that you are going to lose him. That's what I remember ten years later.

Loretta: Well, that's acting. It has nothing to do with timing or anything. It simply has to do with ......certainly, when you're not talking, if you're acting at all, you act best when you're not talking.....because talking will take care of what that's supposed to convey. It was a good thing that this happened to me (the bad review). At that time I thought I'd never get over this and I'm sure, over the years, I have received many more bad reviews than I have good ones. I don't know whether that's' true or not.....but I've had enough bad reviews.

Before I went into television, I was not what I call a flamboyant actress. Katie Hepburn (Katharine Hepburn) has always been a magnificently flamboyant actress, and you look at her......I don't care what's going on. You look at her. That was her big gift, I think. And Bette Davis, also. Not only did you look at her but she was so perfect in everything that she did, in the parts that she played, that she demanded that you look at her.

Ed: I think the same thing is true for you....

Loretta: Well you do now because you're interested in me. But before we met...?

Ed: Yes.....

Loretta: That's good. I'm glad.

Bet: You know you do the same thing. You're not as flamboyant......but, Gretch, you are the shining light, in other words, everyone else is a small thing. See, this is the magic of your performance......that's the whole answer. You either do or you don't have it. And it's a gift, Gretch.

Loretta: Oh, I know it's a gift. Nobody has been able to define it even. Who knows what made Spencer? Who knows? What can you say?

He wasn't very attractive or anything. I mean good-looking. It fascinates me to this day. I cry all over again in those scenes. And it's only because those two people were so emotionally ......

(Loretta's mind going back to comments Bet had made about Loretta's "*star*" persona in years past) Bet, you used to tell me I was a phony during my movie star years.....

Bet: ....Oh, Gretch.......... I don't know.......(phone rings)

(Onto a new topic after Loretta was through with her phone call)

Ed: Did a producer approach your mother about a story of the girls...

Loretta: No. A lot of writers wanted her to write her story, and she said, "Oh, no, that would be vulgar. Ladies don't do that."

Bet: She thought that any publicity was vulgar.

Loretta: She said, "You know, fools' names like fools' faces are always seen in public places." I looked at her and said, "Mom, I'm an actress." She said, "Well, nevertheless.........."

(A Couple of days later, coming back to the topic of how Loretta annoyed Bet with her star behavior)

Loretta: I tried to find out from Bet, but she has forgotten what it was about me that annoyed her. Since I wanted to be *liked* by other people, I really wanted to know what had offended her so.

Ed: I found that an interesting scenario in the kitchen. I know you love each other as sisters and I can see why….I'm very impressed with your sister…..but you kind of intimidated her when you asked her that question.

Loretta: I think I always did. I think I always intimidated Sally.

Ed: I could tell because her voice became soft, and she didn't know what to say, and then the phone rang and you were on the phone and she said….something to the effect of….that you were a movie star and there were certain ways, certain things a movie star has to do to be a movie star, and you just didn't turn it off when you came home…..to me that answered the question more…

Loretta: Well, it does ….but it doesn't help me because I am a movie star, and I don't know what it means, "acting like a movie star". Because I'm not *acting* like a movie star….*I am* a movie star.

Ed: Ah ha…I see the distinction…..or there isn't a distinction, that's what you're saying… but allow me one last question on this topic: Isn't there something inherently superficial in "acting like a movie star"?

Loretta: No, it isn't superficial ..... at least when you're around fans. It's just that some people expect you to be a "movie star".....and tell amusing stories, and it's a vicarious thing with them...

If you and I were talking here, and suddenly, a fan walked in, I would certainly not go on talking with you as relaxed and easy as I am now. I would be "Loretta Young" to that fan. And I would try to be what that fan thought he was going to get from me, see. Uh. If that's phony, that's phony. I don't think it is because it's "Loretta Young" and I AM LORETTA YOUNG.

(Ed refers to the conversation he had had with Bet while Loretta had been on the phone)

Ed: Another thing she said, she and Polly Ann were very close. There were no secrets between them. They almost could read each other's minds......but that you were so secretive...

Loretta: You know why? Because they didn't need me, and I was pushed out...

Ed: You were conditioned early.....

Loretta: Sure. There has never been the closeness between Polly Ann and me and Sally and me or Georgiana and me.....that there is between Pol and Sally. I accepted that a long time ago.

Ed: Ah, ha. I think what's so amazing, that being the case, how much you really enjoy each other's company as you do. She wouldn't come over here to see you if she didn't want to be with you.

Loretta: The family...... I *like* all my family which is no credit to me. They are very *likable.* If they weren't, I probably wouldn't ....but Polly Ann is charming and Betty Jane is charming. I don't see as much of my brother because he lives in San Marino, and I don't see as much of Georgiana because she and Ricardo are *very* social...but not too many months go by when I don't go to their house for dinner or they come here.

Ed: The point is that they are there if you need them......

Loretta: That's right....I think one of the reasons I haven't moved away from Beverly Hills is because my family is here, and I know they're here if I need them....

Ed: And you're there for them...

Loretta: After both Carter (Polly Ann's husband) and Norman (Sally's husband) died, they were both lonely. So I said, "Polly Ann, I'm going to come over and stay a week," or "I'm going to stay with you, Bet," and I'd just go over and live with them for a while until that time passed.

(Back to MAN'S CASTLE)

Loretta..... really a wonderful period in my life. I was on my way, I think, in the picture industry. Frank Borzage, the director, had already done SEVENTH HEAVEN with Janet Gaynor, and everyone had already won their awards so he was one of the top directors and one of the sweetest and most sensitive men I have ever worked with in my life. I don't remember how he directed people because I don't ever remember him telling me to do anything or not to do something.......of course, you didn't have to tell Spencer what to do or not to do......he was wonderful to work with.

Frank Borzage just kind of pushed you in the direction without ever saying.....he'd either smile a little bit when you were doing it right......

He was Italian......but he had blue eyes, and he had more hair on the sides than on the top and it seemed to me to be reddish. Not slender. I felt that I was doing this on my own. I thought, "Gee, I'm not doing badly. Why am I under contract to all these bosses that seem to misuse me....?"

Ed: I think you were 20...

Loretta: It was at Columbia Studios that I liked because it was a small studio, and Harry Cohn I liked very much.....

Ed: No confrontations...

Loretta: Oh , no. You could have had anything you wanted out of me in those days. Let's see......I don't think so. It could have been that the director was important enough that he directed and produced it...

Ed: Critics didn't like the picture.....

Loretta: Oh yes they did...

Ed: Variety didn't......"Tracy was too unsympathetic .....Loretta Young does a noble job as a little girl who stands nearly everything......."

Loretta: Most of the reviews were marvelous. It's a classic. You can't.....I mean, the characters are unsympathetic....It's like saying Scrooge is unsympathetic. If that's the way he's written ...you know.....

(talking about her own performance) Her performance was good and steady as a mouse who found security......even when she said, "Even if you go away now, you're a prisoner inside of me, you'll never get away. " That was a mousy quick thing......hurry and get it out quick before he hits her. I believed both of them. He was too tough, and she was too mousy.

The reason I like MAN'S CASTLE ....frankly: Spencer Tracy. We only did this one picture together, and I'd given my eye tooth to do twenty with him.......absolute pleasure to work with. You never knew when he was rehearsing or when the camera was going or anything.....he was just the same way. But he knew exactly where he was going all the time. He was such a good actor.

There is a scene at the end of the picture. The Breen Office made them cut it because she has to be married before she has the baby. She's pregnant. But it doesn't make any sense. The whole story is that he doesn't want to be anchored. He doesn't want to get married. This is way at the end of the picture. This is why she is crying because he's marrying her just to……….

Ed: Glenda Farrell, did you like her?

Loretta: Very much. When I married Tom I didn't know that he had been going with her for two years in New York. We had worked together at Warner Brothers on a lot of things. I liked her. She was a nice woman. Very professional. She ended up marrying a famous surgeon.

Ed: Did you think Spencer Tracy was an intelligent man?

Loretta: I thought he was. But then I thought everything about him was right. He had a lot of common sense.

(Circling back to when Loretta's sister had been part of the conversation)

Bet: He was so handsome. He'd come to the house, and I'd say, "I'm going to take acting lessons." He'd say, "Why for God's sake?" He was furious.

Ed: Was he brash, or was he shy?

Loretta: No, he wasn't brash and he wasn't shy. He was perfectly charming and normal and a lovely sense of humor and very sensitive, I thought.

Bet: He was so wonderful and so understated in every way.

Ed: What color were his eyes?

Loretta: I don't know....

Bet: I think they were blue or gray. He had red in his hair.

Loretta: He was always stocky. They were not blue. Hazel or gray. Spencer grew on you very slowly but very surely. He was just kind of there and little by little he just......the others....Tyrone Power.....Clark Gable... had the looks that just knocked you dead.

(About Louis B. Mayer)

Loretta: You can say what you like about that man, but he was a family man, and he wanted decency and family pictures.......What he did in his private life was his business .....I found him very warm and kind to me.

Ed: Was he a gentleman?

Loretta: To me he was. Yes. Yes, he and his whole family had good manners.

Ed: Would your mother have thought that he was a gentleman?

Loretta: No........though he was more of a gentleman than Darryl
Zanuck because Mr. Mayer always stood up behind his desk
when a woman walked in. Zanuck...... a very small man.....with
his little riding crop......he did play polo so that it was not an
affectation ....I disliked him intensely. He was a wonderful
producer for men's pictures, Eddie Robinson, Jimmy Cagney,
stories out of the headlines.......

When Zanuck left Warner Brothers, he took certain actors with
him. He took George Arliss and he took Constance Bennett.....or
did she freelance? Warner Brothers couldn't *give* me to him; I
had to make my own contract with him. Before I signed with
him, I did MAN'S CASTLE. It must have been that way. But I know
when he left, there were certain Warner Brother's stars that
went with him....I must have right away.......after I freelanced for
MAN'S CASTLE......

Part Six: 20th Century

Ed: What was your first picture for 20th Century?

Loretta: THE HOUSE OF ROTHCHILD

Ed: Are you sure of that? It looks like the first thing you did was THE DEVIL'S IN LOVE

Loretta: That was at Fox....

Ed: Not 20th Century-Fox? ..... you're right...that was at Fox...

Loretta: Just Fox? What year was that?

It looks like HEROES FOR SALE was the last First National/Warner Brothers release. Released in July of 1933, and in August of 1933 was THE DEVIL'S IN LOVE for Fox.....

Loretta: I could have been loaned out for that. I could have been loaned for MAN'S CASTLE by Warner Brothers. I thought that I freelanced but I could have been loaned out.

Ed: .....that would make more sense, frankly......that you were loaned out .....and when it was time for your contract to end at Warner Brothers.....Daryl Zanuck just made you a better offer.....because I doubt they'd just let you go.....they sure were working you hard and giving you leads......in addition to HEROES

FOR SALE and THE DEVIL'S IN LOVE, THEY CALL IT SIN…….they were all released within a month…..

Loretta: Warner Brothers wanted to pick up my option, but they didn't want to give me a raise. I said, "No. I want a raise." David Thompson was my agent by that time. He had been with First National and so he knew me, and he must have peddled me around……I'm sure about this now…. I remember thinking, "Well, it's only a $100 raise, what's that to the studio?……I want my money." Common sense….

Ed: He was your first agent?

Loretta: Yes.

Ed: When did he come into your life?

Loretta: I guess when he left First National. Before that I didn't have an agent……didn't need an agent. But when he left, he must have said, "If you ever need an agent, Loretta…"

Ed: So you think he came into your life at this juncture?

Loretta: Could be. I know he went out of my life when Zanuck threatened me with extinction.

Ed: What is your first memory of Daryl Zanuck?

Loretta: I remember seeing him in the Green Room at Warner Brothers and thinking he was a pugnacious little punk. He was yelling and screaming all over the place. The Green Room was the lunchroom where the executives and the stars ate. They didn't deign to eat in the commissary with the rest of the "common folk".

Ed: Are you sure THE HOUSE OF ROTHCHILD was your first film for 20th Century and not BORN TO BE BAD?

Loretta: Yes. Because I remember saying, "There are only two conditions, Daryl, that I want. I do not want to do a picture with George Arliss, and I must have a vacation every year, at least six weeks. And the first picture I did was with George Arliss, and I didn't get a vacation for two years.....

Ed: This says that in July of 1933, you signed a contract with 20th Century beginning at $1731 a week to end at $3360 a week. That was a seven year contract.

Loretta: I doubt that. I never made more than $1500 with Zanuck at the end of my contract. I don't think. Although I didn't take care of my money.

Ed: That would sound like a more sensible contract. David Thompson would be doing the negotiating at this point.

Loretta: I don't know. I wonder where you could find that? Look for a contract for me. I think they're buried in a vault in New Jersey some place.

When I was seventeen-years-old, Mama signed a contract. She said to me, "The next time, you have to sign the contract. You'll be old enough so that you can sign it yourself."

Ed: You were 20 at the time you signed with Zanuck.....

Loretta: Well, then, I must have signed it myself. Or do you have to be 21?

Ed: ....well, maybe 21.

1934

HOUSE OF ROTHCHILD

Why didn't you want to work with George Arliss?

Loretta: Why? Arliss was such a genius, and I was such an idiot. I didn't know I could learn anything from him. I just didn't want to play any more ingénue parts which was dumb of me because I was perfectly cast in that picture, and I looked marvelous. I was just mousy enough and pretty enough to be the daughter of Rothchild as they wanted to present her.

It was a wonderful picture, a good picture. I've had people mention THE HOUSE OF ROTHCHILD to me when they don't mention, let's say, THE FARMER'S DAUGHTER. Maybe they were English people, and they loved George Arliss and they loved the Rothchilds.......

Ed: Boris Karloff....

Loretta: I never worked with him, did I?

Ed: He was in this movie....

Loretta: He was in THE HOUSE OF ROTHCHILD? I never worked with him......he was in scenes that I wasn't in. George Arliss. I found him to be a perfect English gentleman. A little aloof, rather cold, rather objective.....brilliant. His wit was wonderful and quick. He kind of looked like he was looking down his nose all the time, and he probably was.....

Ed: What made him such a good actor?

Loretta: He seemed to know *exactly* what he was doing at every single moment of the picture......and he did.

Ed: Robert Young was in this picture....

Loretta: Uh, pleasant and friendly, but no romance. I didn't appeal to him, and he didn't appeal to me. I don't know whether he was married at the time. I think he was borrowed from Metro to do it. His part wasn't much....

Ed: What was he like?

Loretta: I wish I could remember more about him. But what I'm discovering is that, in those years, unless it had something directly to do with me or my emotions, I block it out.

Ed: You had a lot of other things going on. Spencer was probably in your life at this time.....

Loretta: Oh, was he ever! Yes!

Ed: Did Spencer ever come on your sets?

Loretta: Spencer? No. That kind of thing was unprofessional. You just didn't....

Ed: I found another source that says you started your seven year contract at 20th Century at $1731 a week to end at $3, 365 a week.....

Loretta: I forgot that. Yes, that's right. Well, that's better. I feel better about that....

I had the same star dressing room at Sam Goldwyn's when I made THE HOUSE OF ROTHCHILD that I did when I was doing my TV show. The same one.....at one time Frank Sinatra was right across the way from me....

Ed: Why was THE HOUSE OF ROTHCHILD shot at Sam Goldwyn's? That was a different studio than 20th Century......

Loretta: They were. But when Daryl first left Warner Brothers, he produced movies at Sam Goldwyn's for a year or two, and then when it became 20th Century-Fox, he moved to the Fox Studios on Pico Avenue.

(Reacting to a review (now lost) of THE HOUSE OF ROTHCHILD)

LORETTA: They're talking about my looks only. That's all they had to talk about.....poor thing. It's a fair assessment because I did look pretty; the costumes were lovely, and I did wear a blonde wig in it.....

Ed: Did it mean anything to you that it was in color....

Loretta: No, I'd forgotten that it was in color .....

Ed: ....just the end of it.

BORN TO BE BAD

Ed: This review agrees with you: "BORN TO BE BAD is so bad that we can't understand why they ever thought to make this movie in the first place...."

Loretta: (laugh) (laugh)

Ed: but it did give you a good review...

Loretta: It did?

Ed: .....but Cary Grant

Loretta: He was terrible.....well, he was boring in it. I don't know, I think I was terrible, too....I wasn't terrible, I just wasn't what the script called for.

Ed: ...and they didn't like the little boy in it either......

Loretta: I didn't like the little boy, either. Did you?

Ed: ...No. He always had that sneer on his face. It was just too hard to care about him. I never saw him again in anything else....

Loretta: I didn't either. Little Dickie Moore was adorable. He could have done anything, and you would have loved him.......

Ed: Did you feel anything for Cary Grant?

Loretta: Didn't mean one thing to me. I don't remember who I was interested in at the time. Who could that have been?

Ed: .....could have been Spencer......Sure. You met him in 1933 .....Early 1934.....

Loretta: I know I was in Honolulu on a vacation. I'm trying to think who was there.....but I was there so many times......

Ed: You associate that with this picture?

Loretta: Yes, because I was there on a vacation, and I got a telegram from Zanuck's office to return immediately. That took a few days because we had to go by ship……. But the script was waiting for me when I got home.

So I read this thing, I guess, and I made an appointment to see him. I walked into his office and said, "Daryl, I can't play this." He said, "You're going to play it." Jean Harlow was set for it, and she died. He said, "You have to play it; you're an actress and you're going to play it." I said, "Well, this says she walks into the room, and she's so sexy that the men just drop over dead." If I have appeal, it's not that. I'd done a picture with her (Jean Harlow) and that's what it's all about …..it was PLATINUM BLONDE…….

(Current note from Ed: I immediately researched when Jean Harlow died; it was in June, 1937, three years after Loretta made BORN TO BE BAD. I shared that information with Loretta. Back to Loretta's comments)

Daryl said, "No…..you're going to do it. Go on." I didn't want to get off salary again. I'd done that too many times with him.

Ed: You had just started with him. This was 1934…..

Loretta: No, he had been at Warner Brothers.

There was a scene on the telephone, and she answers it wearing a pair of step-ins and a bra; and my figure wasn't anything to speak of either……..so we made a test and they said, "Can't you make them any skimpier?" I said, "Sure, cut them down to nothing, and you still won't see anything……"

So they made them skimpier and skimpier. I noticed when watching this scene ..... instinct ..... I came out in this thing, and I had a bathrobe over one shoulder, still trying to hide......

There is one scene in the picture that is very good ....she's sick in bed at the house. The rest of it was just kind of ......I was miscast in it......but there are some bad women that look like angels. So, in another way, it was very good casting. Good-looking women get away with a lot of evil things because people can't believe...

Ed: What were you saying the other day about Cary Grant and a sun lamp?

Loretta: I don't think he ever wore make-up. I'm not conscious of him ever wearing ....he always had a beautiful sun-tan. He told me that every morning, just after he took a shower, he spent four minutes under a sun-lamp, and apparently it was over his whole body, I don't know. When we were on the picture, he had a little sun-lamp in his dressing room; so in case he missed it in the morning, he got it sometime during the day.

Ed: This is something kind of juicy but I'm going to read it to you anyway......"BORN TO BE BAD. It ran into problems in telling the story of a woman who is emotionally scarred by past experiences and determined to survive on any terms." That part seems accurate...."The script called for Young to be a model who does not wear underclothes when trying to get buyers interested in products. With the Hays Office in full power in 1934, Zanuck was forced to drop this element which resulted in the scene not making any sense." I kind of know what he's talking about.......

Loretta: What scene?

Ed: ....you're all dressed up and you walk into a nightclub or something ....There isn't any continuity and you're wondering....what does this girl do for a living? Actually, this is more respectable than what I thought she was supposed to be doing.....

Loretta: Not at all juicy. I think this could have come from the fact that Jean Harlow was supposed to have played the part, and she never wore underwear of any kind. They're just confusing the script with her....

Ed: We did establish that she had not died for another three years after this movie......

Loretta: We did, huh? Well, she turned it down or something.

Ed: That could easily be. This was one of your first films for 20th Century .....you were not in a position to be negotiating at this point......

Loretta: No, I just did what I was told. Well, then maybe it was. Maybe it was written for Jean Harlow, and she didn't do it, so he put me in it. And she didn't die for three years afterwards......

In those days, I tried saying yes to everything because he was the producer and running the studio and then, little by little, it just wore me down to the point where I just saw him make so many dumb choices for me that I just finally had to get away from the contract.

Ed: I thought you pulled the performance off...

Loretta: To look at it now, it is not nearly as bad a picture as I thought it was then. I remember one review that was so funny: "Last night we saw a preview of a picture with Loretta Young and Cary Grant. It was called BORN TO BE BAD......and it was." That was the whole review.....

Cary wasn't very good in it. This was a straight leading man role, and Cary is not a straight leading man.

Ed: That was a Cary Grant I'd not seen before.

Loretta: No. See, I was under contract to the studio, and they hired him to come and play the leading man. He must have needed a job badly.....the money, I mean, because that was no part for him.

What I remember mostly was that he was interested in Virginia Cherrill. I think he was married to her, so I was just a little spec on the wall. Of course, it was easy for me to have a crush on every leading man I worked with. No reason why I wouldn't. See, I wasn't married and therefore, looking at every man with possibilities. But that's all I remember. Cary always liked me and

I always liked him. I'm sure if he had liked me enough, I could have been madly in love with him. But he didn't, and nothing turns me off quicker than somebody who's not infatuated or doesn't think I'm divine.

CARAVAN

Ed: This is a big favorite of yours, CARAVAN....

Loretta: *UGGGH*!

Ed: Produced and directed by.....

Loretta: Eric Charell......He had made something about horses in Germany, a smash success. He was German. A pleasant enough man, and I guess a good director for big extravaganzas....His brother worked with him. I remember on that picture, they made the English version and the French version at the same time with Loretta Young in the American version and Annabella played my part in the French version, and, of course, Charles Boyer was French in both versions.

I felt so sorry for Annabella because they imported her to do this, and she had to......I had all the clothes made just the way I liked them, and so all they did was copy my clothes for her. She had no choice in anything......she just wore what I wore, see. And she was an important actress in France at this time. I would rehearse a scene and do what I wanted to do, and she had to come in and stand in exactly the same place and do the same thing as I did. I would have crabbed about it, "Well, I don't want to do it that way,"....but they didn't want to realign the camera for every shot.

Ed: What was Annabella like?

Loretta: She didn't speak English...so I didn't spend too much time on the set....you don't.....

Charles Boyer was absolutely perfect. He was always a friend of mine, never a romantic interest. We did two pictures together, SHANGHAI and CARAVAN..... He always struggled with the language and with the accent.....he had big soft brown eyes. His mother was absolutely gorgeous ....that's where he gets his looks.

Ed: How about the director, Eric Charell?

Loretta: He certainly wasn't bad, but the whole picture I thought was so stupid. It was the only preview of my own films that I walked out on, and I got called to the front office the next day and bawled out.

Ed: Where was the preview?

Loretta: The Village Theatre, Westwood. It was a silly story....fairy story......musical comedy...

Ed: Review: "....Caravan is big, beautiful and BORING!"

Loretta: That's it! Big, beautiful and boring. Absolutely.

Ed: Review continues, "Loretta is charming as the countess......Boyer.....badly overplays his part."

Loretta: That would be Eric Charell directing him. He'd just done the WHITE HORSE INN in Germany, and he came over and directed the same way. Well......in movies you just ......

Ed: Anything going on in your private life associated with CARAVAN?

Loretta: There was a scene where I was supposed to be a ten-year-old child. They were testing people, and I said, "What about my sister Georgiana?" "What does she look like?" I said, "Oh, she's very pretty."

My hair was blonde for that picture and when Georgiana came over, her hair, of course, was dark. So I said, "Georgi, do you care if we bleach your hair?" "I don't care, Gretch; I don't care." Of course, she was just doing everything I told her to do. She would do anything the director told her to do, so I'd just stay on the set with her. I'd like to see the picture again just to see what she looked like because she was darling.

I can still see Georgi, her hair was growing out. Mama wouldn't do anything about it.....and there was big black hair and then blonde ends. She was just awful for about six to eight months and we finally got it off her head. I think that's when Georgi decided that she didn't want to be an actress.

I thought the clothes were....they were fairyland clothes.....there was one big dress......marvelous looking.......rows and rows of white net....she was a princess in a kingdom....

THE WHITE PARADE

Loretta: Funny, I don't remember too much about that. I remember I was thrilled to death at the preview because it was beautifully received.

Ed: What about Irving Cummings as director?

Loretta: He was a big old bear.....he was very charming......an actor himself.......Polly Ann was in THE WHITE PARADE.....she played one of the nurses. I think I have a copy of this picture here.....

It's funny, because at the time, everything about them (Loretta's films) seemed so vitally important.....I wonder who produced it.......

Ed: Jesse L. Lasky production...

Loretta: He was charming. I liked Mr. Lasky....

Ed: Didn't he ask you to do something with Spencer Tracy after you had broken up?

Loretta: Yes, just after I had broken up with him.....I didn't want to start it over again.....

Ed: Astrid Allwyn....she was the one you supposedly had that fight with.....

Loretta: No. Not at all. Never. I never fought with *anyone* on the set like that. If I didn't like someone, I kept it to myself. It's just not professional. You just don't do that....

Ed: ....No one did?

Loretta: Not any professional....

Ed: Ever see it on any of your movies?

Loretta: No.

Ed: Review: "Loretta Young is altogether convincing as the sympathetic female motivator who has dedicated herself to her profession.....she can be articulately inarticulate in her histrionic opportunities...."

Loretta: What does that mean?

Ed:.....able to communicate it...

Loretta: Isn't that what acting is?

1935

CLIVE OF INDIA

Ed: United Artist.....Director Richard.....

Loretta: Boleslawski. A darling, darling great big blonde man and charming. I don't think he paid too much attention to directing Ronnie (Ronald Colman) and me. It was a big picture. It had a lot of people, a lot of sets, a lot of costumes. I remember one time ......Ronnie..(laugh)...it was a scene when he comes home from India, and I had a hoop skirt and it was seven feet across. It was four feet across normally; I want them to be six or seven feet....just to be different, I guess. Of course, the bigger the skirt looked, the smaller your waist looked, too.

There was a staircase. I'm wearing this brown velvet dress. He was supposed to sweep her up in his arms and carry her up the stairs.....at rehearsal he picked me up. I said, "Oh, Ronnie.....put me down, put me down." He said, "No, no, it's just fine, " and he carried me upstairs. I said, "Ronnie, this is just a rehearsal...." He said, "I can carry you up the stairs."

Thank God I didn't let him do it again (in rehearsal)..... by the time they got the take, I thought the poor man was going to have a heart attack in the middle of the stairs because, not only me, he had to pick up these hoop skirts, too, that weighed a ton. And he wasn't a big strong athletic man...he was just a bit taller than I was.

Ed: Considerably older, too...

Loretta: I'm sure he was....

Ed: You were 22 ..... he was 44.

Loretta: It didn't make any difference to me, I thought he was gorgeous. At 44, a man is gorgeous.

I think of all the close-ups that I've seen of myself.....and of him...the first close-ups introducing us to each other were just gorgeous in that picture. J. Marley, I think, photographed it. He was one of the best in the business. She (Loretta's character)comes all the way from England. She's the sister of his best friend, and he had seen a medallion, a painting of her ...and then she comes out to marry him.....they're engaged, just long distance.

She's in the room, and he comes into the room, a hoop skirt again, and I swung around to look at him, and he stops dead and then they come to a close-up of him.....the most gorgeous thing you've ever seen and then a close-up of her .... and you wouldn't believe it was so beautiful. Innocence.....they were absolutely beautiful, those pictures. I don't remember much about CLIVE OF INDIA because it was a man's story, and I was playing Mrs. Alexander Graham Bell (meaning a support role to the leading man). But those close-ups were beautiful.

Also, I got ringworm on that picture. I had some still pictures made with this beautiful little kitten. One of the photographers came on the set to do a portrait sitting of me, and I had a great big dress......somebody said it would be a lovely idea to have a kitten.....so they went out and rented this little kitten, and I had it on my arm.

They were darling pictures......and two days later.... I asked, "What is that!" I had ring worm for about three months. They burn it ..... they cut it. A cat may look cute, but if it's got ringworm, don't put it on your skin anyplace, because you'll get it....

CALL OF THE WILD

Loretta: I didn't want to do that picture because I thought it was not a big enough part for me. Boring I thought. And same old leading lady stuff I'd done forever. Frankly, I had read the story as a child, and I knew it was a dog story really, the dog and the man. I wanted something beyond looking pretty and saying, "Yes," and "No."

(Ed and Loretta looking at a picture...)

Loretta: This is Reggie Owens. And I guess this is just the camera crew....This is Jack Oakie and Clark and I. Do I have a billy club in my hand? They used to shock me......finally, the electrician gave me a little billy club and that billy club went everywhere with me.

(End of picture gazing)

Frances Early went with me as a companion. And she was just darling. I was just crazy about her. She is a friend of Sally's.

Ed: What was Jack Oakie like?

Loretta: Darling. But always kidding. Never serious. I never saw him serious.

Ed: I always felt that there was something sad under his playful persona.

Loretta: Isn't that often the case with the happy-go-lucky types?

Ed: Yeah, that's a good point. .... How long were you up there?

Loretta: Nine weeks! And we got about six days work out of those nine weeks. It was so COLD! The main lodge had burned down, and we were living in the summer building which housed the servants, the maids, everybody. The studio was very foolish sending everyone up there knowing what the weather was like. It was 10 degrees below zero sometimes. When you come from Southern California, your blood isn't used to that.

Anyway, for the first couple of days, nobody could go outside, and your nose is closed to here and your eyes are closed.....it was so cold. You wore glasses for protection and then they'd say, "We're going to shoot now; take the glasses off...." You couldn't breathe!

The rooms we stayed in were only big enough for a bed. Fannie and I had a double room so there were two beds, a thing between it, a dresser, that was it. And a closet. It was just paper thin because it was for the summer time. They had tiny kerosene lamps, those little round things with the holes at the top and the smoke and.....and, oh, terrible. And tiny little halls with windows at the end of each hall and a window in each room. It was really nine weeks of absolute torture, physically speaking, for creature comforts.

The building where we ate, another temporary building, was about a half a block away and they strung a rope from one building to the other so you wouldn't get lost in the blinding snow. And they had a recreation room, which......... finally, I think there were too many men on our location and only about five or six women. They got rowdy and the studio was annoyed and decided no liquor. Well, it was so cold up there they *had* to have liquor.

The studio decided that only the cast could have liquor. Well, first of all, I didn't drink anything, and Frances didn't either to speak of. Jack could put it away if he wanted to, and Reggie was a nominal drinker, and so was Clark.

Ed: He wasn't a hard drinker? Clark Gable?

Loretta: Oh, I don't think so. Not nearly as hard as John Wayne. At least not that I saw.......anyway, when Clark heard about this, he hit the ceiling. He said, "What the hell do you mean only the actors? These poor guys are there in the cold......."He called the production manager, and I could hear him because I was in my room and the walls were so thin. He said, "I want ten cases of scotch. I'm ordering this myself. I'm going to drink it all. Jack

Oakie wants ten cases of bourbon. I just asked Miss Young.....she wants some gin and vodka." He ordered ten cases of everything......of course, they wouldn't say no to him.

Ed: Right....

Loretta: So they did. They ordered all this liquor and every night when the crew would come from work, the fellas would line up and take what they wanted. And we'd just pass it out.

Ed: This wasn't Warner Brothers?

Loretta: 20th Century......it was Daryl Zanuck, yes, 20th Century before he went to Fox.

Ed: Oh, I got it. I knew it was the end of something. Okay, that's it.

Loretta: Before he went to Fox. And every man grew a beard. They had to. And they'd come in at night with ice cycles hanging on their beards, and if they had eyebrows, the same thing.

One day, they finally said, "Well, we're going to a covered set." The covered set was (laugh) me, in a blanket, because I had fallen in the water, and they built this big fire, and she's trying to keep warm, see.

Ed: ....and she has to speak very philosophically......

Loretta: (shivering) va-va-va-fa-fa..... At least I had a fur parka on before, but for this I had a little blanket around me. I tried saying my lines for about an hour. Finally, I started to cry. Tears just rolled....

Ed: Oh, I know what you mean. I've lived in cold weather. I know what you're talking about...

Loretta: Bill Wellman said, "Oh, for God's sake, we've got a crying actress on our hands..." I said, "I'm sorry, I can't act. I'm going to my room." I just left and put my parka on and went to my room, got into bed and stayed there.

Sometimes, we went ten days at a time without any work done, and everyone was going stir crazy. One day I said, "If we're not going to shoot tomorrow, I want a car and driver, and I'm going to Seattle to see my grandfather (Royal). Clark came right behind me and said, "What's more, I'm going with her." And Jack Oakie comes up and says, "What's more, I'm going with them." And Reggie comes up and says, "They're going to make room for me, too."

They said, "Wonderful, take the day off." So we did. Clark and Jack and I wound up together. I called Grandpa and arranged to meet him for both lunch and dinner the next day. So we had lunch, Clark, Grandpa, Jack and I. I don't remember where Elizabeth was, his wife. She was a ding-a-ling. She wasn't with us. I did a little shopping, and then we all went to dinner. By the time we got back to Grandpa's apartment, there was a message for us, "Come back; they're going to shoot tomorrow." It was a three hour drive. I said, "Oh, Clark, you know they're not going to shoot tomorrow."

Anyway, we had to go back. Of course, they didn't shoot the next day. Wellman said, "I have to stay up here. I don't know why you four can have such a good time. No, I want you back here." Petulant, you know....

Loretta: He treated his assistant director so badly on CALL OF THE WILD....I don't know why those men didn't kill him, but they were afraid to hit him because they were afraid that they'd kill him, and they'd go to jail for manslaughter ......He had a plate in his head, and he knew that nobody would touch him.....

Ed: I'm curious. I know you lived with this all your life, but when you're going out to eat at these places in Seattle, wasn't it a big deal for Loretta Young and Clark Gable to be in a restaurant?

Loretta: Oh, yes. Sure. The whole restaurant stopped, of course. And Grandpa was very proud introducing me, "This is my granddaughter..." And Clark Gable, oh my......of course, the women just UAAAA! all over the place.

One afternoon, Franny and I came back from lunch, and all these guys were down at the end of the hall. I heard them laughing and we went down, and I asked, "What's going on?" Jack said, "Come here. You got to see this." Clark said, "You won't believe your eyes." I looked out the window. Buck was this beautiful big St. Bernard. They had a stand-in for Buck who did all the long shots, and Buck did the close-ups, see. They treated that dog.....you never saw the kind of superstar attention that dog got. He had a heated trailer to wait in. We didn't! We were lucky to sit in a sleigh with a blanket around us. That dog must have weighed 200 pounds, and I weighed 109. And during our close-ups together, I swear the trainer trained him to just lean on me and push me out of the camera line. I finally got to the point where I said, "I can't handle it."

Anyway, we were all fed up with this dog........I parted my way to the window so that I could see what was going on. Here is Buck, out in the snow, and one man is patting his head and they are giving him an enema. I burst out laughing. I said, "That's the worst!" This dear dog......they wanted to keep him healthy and they were so gentle with him...........Oh, we got to laughing so much.....

We were there for eight or nine weeks. They finally brought us home. I know I did the water stuff on the back lot down here because I said, "I simply will not go into that water. I'm not going to kill myself...."

(Loretta discussing her relationship with Clark Gable versus Spencer Tracy)

Loretta: With Spencer, I felt much more serious because I didn't know the situation when we met, and then it went on for a long time; and I was involved with him before I really realized that he was married and that was it. I think we went together for a year and a half or two years, or maybe I've said it so many times, I just think it. With Clark, I knew he was married. I understood that he was unhappily married.

Ed: Which marriage was this?

Loretta: This was to Rhea Gable. Nevertheless, we never went out together. Well, we couldn't. He was married. However, when you're working on a picture, and you're that close together, you don't have to go *out* together......you are together, particularly when you're on location because you eat three meals together and you sleep in the same building.....not together. You're acting together all day long, and this goes on for nine weeks so there's plenty of time.....you could get fascinated with somebody. And I could very easily, I'm sure.....because he was fascinated with me. I don't know if I was really in love....I think I was still in love with Spencer, but apparently not enough to...... I don't know. There were so many barriers between us (Loretta and Gable). I was closer with Spencer....

SHANGHAI

Loretta: With Charles Boyer...

Ed: James Flood directed.

Loretta: Walter Wanger produced...and the clothes in that were beautiful....I got them from a little shop on 7th Street....

Ed: Was that shot at Paramount?

Loretta: It wasn't shot at Paramount. It was shot at a little studio.

Ed: It says, "Romance between a half caste; half Russian, half Chinese and an American girl....."

Loretta: ....actually, the absurdity, the reason why they couldn't get married or couldn't be in love was because his mother was a Chinese princess.....that's absurd. That was the big tear. That's why they couldn't be together.

Ed: I don't get it. Just because his mother had been Chinese?

Loretta: Well..... "never the twain shall meet" in those days...

Ed: Review: Both Boyer and Miss Young give remarkably good performances throughout....."

Loretta: ....well....

Ed: ....and you got top billing this time....whereas you didn't the first time with Boyer on CARAVAN.

Loretta: I made THE CRUSADES right after this....

Ed: Where did CALL OF THE WILD come in?

Loretta: Before.

Ed: Before SHANGHAI?

Loretta: Yes.

Ed: Because it was released a month later.

THE CRUSADES

Loretta: I remember when I walked on the set of THE CRUSADES.....we were two or three weeks late on SHANGHAI, Mr. De Mille said, "Well, my dear, I don't know whether to kiss you or kill you." That's a terrible beginning with Mr. De Mille because I had been a patsy to one director, and I didn't want to do it with another. So, I said, "I suggest you kiss me....because I'm not feeling too well, and I might burst into tears." He kind of smiled, and he said, "In that case, I'll be very gentle with you." From then on, he was. He was just marvelous.

Ed: Did you say in your FILMEX speech that he was one of your three favorite directors?

Loretta: I thought that he did what he did marvelously. I said to him one day......we were rehearsing.....I asked him, "Is this what you want?" He said, "Oh, Loretta, I don't know what I want. I've got thousands of people; that's why I hire very good actors......you know better what you want than I......I'll tell you if I like it or not." I asked, "Well, do you like it?" "Fine." That's all the direction he ever gave you.

That wasn't what I was fond of. What I thought he did a marvelous job of was presenting pageantry, evil versus good, and vice versa. He always gave enough of the evil to stimulate you and then prove it wrong.......

Ed: He wasn't one of your favorite directors as a performer......

Loretta: Oh, no. Because he didn't direct you. It was all kind of pageant with him. You know, if you looked like Berengaria (her character in the film), whatever you did was Berengaria.

One night we were on the back lot, and he had two expert archers, and there was a scene where Berengaria was supposed to go out on the battlefield and an arrow goes right by her. It was just when I was walking forward he wanted to do that.

I said, "Mr. DeMille, I'm very nervous about this." He said, "You don't have to be." I said, "Well, I really am, and I don't think I want to do this." He said, "I'm going to shoot the arrow so you know I'm not going to hit you......"

Ed: (laugh) (laugh)

Loretta: I looked at him and said, "*You're* going to shoot the arrow?" He said, "Yes. I'm very good at it." I said, "Oh, Mr. DeMille!" He said, "Don't worry, just go out there. Trust me. Trust me." Well, I did......He just missed my nose.....I could hear it go by, and the quiver on the wall when it hit. I just stood there. I thought, "If he says, 'Cut this and do it again,' I'll kill him!" I finally said, "I'll never do that again." He said, "You don't have to. You were perfect and so was I," and off he went. He was an excellent archer. But he was just enough of a show-off that I was saying, "My God, if he had missed a quarter of an inch, there goes my face,"....... you know.......

But no.....as a personal director......no.

Ed: He was more like the producer, wasn't he? In terms of the kind of material he dealt with and the proportions of it.

Loretta: Well, he saw the whole thing. He was the director-producer. I mean, he didn't have any producer above him, and he also did a lot of the writing and acting and everything else (laugh) (laugh).

There was also ......there were two girls sitting outside my dressing room......it was hot and it was lunch time...

Ed: Paramount......

Loretta: Yes..... 12 o'clock or 1 o'clock and my door was open, and I was inside. One said to this girlfriend of hers..... "I wonder when that old bald-headed, son-of-a-bitch is going to call lunch"..... And out of the blue ......over the microphone loud speaker comes, "Young lady! The young lady sitting by Miss Young's dressing room door.....would you mind repeating what you just said?"

Of course, she just froze and got scared. I thought, "I wonder what she's going to do. Maybe she can't." I don't know how he heard her unless...... unless he had microphones stashed all over. ....He had a megaphone himself. He said, "Young lady! I repeat, would you kindly repeat what you just said?"

I said, "You better do it. He won't let up on you." And so she stood up and said, "I just said, 'I wonder when that old....bald-headed son-of-a-bitch is going to call lunch." He said, "*Lunch*! ....back in an hour!" That's all he ever said to her. (laugh) (laugh)

Ed: ...ah, great.... What about Henry Wilcoxon?

Loretta: I thought he was marvelous in the picture, and I don't think he has ever done anything as good since. He was perfectly cast in it, and he looked exactly like Richard the Lion......his face kind of looked like a lion. He was a great big man. The chemistry between us was very good......on the screen.......

(laugh) I remember one time we were doing a scene, and I thought I was acting.....I don't know what I was doing. We were talking to each other, and I paused.....he stopped and said, "What's the matter, did you forget your line." I just looked at him and burst out laughing, and I said, "No. I'm acting." And he said, "Oh." Mr. DeMille asked, "Why's she laughing....what did you say?" Then I had to repeat it for the whole company. Of course, they just fell apart. From then on.....he said to me...."You can pause for ten minutes, I'm never going to open my mouth, ever....."

He was very serious. We were all very serious and working very hard. DeMille took himself quite seriously, and therefore everybody else had to, if you wanted to get along with him.

There wasn't too much joking on the set.....

Ed: Specifically to that set....... or is that what you're saying about most sets.....

Loretta: Well, no. There was not much practical joking. There is a great difference. Tay Garnett was laughing all the time, and his pictures show it. That came right through. They were so easy and so much fun. He did LOVE IS NEWS and CAUSE FOR ALARM. We had a marvelous time making LOVE IS NEWS because Tay was fun to be around. He did not take himself too seriously.

Was THE CRUSADES in color?

Ed: No....

Loretta: Should have been. I remember still pictures of myself in color in CRUSADES that were gorgeous with that honey-colored silk hair, it went below my knees and there was a green dress .... I can still see that beautiful color. The wedding outfit in CRUSADES was cream colored with pearls all over and the crown and cream-colored hair....Oh! Gorgeous!

Ed: These pictures that were black and white.....how did they choose colors?

Loretta: They didn't. They just used anything. Red was not particularly good because it went to no-color. I know the red dress that Bette Davis wore in JEZEBEL was a kind of maroonish brown, because I borrowed it from Western Costumers to wear in a show I did about Charlotte Bronte.

Ed: For television?

Loretta: Yes. And it was a strange color, but they tested all colors and that looked red. Red just loses it.....hardly any outline in black and white (films). The cameraman didn't like stark white because it might vibrate.....and red would bleed in color (films) so they didn't want it to run in your face. Now they seem to photograph anything. The film is so much more sensitive now. On location the last time (LADY IN A CORNER, TV movie, 1989) there wasn't any more light than in this room now. Maybe a reflector or something. I asked, "Where's your lighting?" He said, "It's all in the film now." It's so sensitive. And it's wonderful to work that way because you don't have to keep in your key light.

Ed: Key light?

Loretta: The source of light. The major key light. I'd have to look in that direction because if I didn't, say, whatever nose I had, I'd lose it.

Ed: The cameraman would be controlling the light directly on you......

Loretta: Yes. And then they have fill lights on the side. And sometimes they'd have what they call an eye light on the camera, and it just picks up the eyes, and I don't know whether it takes circles away or what it does. I think it depends on the height of the key light.

Ed: Where was it best for you......shooting down a little?

Loretta: A little……a little

Ed: In color, how did that change in terms of make-up?

Loretta: Not much. I think you wore less in color. I know I wore less than I did in black and white. Lipstick had to be lighter, or course. Lipstick should always be lighter than what we used to wear, anyway. That blood red just looks awful. I like the way women look today. They don't look like they have any lipstick on but their mouth is there. I like that look.

Ed: …..your lips now, very natural…

Loretta: Oh, I've licked all the lipstick off. I put it on this morning, and I haven't put any more on….what time is it…..5:00? It's worn off.

1936

THE UNGUARDED HOUR

Ed: Sam Wood was the director. Did you get along with him?

Loretta: Well, who wouldn't? He was a wonderful director, and it was just a little program picture…

Ed: Tell me more about Sam Wood…..

Loretta: Tall, kind of gray hair, and ......been with them (Metro-Goldwyn-Mayer) forever. His reputation was excellent.

Ed: ....kind of an Agatha Christie kind of script. English accent......

Loretta: Oh, one of my phony English accents. I was Lady.........The only accent that I really got and I got it so well, I couldn't do any other one.....and that was THE FARMER'S DAUGHTER. But then I had an expert teach me. She took it away from Ingrid and gave it to me and she, herself, was Swedish, so it worked very well......

Ed: You had a different look in UNGUARDED HOUR.....your hair pulled back. Very pretty but a different look.....

Loretta: I don't know. Adrian's clothes were very high-style and I thought they were wonderful.

I think it was UNGUARDED HOUR that I was doing.....Spencer was doing SAN FRANCISCO with Jeanette McDonald and Clark, and both of them (Tracy and Gable) walked (laugh) on my set. Anyway, I was delighted to see them and, of course, very flattered that they would openly walk off their set and come over. Everybody stopped what they were doing and everyone had a good time. Anyway, it was very pleasant. That's all. They just came on the set to say hello.

Part Seven: 20th Century-Fox

PRIVATE NUMBER

ED: 20th Century-Fox

Loretta: ....with Bob Taylor. Patsy Kelly....we worked a lot together. Basil Rathbone played the butler...

Ed: ....it says: "Robert Taylor and Loretta Young are a hot combination at the moment...."

Loretta: Well, we weren't too hot because we only did that one. He was under contract to Metro and I was under contract to 20th Century-Fox, but we worked well together. It was the story of a maid who falls in love with the young man of the household. I think Constance Bennett had done it originally, and it was a remake, and I don't remember much about it except I was smart enough not to get a crush on Robert Taylor because he was going with Barbara Stanwyk at the time, and I didn't want my heart broken......he wasn't one bit interested in me.

Ed: Robert Taylor seemed like a ......

Loretta: ....a robot.

Ed: ....like a farmer.....and to me, that's a good thing......something earnest about him....

Loretta: He was very good-looking for the day. As I look back on him, he was too "candy box cover". He had a widow's peak, and it was black hair, looked like it was drawn on, but at that time he was......

I felt kind of sorry for him because I remember one night, I think it was Mervyn LeRoy's house for a big dinner party, and he was always kind of isolated. The women didn't pay too much attention to him because Barbara had him......and boy did she have him....and the men were jealous of him so they didn't pay any attention to him.....and so usually, unless he was sitting right there with her......he wasn't a very good conversationalist. I think he was just too good looking.

Ed: He was very conservative, politically.

Loretta: Oh, yes. Well, we all were.

Ed: Here is something I read....... Robert Taylor.....you used to drive him crazy because you'd go to the mirror right before you'd do a scene.....

Loretta: Yes, I knew it drove everybody crazy...

Ed: But he thought it was worth it when he saw......

Loretta: It must have been very annoying because they'd say, "Ready..." I'd say, "Fine, two minutes" ......and I'd go to the mirror and check my hair because I did my own hair....."Okay, ready." But they had that split second where they're standing there, doing nothing. So I can understand how it would have been very annoying.

Thank heaven nobody told me that it was annoying. Otherwise, I'm sure I would have felt uncomfortable doing it, and therefore not have paid so much attention.

Ed: ....so interesting.....

Loretta: It's true. I was a star. And everybody can wait. That's why you're a star.

Ed: ....it's just what happened......not a power play.....

Loretta: Oh, no. Oh, no. If you are a star, you don't have to act like a star. You *are* a star. You know that by how much money you get; you know that by where your name appears....

But, really, every other star went to their dressing room to do it. I saved them a good 20 minutes. There was a mirror right there, and I took one quick check.

A star cannot claw its way and stay there. It has to be molded, and what talents you have have to be used to the best of your ability.....and then somebody has to keep you there because there are too many barracudas in the sea.....

Ed: That brings me to a "Star" kind of question........at what point did you have the prerogative of choosing your own cameraman?

Loretta: It must have been at Twentieth....I know when I did CALL OF THE WILD and ROTHCHILD and I didn't have that prerogative yet......but it must have been at 20th Century-Fox. I don't know why......I guess because other stars were doing it ......because I was never displeased with how I looked. I always thought I looked pretty good. I don't know why that made such a big difference .....I guess it made me feel like a star. I can understand the director....that's different. Because they can make or break your performance.

Ed: So eventually, you were able to choose the cameraman and the still photographer?

Loretta: Yes, and the director. Once you decide on that, these are what they call "brownie points" that the agent knows what to ask for. When I started freelancing, it was very simple, because if they wanted *me*, they accepted all these little do-dads that went along with it.

RAMONA

Ed: I read that they held it up when they decided to make it in color..... 20th Century-Fox's first three-strip color..........

Loretta: Oh, really? Good. Because it made the picture. Otherwise it wouldn't have been anything. It was such a pretty picture.

I loved RAMONA.

They called me and said I was going to do RAMONA and I said.....".Great." That's all I remember. I heard later that Rita Hayworth had asked to do it, but she wasn't under contract to Zanuck. Rochelle Hudson also wanted to do it, but I'm awfully glad she didn't, because she wouldn't have been good at all. I was very good in it.

The first three or four days' rushes came in, and I wore a black wig because she is Indian, and I used to take these little soft hairs out around here and push them back over the wig so you wouldn't get that hard wig line. And there was a little halo around here. They sent this woman down.....I don't know.....electrolysis or something to take out all those little red hairs that showed. And I was going to let them do it, like a fool. All I had to do was pull the wig down a little bit further and not pull them out, see. Those first three or four days would have to be reshot.

Anyway, this woman came down to Escondido where we were on location, and she said, "Just lie down and just relax a little bit," and she started putting needles in my head and turning on the electricity. She did it once, and I said, "That's it. Please take them out, take them out, please." She took them out. And, I said, "Shave me, but she's not going to do that with me." Lucille was her name; I had her for years. And she did something or other; I don't know what she did. And then she put a few pencil lines and that took care of it.

We went down on location to do that. That wasn't long after Judy was born. I remember I had a bungalow, and they put in a cook.

Pat Palimount was my driver. We had a trailer, and we went back and forth all the time. We were there for ten or eleven weeks. It was a wonderful location. I enjoyed it. They'd start at 7:00 in the morning. They wanted the morning sun. I said, "I don't care how early, but I will only work eight hours.....so if you want me by 7:00, then I'll go home by 4:00. Eight hours.....that's it." "Fine." They agreed to that.

One day, it was about ten minutes to 4:00, and I said....to the assistant director..."You better hurry up because in ten minutes I'm leaving." "Well, we've lined up for another shot." This was a wonderful director, Henry King. He did SONG OF BERNADETTE, wonderful. And he was a very important man anyway. He behaved like a director and looked like a director, a big fellah.

Ed: American?

Loretta: Yes. He picked on, I thought, Kent Taylor, terribly, because he wanted him to be a better actor than he was. He shouldn't have cast him then....He was wonderful looking, and I thought he was adequate for the part. There was no big acting to do in it as long as you looked it....

Anyway, I said, "You better warn him." He said, "I'm not going to warn Henry King about anything." I said, "Well, I'm warning you.....at 4:00 I'm off." Now, when I left the set (laugh) four, five, or six people trail along after me. Pat would go get the car...that's one....Then the hairdresser, Lucille, two. Then Carrie Cline, the wardrobe lady....then my stand-in would leave. Then my make-up lady would leave......because they all just worked for me. So they'd all just trail.....when I left. You knew I was leaving because this whole entourage went along, see.

Henry and Don Ameche were coming to my bungalow for dinner that night. I had gone home and had a nice nap and a bath, and by the time they got there around 6:30, we all had a little glass of wine and Henry never said one word (about Loretta's leaving) all during dinner. We talked, and we laughed. Finally, everyone went home around 9:00. They had to get up early in the morning. Henry said, "Loretta, can I speak to you for a minute?" I said, "Yes, Henry." So he let everyone go home, and he shut the door, and he said, "Now, sit down." He said, ..."Nobody *ever* in my entire career as a director, has *ever* walked off of one of my sets without my knowing it, and I want you *never* again, as long as you live to do it to me again. I was thoroughly embarrassed. You had no right to disregard my position as a director......"

Well, he went on in the most precise, honest, factual way, and I looked at him and said, "Henry, you're so right. I'm so embarrassed now. I don't know what I was thinking of." He said, "I do. You were thinking of yourself.....and, if you are going to work with me, you have to have more respect for me and the company. I stood up like a fool and said, 'I'm ready for Miss Young now,' over the loudspeaker and was given the reply,'Miss Young has already left the set, Mr. King!' What position do you think that put me in?" I said, "Not a very good one, I must say. And, I'm sorry; it won't happen again" .....and it never did. We were equally careful not to infringe on the other person.

He did it so quietly and so honestly that it was a great lesson. Not only did I not do it to him, but I never did it to any other director. Even on the television show......the first person I would say good-night to.....was the director. "I'm going now, okay?" "Yes, okay, fine."

There was another bad moment with Henry......We were on location, and the property man had the wheat fields just right, and if they weren't, they'd put a little thing in it and string it up. I didn't know it was going to be photographed later, and when I got out of my car with my entourage following, like little chickens, we made this big path all the way through the wheat field......just ruined this whole beautiful wheat field. They had to go back with their sticks and strings and do it all over again.........

Ed: What was going on in your personal life.......

Loretta: I was going with Eddie Sutherland at the time. I was going with him .....only because there was no one else who interested me, and he was, as I said......a charming man, lovely manners, a nice escort. Very well respected in our business and that was it. But I was never in love with Eddie Sutherland, or never did I have a crush on him.

Ed: Was that whom you were rushing back to in the trailer.....

Loretta: No, I wasn't rushing back to a man, I assure you. I was rushing back to get a break from the location. The trailer! I thought I was going to get a nice nap on the way back, and it threw me all over the place. It was just awful. I only tried that once. I didn't do it again. But every two or three weeks, I would just leave on purpose.

My eyes were burned by plate light, they tell me when I was a child, and I had to spend two weeks in a dark room with meat on my eyes. Plate lights were those things that spark. I was burned twice.....again on CALL OF THE WILD in front of an open fire. We got on RAMONA and in those days, color.....well, the little eye spot which they used in the camera just to pick up the little sparkle in the eye......it was an open arc right over the camera, and it got so my eyes would just turn red ......just like that.....and I was using 1/1000% adrenaline in my eyes to squeeze the blood vessels out for close-ups. I got so I couldn't get through a close-up....the blood just ran right back into them again.

Finally, I got a cold sore so it gave us about ten days of not working. And it was the only thing that seemed to save my eyesight, because when I finished, I went to the doctor and he said, "You have to retire for a year.....your eyes are so mistreated at this point, with all the intensity of the light......"

I said, "I can't retire for a year." He said, "You have to. You won't have any eyes left." Anyway, I think it was four or five months before I went back to work......"

Ed: I thought you were beautiful in RAMONA....

Loretta: I think so, too, now.

Ed: Any favorite scene in the movie?

Loretta: There's one lovely scene......when the girl first finds out that she's not her mother (referring to the woman she grew up thinking was her mother). It's a whole close-up, and I was backing up, and the camera went with me. It was the purity and innocence on her face that was attractive......

Ed: ......really you hanging by that tree......or a double?

Loretta: Oh, that was me. That wasn't anything. I thought, really, between you and me, the only good scene in the whole picture was the last scene when he (Don Ameche's character) gets shot. I mean .... it was wonderful because it was so ruthless and cruel. It just destroyed their whole lives. He was so cold with it. I think it was John Carradine, wasn't it?

Ed: Yeah. What about Don Ameche?

Loretta: I thought he looked marvelous. I liked the black wig on him and the thing around it....

Ed: I thought he looked more Mexican than Indian......

Loretta: Yes, he did. Well, he is Italian, so. He certainly looked like Alessandro.

Loretta: After RAMONA, Zanuck wanted me to do LLOYDS OF LONDON. This was another second lead, or another half-baked lead. I was looking for women's roles, and he was just using me as the leading lady……..

Anyway, I walked out of it. I wouldn't do it. Of course, he took me off salary. That's what they'd do. I don't think they could keep you off indefinitely. They could keep you off for the period of the picture, though, then tack it on to the end of your contract.

LADIES IN LOVE

Loretta: Oh, we had the best time. There was nothing exciting about that. Janet Gaynor, perfectly professional.

Ed: She had top billing….

Loretta: Ah, ha. She had it in her contract. She came to work at 9:30 and she quit at 5:30…. *but* she was ready at 9:30. No curlers in her hair……she was on the set, ready to work. I think the rest of us resented for the first couple of days when they let her go at 5:30, but they managed this without too much trouble because they would do her close-ups first….the director was a very sophisticated man…..Griffith. He knew how to handle little sticky situations like that….

Constance Bennett was a *big* star but I knew and liked Connie, and she knew and liked me.

Ed: ……on her way down…

Loretta: Yes, she was…..

Ed: You were billed over her.....

Loretta: But she had been a big star, and she still wanted to work. The parts were good and Simone Simon played a young girl in it, and she behaved perfectly normal and nicely on the set, too. I think everyone was so careful not to be the bad guy that it all worked well. Tyrone Power was my boyfriend in the picture. Paul Lucas played Connie's friend, and I think Don Ameche played......it was a nice little picture......there was nothing extraordinary about it.....

Ed: Simone Simon.....Daryl Zanuck. His little pet. She didn't go anywhere, did she?

Loretta: No, of course not. He didn't know what to do with women. She could have succeeded at Metro because she was a good actress.......but you have to let it develop. You can't shove it down the audience's throat.

Ed: Was it a success?

Loretta: Oh, I think so.

1937

LOVE IS NEWS

Loretta: Tyrone Power. All we did was kid and laugh and make fun, and the camera rolled all the time.

Ed: Were you dating him at this point?

Loretta: Oh, yes. As much as I could. As much as he'd ask me. In those days, the woman......you had to wait until the guy asked you, see. But believe me....I wouldn't have given him one moment's peace if I hadn't been embarrassed. But you had to sit and wait until they called you. You didn't even make suggestions such as....."Well, there's going to be a party next Saturday night.....are you going?....would you like to escort me?"

Anyway, he was also interested in Sonja Henie at that time, I believe. She had just come under contract to the studio, and the studio pushed it, I'm sure, because the studio department needed anything at all to build us all up.

Tyrone dropped me in a puddle (while filming) and really did drop me in a puddle. He said, "You know, it's only two feet." You can hurt yourself just as much from two feet as you can from ten. I was smart enough to turn on my side so that my hip took it, not my backbone.

There's a very interesting scene .... the last scene in the picture. Tay Garnett was really such a professional and a wonderful director, and he knew when he had something good that just happened. We were on location at Warner Brothers on their back lot. I came down half a block and then a full block and then into a drugstore and into a telephone booth. She was running away from him, and he was following her. He had all the pedestrians and the traffic ....and the camera was on a boom, and when it came into the drug store and into the telephone booth, it came up into a close-up of these two. All one shot, and they had lined it up all morning, all afternoon, and it was about 4:00 in the afternoon. The cameraman said, "If we don't get it now, we're not going to get it because the sun's going." "So, all right, fine."

We rehearsed it plenty of times.....we were shooting it......right in the middle of the thing I fell, and Tyrone caught up with me ......he was not supposed to. So, anyway, instead of stopping, he got up with me and tried to help me up. I said, "Oh, leave me alone.....just don't bother following me....."I took off again. The cameraman was smart enough to just hang in there, and Tyrone took off too, and he let just enough distance to allow me to stay ahead.....the camera just went on, and we went into the phone booth and the camera came into the phone booth, and we finished the picture.

Somebody said, "We have to take that again." I said, "Why?" and Tay said, "Why?" and Tyrone said, "Why?" The assistant said, "Well, you fell down." Tay said, "Yeah.....so?"

Ed: You did that final scene at Warner Brothers.......but it was a 20th Century-Fox ......

Loretta: Because they would rent different locations from different studios. They had a New York street at Warner

Brothers that he liked better than the New York street at 20th Century-Fox, so we just did it over there. I'm sure they paid for it.

Ed: George Sanders was in that movie......

Loretta: Don Ameche was too.

Ed: Don Ameche was Tyrone Power's boss.....also Stepin Fetchit.....

Loretta: (laugh) (laugh) He was darling. Wasn't Stepin Fetchit in KENTUCKY, too? I don't remember him in this picture, but I just loved him. And he was just the way he was. At least that's the way he acted in the studio. Maybe he was in character and didn't want to get out.

Ed: "Miss Young looks and plays well with Power...."

Loretta: We had a marvelous time on that. I was just Barbara Hutton (Woolworth heiress) as far as I was concerned......

Ed: .....but more of a sense of humor....

Loretta: Oh yes. She (Loretta's character)played all sorts of jokes on this poor thing. In fact, she announces to the press that they're engaged. Imagine having the guts to do that?

Ed: You were twenty-three when you made this movie. You had such sophistication......Somehow you had leaped......from TRUTH ABOUT YOUTH. You would have been seven years older.....

Loretta: Seven years as an actress is a *long* time if you're working all the time.......

Ed: Twenty-three is still pretty young....

Loretta: Oh, yes. Well, it is.....but not if you've been working since you were twelve or four, see.

Ed: To me, that movie is kind of the beginning of the person that I know as you.

Loretta: Probably. Yes. She was more sophisticated and more.......And she dared to do a lot of things that were not just a leading lady part. That's probably why I liked it. The clothes were marvelous, I think. Irene did the clothes. Was that before or after IT HAPPENED ONE NIGHT? We used to kid about the stories being so much alike, which they were......

Ed: It was after........

Loretta: Well, you get a good picture and ten or twelve people go out and make the same story with different casts.....same story.....

(Doing still pictures from movie scenes)

Loretta: After each scene set-up that you would do, whether it was a long shot, medium shot, close-up, after each one, they'd take stills....

Ed: What did they do with all those pictures?

Loretta: Oh, use them in movie magazines....

When the still man would come in, everybody used to moan and groan, "Ahhh, here comes the still man...." I don't know how the poor thing had any ego left .....but I was very interested in all the stills, and each day before he would go to the publicity department, he would bring them to me, and I just loved them....and I'd order as I'd go along....

(Referring to still pictures with Tyrone Power)

When you're doing still pictures and there's music playing, and if you have a crush on him anyway and he has a crush on you.....there's an aura. Of course, I don't think anybody can look into the camera and be romantic because you're looking at the camera, and the people are looking right back at you and you're going to be conscious of them. In a romantic shot, your mind needs to be someplace else.

Ed: Did you ever wear costumes from movies into the gallery (studio photo gallery)?

Loretta: Oh, yes. For poster art. After the picture, usually the whole cast, you had the whole day. If Tyrone Power and Don Ameche and I were in a picture, we would go to the gallery and do portraits of all of us in the morning ....of each of us together and then separately for that one picture and in the afternoon do poster art, and that usually involved the three of us until we were exhausted.....

Of course, I had *my* hairdresser and *my* wardrobe lady and *my* make-up person there.....Tyrone had his....the place was jammed with people. I don't know how anybody could concentrate. It would get so that when I was doing portraits, I would go alone.....the less people there the better....for portraits because you could concentrate a little bit more....

CAFÉ METROPOLE

Loretta: That was another love story with Tyrone, and I was just pleased to be around him. I think at that time we were dating...

Ed: Any run-ins with Mr. Griffith?

Loretta: Not that I know of. If there were, I've forgotten them.

Ed: Adolph Menjou....

Loretta: He was known for being very stingy. For four or five pictures, I had been paying for coffee and donuts for the crew, and everybody expected it. If they were going to work on a picture with Loretta, they didn't bother eating breakfast at home because they could get it on the set. One time, Adolph Menjou was drinking his coffee and eating a donut and I was sitting right next to him. He said, "I don't know where in the hell this coffee and these donuts come from. Some jerk must be springing for this." I said, "I'm that jerk. I pay for this." He said, "Oh, Loretta, you shouldn't be doing things like that. You're never going to make any money doing it that way," and he continued to eat them every morning after that.

He dressed beautifully, and one day he announced that he'd be bringing some suits to the set. He brought them and put them on a rack, and he had price marks all over them. He was selling them. He wasn't giving them away.

Ed: Gregory Ratoff was an actor in this one.

Loretta: Yes. He was good, too. I knew Gregory well. He was one of Daryl Zanuck's pets, part of his entourage. Daryl could be very cruel to those men.....but through him they got a chance to be a director ......

Ed: Gregory Ratoff was Russian, right?

Loretta: Yes.....gray hair and pudgy and kind of watery eyes. Married to a perfectly beautiful woman, an actress......Eugenie Leontovich. I first saw her in a play in London.....

Ed: Was CAFÉ METROPOLE like GRAND HOTEL?

Loretta: It was, kind of. But it wasn't nearly as good as GRAND HOTEL, of course......

Ed: a hit?

Loretta: I don't think those pictures ever were a failure because they didn't cost that much. It was a program picture. It was romantic, and people went to see them. People used to just go the movies, you know. They didn't pick a movie, they just.....

Ed: Ratoff was the original author......he had a leading role.

Loretta: Yes, we had scenes together....

Ed: Review: "Loretta Young was the headstrong heiress..."

Loretta: I told you, it was the same story, just different casts......and sometimes the same cast....Tyrone.......see, the pictures that we played together were ......kind of little nonsense pictures. Love stories. Unimportant love stories. Kind of light things. Uh, supposedly comedies.

Ed: LOVE IS NEWS sure was... You know, that reminded me of a Cary Grant/Katharine Hepburn type of movie.

Loretta: Well, they were all trying to copy them I think at that time, to tell you the truth. I think it started with THE AWFUL TRUTH with Irene Dunne and Cary Grant, and it was that kind of charming but flip sort of comedy.

(Loretta on Daryl Zanuck)

Zanuck was a *wonderful* executive of a studio because he was ruthless. So he ran a very tight, very good studio. He was a fine showman. He started a whole era in the motion picture industry.....LITTLE CAESAR and all those....

Ed: ....as a writer at Warner Brothers, right?

Loretta: Yes, he (Zanuck) wasn't a very good writer, but he had ideas anyway, and when he went from First National to Warner Brothers, he did run the studio. He was ruthless. No emotions, no sentiment, no feelings at all. He'd say, "You're fired," "You're in," "You're out......" It was just like that.

We didn't get along at all, not at all. All we did was fight when we met. I would be at his house for these Sunday night suppers, but that was his wife's doing and only because I was in the *in-group* at the time.

Ed: Why did he sign you on?

Loretta: Because I made money for him, and I was cheap.

He never made a good woman's picture. He was absolutely insensitive toward women. In his private life, he chose little things (young women) that he could use and misuse. For some of them, that's how they got to be starlets; they weren't in it for the relationship. Finally, I guess he got tired of playing around, and Virginia, his wife, in the warmth of her heart, took him back and nursed him until he died.

(Loretta on Shirley Temple)

Ed: Did you ever have anything to do with Shirley Temple? I know you never made a movie with her.....

Loretta: No. She was adorable, wasn't she?

Ed: But you were there at the same time.....

Loretta: Ah-hum. She was a little queen. We all realized that she was unique, and she was. There had never been anyone like her before, and there never will be anyone like her. She couldn't do anything wrong. She could sing, right; she could dance, right, she could act, right; she could look cute, right. She was right as a child; then she lost it. She didn't lose it.....she just didn't grow into.....children usually disappear into a grownup......she didn't.

Ed: I guess I'm curious. Were you at all jealous of Shirley Temple?

Loretta: Oh, no....

Ed: Because she was the biggest money maker at the studio....

Loretta: Oh, that didn't make any difference. We didn't care about that. No, I was having a good time doing what I was doing. Strange enough, if you're happy doing what you're doing......oh, it doesn't matter what anyone else does......how big or how anything....as long as you're fulfilled inside. And I was doing what I wanted to do.....except I wanted bigger and better parts, so the minute I could get out from under contract to 20th Century-Fox, then I went on to get THE FARMER'S DAUGHTER and THE BISHOP'S WIFE, RACHEL AND THE STRANGER, and parts that I liked.

LOVE UNDER FIRE

I was very fond of Don Ameche, liked him very much, but could not work up a crush on him because I knew it would lead me nowhere. As I look back on it (LOVE UNDER FIRE), it was not one of my more exciting pictures because I knew that Don Ameche was happily married..... You can work up a crush or you can let it go....Don Ameche was not repulsive to me in any way. In fact, I probably could have had a fat crush on him, too. But why it wasn't more romantic was because it was not allowed in my mind to be a little bit in love with him.

I've heard actors say, it's just a job. "When you kiss someone, don't you feel anything?" "Oh, no, it's just a job." It's not quite true. At least it never was with me. Maybe if it had been, I would have learned to be a better actor, but....

Ed: Do you really mean that?

Loretta: People live in dreams and fantasies a great deal of their lives. Being an actor is a marvelous opportunity to actually do them and not be responsible for them, because you can only make love for three minutes as long as the camera is rolling, and passionate love if you want, and the minute the camera is over, no responsibility whatsoever. You call that just a job? Well, it's not quite "just a job," is it?

So then, for a romantic personality to begin with, to be presented with that kind of opportunity when you work with marvelously attractive males....the pick of the lot, usually, and they like you because they have to like you, because it says to in the script....

When you've made eighty or ninety motion pictures like I have made....I see now that most romantic actors do fantasize and do have a romantic, at least a tropism toward the other actor. You cannot tell me in WUTHERING HEIGHTS, no matter how much in love he (Laurence Olivier) was in love with Vivien Leigh, that he didn't have a tropism toward Merle Oberon.

Ed: Tropism?

Loretta: It means a going toward. You don't have to reach it. It's not even a consciousness...it's something that's instinctive almost before you know it. Then it turns into a yearning after it hits the mark.

WIFE, DOCTOR, NURSE

Loretta: That was Warner Baxter, Virginia..........beautiful blonde girl.......Bruce. She was really just darling. I was very fond of Virginia. She was scared to death of me, I think. In fact, she told me she was. I said, "Virginia, don't be. There's nothing to be scared of." She said, "You're so sure of yourself." She was very shy. She was a loan-out from Metro. She had been married to John Gilbert, I think.

She played in THE GREAT ZIEGFELD. She was "The most beautiful girl in the world" on the top..... a beautiful blonde girl. She was darling. She really was. She had been married to Ali Ipar who was in prison in Turkey for years, and she did everything she could to get him out. He was a Turk. When he finally did get out......she had waited all these years for him......I think he went off with someone else finally.....

I think she died at the Motion Picture Home. I think so. I think she had a sad and unhappy ending. Sally told me that she had invited her for dinner one night when they lived on Foothill and that she had sounded like she was pleased to come....Sally said, "Bring anyone you like." She said, "No, I'll just come alone, Sally." She did, but right after dinner she said to Sally, "Do you mind if I go home? I'm very uncomfortable." She was always uncomfortable. She was uncomfortable around me, and I think I made two or three pictures with her. I said, "Honey, just go along with me. I can't help it if I talk faster than you do....."

Ed: Warner Baxter...

Loretta: Very nice. Very pleasant. Charming to work with but I felt he was too old for both of us (Loretta and Virginia Bruce), but he had been a big star and we were just up and coming, see...

Ed: Walter Lang.....

Loretta: I loved Walter Lang, the director. A darling, darling man. He was married to Fieldsy who was secretary to Carole

Lombard, and they were all very sophisticated people. We did two or three pictures......SECOND HONEYMOON he did.

Ed: What distinguished him?

Loretta: I don't know. He was easy to work with. He liked me. Very simple: if they liked me, I liked them. I'm very easy to please, apparently.

Ed: You're so honest about that.....

Loretta: He (Walter Lang) was big with dark hair.....jovial....nice. Knew his job. Knew when to compliment you and when not to. He wasn't too sugary either. He was a friend of Polly Ann's and Carter's because he was at their wedding. I was the Maid of Honor, and I wore, strangely enough, a black print dress with a black hat that had all kinds of flowers, same colors that were in the dress. I didn't think it was extraordinary, but I guess it was because the best woman wears pink or blue or lavender, or whatever she wears....

He said to me......I came up to him, and he said, "I've never seen anything so great-looking as when you walked down that aisle in that *black outfit*! If I wasn't in love with someone else, I could be in love with that," see. But it was always free and easy.

SECOND HONEYMOON

Loretta: Another one with Tyrone. I remember the first line of dialogue.....I was laughing so hard, I could hardly say it. There was a dance......I had a beautiful, white net dress, and I'm out on this balcony and I'm alone.....anyway......he's in this white jacket, and he looks marvelous, and I guess it's somewhere in South America...

Ed: Florida...

Loretta: All right....he comes and sees her, and he just stops dead, and she looks at him and says, "Raoul" (laugh) (laugh). That was his name but I couldn't say it without laughing......and I don't know why. Why they didn't change it, I'll never know....

Ed: Tyrone Power was Raoul.....

Loretta: Raoul. Yes! Raoul! Anyway, he comes over, and they kiss and everything and then you find out that they were married to each other, but now they're both married to somebody else.

Ed: Lyle Talbot.

Loretta: No wonder I didn't like Lyle Talbot......how can you compare the two! Poor fella....sorry, I didn't mean that.......

Tyrone came on the set one day (laugh) (laugh) and they had plucked his eyebrows. He had this beautiful.....one great big beautiful bird went right across the top of his eyes. It was so beautiful. Now there was a blank space there. I said, "Tyrone! What have they done to your eyebrows?" He said, "Well, they just plucked them." I said, "Oh, Tyrone! They'll never grow back. You look just like a lady with her plucked eyebrows..." Tyrone was darling but he was also very vain, and I think that's why he agreed to letting them pluck his eyebrows.

Ed: Was this the movie in which you told me you walked away from the make-up people trying to put make-up on your arms?

Loretta: ......and neck and back and chest and everything. If you've got pancake make-up on it, it looks dull. It's powdery looking. If you don't have make-up on, your own skin shows and it shines. I don't think any men should use make-up on the screen.....

Ed: You never let them put make-up on your back?

Loretta: ....because I kept walking away from them. I wouldn't stand still long enough to let them get it on...... I just kept walking away

Ed: ....that's an impertinent actress.....

Loretta: (laugh) (laugh) yes......(laugh) (laugh)

Ed: Do you think other actresses would have done the same thing?

Loretta: I don't know......

Ed: That's what's so fascinating.......just how willful you were....

Loretta: Oh, yes. Oh, yes. You wouldn't last in this business if you weren't. Because if you did everything you were supposed to do, they would walk all over you, and you'd be a piece of putty, and *that's* what would show on the screen......a piece of putty.

(Myron Selznick becoming Loretta's Agent)

Loretta: I had a big fat fight with Zanuck; I don't know, another picture I wouldn't do. Dave Thompson was still my agent, and he had no clout in this business at all. And Myron Selznick had all the big stars and had great clout, see. Zanuck threatened me, "From now on, you'll go to Western Avenue. No. Better still, *out of the business entirely!*"

Ed: You'll go where?

Loretta: To Western Avenue. Western Avenue was a studio which Fox took over. The whole studio. Sol Wurtzel was head of that. My answer to that was, "Daryl, the only good picture I've ever done at this studio was at Western Avenue, and you were in Europe and Sol Wurtzel produced it. You had nothing to do with it......it was RAMONA!" And with that I walked out the door.

He did. He just cut me off salary. And he could have blackballed me right out of the business. I was seeing Eddie at the time......Sutherland, and of course, I'm telling him everything that happened because he's in the business. He said, "No, you can't fight this anymore yourself. You need Myron Seznick."

I said, "I can't stand Myron Selznick; he makes me sick to my stomach. I can't *stand him*. He's such a pig, and he's drunk all the time. Oh, he's a bore. He's terrible."

I remember one night, I had been dancing around the Tracadero with another friend of mine, and Myron Selznick was sitting at a table near the dance floor. I had on a cross, a beautiful gold chain and a cross as a necklace. The cross, I remember, was made of topaz, big topaz.

Myron was drunk as a coot, which he always was, and he kind of tugged at my dress as I went by. He said, "Hey Loretta, why do you insist upon being so obnoxiously Catholic?" And I was so damn mad at him, I said, "Well, come to think of it, why do you insist on being so *obnoxiously* Jewish?" And I turned away from him, and I said, "I'm never going to talk to that man again." Which I didn't. And he didn't to me except to give me dirty looks.

It was a year or so later when I'm having this conversation with Eddie. I said, "Eddie, no, I won't have anything to do with him." Eddie said, "I'm sorry, but you have to. He's the only person who can get you out of this jam at this studio because this is the third or fourth time you've walked out, and your reputation is getting that you're impossible to handle, and the first thing you know, *nobody* will take you."

"Well," I said, "I won't call him." He said, "I'll call him. I'll have him out here tomorrow morning. But let me call first to see if I can get him." He got him on the phone and said, "I'm at Loretta Young's house...." and he told him in a nutshell what the problem was, and he said, "*Would* you take this on for her?" He said, "Yes. Tell her I'll be there at 10 o'clock tomorrow morning." So he told me. I said, "Now, Eddie, you be here too. I can't handle this. I don't like that man."

"I'll be here," and he was.

The first thing Myron asked when he came in, "Have you got anything to drink in this house?" Well, we had a bar but we didn't have anything in it. The architect had built it into the house. I went upstairs and said, "Mama, he wants some *liquor.*" She said, "The only thing we have is port wine; he won't know the difference. It's alcohol." So, I put the bottle down and he drank it just like it was Scotch. Anyway, he heard the story.

I told him what had happened, how unhappy I was that Zanuck was using me as a stock girl. He said, "All right. What's your goal? What do you want?" I said, "I want to finish my contract and leave the studio. I don't want to work for Zanuck anymore." He arranged a meeting with Zanuck that afternoon.

Myron did all the talking. I think he did get me more money, but that wasn't my concern. I wanted better parts. Whatever the problems were, they were straightened out. What Myron did for me was take the whole burden of even thinking about Daryl Zanuck off my shoulders. Myron Selznick was the industry's first super-agent.

(Transition to Loretta doing product promotions.)

Ed: Lux soap?

Loretta: Yes, a lot of soap ads.

Ed: Print ads?

Loretta: Yes. They weren't anything. Johnny Engstead shot the pictures usually. You just went to his gallery. I don't know when I stopped doing advertising. I don't know why I stopped.

Ed: ......paid?

Loretta: No, you didn't. I think that's why I stopped.

Ed: Was this during the Zanuck years?

Loretta. It was during the Daryl Zanuck years.

Ed: Lux soap and Royal Crown...

Loretta: Yes, that's true. Both of them.

Ed: Anything else?

Loretta: Chesterfield cigarettes. I don't know if they gave me free Chesterfields or not. They must've. I know Lux soap we used to have all the time at the house because they said, "Well, we have to send it to you." I told them, "I don't use it." They said, "You have to use it because you say you use it."

Ed: Royal Crown......ever drink that?

Loretta: They had it in the house all the time. I didn't drink it.

1938

FOUR MEN AND A PRAYER

Loretta: I was in New York and I called the studio and said, "Do you want me to buy some clothes while I'm here?" The wardrobe department said, "Yes, buy anything you want and just let us know." I asked, "What's the limit?" They said, "It doesn't make any difference; just don't buy a sable coat." So I went to Bergdorf Goodman's; the sky was the limit and I bought a beautiful black coat with red fox all around it. I wore it in this picture. I had on a red fox hat.

Ed: I remember that....

Loretta: Well, I knew Jack (John Ford) personally, and I thought he was a marvelous director for men. But I didn't thrill him any more than he thrilled me working together, because he didn't know what to do with a woman. If the woman's part was a prostitute, and he could be rough and tough with it, then he knew how to handle it. Claire Trevor in STAGECOACH, I've not seen a better performance than that. Hers was just wonderful and so was Duke's. But that was his cup of tea. But this was not.....I don't know why he did it unless he needed the money.

Jack was a blowhard. He was the boss.

I told you one day that he didn't like it when I took too long to change clothes, and because I knew he didn't like it, I would just dawdle along......because he didn't inspire me to cooperate with him.......*at all*! Well, his way of hurrying me up was taking this whole dressing room which was on wheels and shake it......which was a stupid thing for him to do......if I had been standing up at the time, he could have knocked me off-----and hurt my back.....it was just insensitive of him.......because he was a rough man. I let out a yell and moaned and groaned as if I'd fallen and broken every bone in my body. I kept it up for three or four minutes. Finally, I quieted down and said, "I'd like the doctor to come over," which he did. He found nothing wrong, of course, and I came out to a subdued director. We both knew I was one up on him.

He drank an awful lot......so did all those around him.

Ed: How did he direct?

Loretta: ...."All right, we're ready to rehearse now...." the actors would feel their way around. "Is that all right?" "Yeah....fine." The men he gave a little bit more attention to.....

It was on that picture......wanting to make his point always and have everybody under his control and a little bit scared of him........a perfect example of what I mean......Richard Greene ...... we had started shooting the picture, and Richard Greene was held up in England doing another picture, I guess. He was on his way from England so he came on the set late. Maybe 10 days late....I don't know.

But anyway we were in the middle of doing something, and Jack says ..... "*Just a minute* ....everybody sit down. *Mr. Greene* has finally arrived from England. Come in Mr. Greene," and this poor fellow, who was scared to death anyway.....he was very young and very....gentle. Jack sat down in a chair and said, "My first question for you? *Are you a fairy*? ......That's the expression they used in those days.... Richard Greene turned as red as.....he didn't know what to say to him.

I said, "Jack, your behavior is entirely uncalled for. Mr. Greene, I suggest you come to my dressing room until Mr. Ford is ready to act like a gentleman."

We went to my dressing room and finally Jack sent a note of apology, but it was very exaggerated.....he couldn't just say, "I'm sorry," ......very obnoxious about it.

Ed: Was Richard Greene a fairy?

Loretta: Oh, no, totally not. That was just for control purposes.

Ed: Back up to when you said you were in New York. Do you remember what you were doing there?

All during my movie years, for instance, when I would go to New York just to play....from the time I was 20 on .... and I'd wear the most wonderful clothes. Lilly Dache was the big hat lady then, and a man named Jake who did furs; they would know I was coming and they'd just send over twenty hats or I could go pick out twenty hats. She'd send them all over to the Waldorf Towers or the Pierre, wherever I was staying....and he would send over four or five mink coats. A couple for the day, a couple for the evening, to wear as long as I wanted, and then if I wanted to buy them......fine.....if not, send them all back.

Ed: What did they get out of it?

Loretta: Publicity. I wore them.

Ed: How's that work?

Loretta: Because I'd be photographed every place and someone would say, "Whose dress is that, Miss Young?" I'd say, "It's Irene's." I bought them all from Irene or Bernie Goodman or from Hattie Carnegie.......

THREE BLIND MICE

Ed: Richard Griffith produced a lot of your pictures.....

Loretta: I guess he did. But in those days we didn't see much of the producer on the set.

Ed: Directed by William Seiter......you got top billing.....Joel McCrea, David Niven....Pauline Moore, Stuart Erwin, Marjorie Weaver....

Loretta: Weaver was the one....we thought she was going to be another Janet Gaynor....

Ed: She got good reviews...

Loretta: She was marvelous in it....

Ed: ....and Binnie Barnes

Loretta: Bennie Barnes was wonderful in it.....I think she played the rich sister of David Niven....

Ed....Joel McCrea...

Loretta: Crazy about Joel. He was married to Frances Dee, who was gorgeous. I think I could have, well.....yes, I'm sure I had a crush on him, but he was married to this beautiful girl, and I knew her and liked her....so......you turn your attention the other way. But he was darling.....darling to work with, too. Very sweet, warm, kind. Perfect for the part.

Ed: I think he was an underrated actor....

Loretta: I think so, too. I think he wasn't exciting enough for the producers to think..."Oh, good, we've a star; we'll run with him." He was just a good solid.....He was like Gary Cooper only a better actor, I think than Gary. But he didn't have a certain.....I don't know.....Gary had, in his younger years, a marvelous combination of a pixy-kind-of-thing and innocence, and masculinity all wrapped into one. A funny combination. As he got older, I thought he lost it.

Ed: ......also said you were instrumental in getting David Niven in the role of THREE BLIND MICE....

Loretta: Probably. He was probably living with us at the time. I don't know. I don't remember being conscious of it.....saying...."Won't you use David Niven in it?" But I'm sure if they said, "What do you think of David Niven?", I'd say, "He's darling...." No, he wasn't living with us at the time. He was already.....he had already done too many things.

Ed: William Seiter......

Loretta: He was just kind of a big old daddy that ran everything. He was not Frank Capra and he was not William Wyler or Bill Wellman or any of the big......but he was a very, very, good director for program pictures.

SUEZ:

Loretta: One of my stubborn periods. I felt the part was too small ......this was what I was always crabbing about at 20th Century-Fox. I was always Mrs. Alexander Graham Bell and I wanted to be Alexander Graham Bell, see. .....I don't know if this was before LLOYDS OF LONDON or after....I walked out of LLOYDS OF LONDON. I said, "No, I'm not going to play another one of these dumb leading ladies...."

Ed: .....made it (LLOYDS OF LONDON) with someone else?

Loretta: Oh, sure. They made it with a beautiful blonde English actress.....(laugh) Madeline Carroll .....and Tyrone Power. Anyway, SUEZ....

Again, I was having arguments with Daryl Zanuck on the clothes. They were marvelous clothes; they were costumes of Empress Eugenie, and over the period of however long it took to build the Suez Canal....hoop skirts were in according to the costumer. The first sequence in the picture was a tennis match......a beautiful lattice gazebo big enough to hold a tennis court and the royal court.......it was the first time Eugenie sees de Lesseps; she's not an empress at this time.....they just fall in love with each other....

There was a painting.....I did some research on her because she set the fashion of that day.

Ed: French?

Loretta: Yes. Nobody paid attention to that. Tyrone was French, too, but we didn't bother with any accents or anything like that.

Anyway, I was doing this research because when you do a picture and your part's not too impressive, you try to find something you can work on. She started the Eugenie hat, a bowler and then she stuck a plume, an ostrich feather that came down and curled way down over her shoulder. She wore this with her riding habit. So, I thought, "Good, I'll just have one gorgeous outfit after another, and I'll play dress-up the whole picture if I can't do anything else."

The studio never curtailed you on anything. You could have sable all over everything you wanted. Anyway, there was a painting of her.....she had on a white dress, and it's off the shoulder as I recall......a great big white hat.....straw hat of some kind, and there are two pink roses. I said, "That's what I'm going to wear at the tennis match, ".... so I just took a copy of it and gave it to the wardrobe....that's what I wanted.

Anyway, Daryl sent word to me that I had to take off that ridiculous white dress because it made me look like a star among a bunch of extras, and they were going to reshoot the whole tennis scene. I said, "Fine, but this is the dress I'm going to wear......she was a fashion setter..." I gave him all the arguments...

Ed: Did you convince him?

Loretta: I must have because I wore it in the picture. I told him, "Don't pull me down......dress up the extras." I think that's what they did the next day. They just put feather boas and flowers and parasols and things......which is true.

Anyway, we did tests of all these clothes. Always. For every picture you tested everything.

Ed: What were you testing?

Loretta: The clothes. To see if the director and the producer and everybody liked them. It was always my choice. I guess the directors okayed the sketches. I never heard if they did or they didn't. But, if they didn't, I never paid any attention to them anyway. I said, "Well, that's what I want to wear, so…"

Ed: ….tests were filmed tests?

Loretta: Yes…

Ed: What was the difference just seeing the dress and seeing it on film?

Loretta: A lot of things look nice to the eye and they don't photograph…..so, it was very important how the thing photographed, not what it really looked like.

Anyway, we did these tests…the producer saw it, and everyone was pleased. On the first day I wore this big white outfit and, of course, it was gorgeous. Also, in this picture……I did something very stupid…just for meanness….just to get back at Daryl I thought. It didn't hurt Daryl……it just made me look like an idiot.

I had long nails, and I agreed to take off the red polish because they didn't have nail polish in those days, but I said, "I'm not going to cut my nails." He said, "You have to put something on them so I don't see them. I don't want to see them." Anyway, I had these long finger nails, and I put natural polish over them. Of course, in the long shots, it just made my fingers look long and tapered; it was quite beautiful, but in the close-ups with Tyrone

Power, I'd get my hands all over his face, just so they could see these long fingernails, see. Who I thought I was hurting, I don't know. I was irritating anybody who was paying attention, "This is *my* demonstration that I don't want to play this part..... *I don't want to play this part*," I thought.

One of the critics, I think it was Hedda Hopper: "Loretta Young lost her mind with those *fingernails* playing Empress Eugenie.....didn't she know they didn't wear long fingernails in those days?" That was her whole review of me. And I deserved it because it was a stupid thing for me to do.

Ed: What Hedda Hopper also said was that it was the worst movie she ever saw...

Loretta: Really? I thought CARAVAN was much worse. I must say it wasn't very stimulating or anything. We looked like a bunch of high school kids who never aged in it. The director never bothered to say, "You're forty-years older now, so you have to look older." Nobody said that. They were out more for entertainment than reality. I think today, sometimes they go too far with their reality. But surely, there's a happy medium somewhere. You don't have to be a candy box cover which we were a lot of the time....In SUEZ, I looked exactly the same after forty years. Tyrone had a little bit of gray in his hair, that was about it.....that doesn't show age.

Ed: What was Zanuck's demeanor?

Loretta: We very seldom met, "Good evening, Loretta....." He didn't waste time on me at all. And, of course, I wasted no time on him. I was much more interested in Tyrone Power..... Daryl and I irritated each other. Chemically, we just didn't get along at all.

Ed: Why didn't you like Annabella?

Loretta: No reason. *No* reason. I found her.....I don't know. I felt a critical eye from her all the time, and she probably felt the same from me. It wasn't important....we didn't do scenes together....it was unimportant that we got over it. It was probably a little envy on both our sides.....

She's here in a strange country......two leading ladies and she gets him in the end. That probably annoyed me.

Ed: You were billed over her...

Loretta: Yes. Well, also, the reason I didn't get him was because I was already married to the Emperor of France. I just didn't understand anything about her. I found nothing bad about her.

Ed: This was one of the few people you felt this.....

Loretta: Yes, antagonism. Not quite..... a critical eye. Discomfort. We were always polite to each other. We never knew each other personally at all.

Ed:.....married to Tyrone Power at this time?

Loretta: No. Not at this time. They were married after SUEZ, I believe. French women, they usually get what they go after....

Ed: Were you still dating him?

Loretta: Oh, yes! If I could. I would date him anytime. As long as we were working together, we were "dating." But not steadily. I would go out with everybody else, and so would he.

Ed: Never steadily?

Loretta: No. I don't think he dated anybody steadily either until he got married, and then, apparently, he didn't because he dropped Annabella, and married the other one, and then he dropped her and married another one.....

I don't know....Annabella's accent was the only French person's accent that I found displeasing. An accent, she can't help that. I saw her in a French picture one time, and I thought she was darling in it. That's what I expected her to be and she wasn't. She played a boy through most of it. I don't know the name of it. But before they did SUEZ.....

Ed: .....how different?

Loretta: ....oh, she was fun and cute.....on this set all I could see was a little pouty.....like Simone Simon.....pouty. I think they think it's sexy.

Ed: Here's a real negative critique from the director, Allan Dwan...."Loretta fitted the part of Eugenie like a glove, an ambitious woman who took advantage of the situation and married a king; never mind the young man who loved her and whom she loved. Will to succeed took precedence over love. She understood that. Loretta was always above everything, you know, and she used the qualities of Eugenie of having complete control over the situation, for being vastly superior to everyone....

Loretta:.....that's probably true....

Ed: "....It came naturally for her to make you feel that everyone she came in contact with was far beneath her....."

Loretta: Well, I'm sorry if they felt that way. I don't think I was conscious of that because I was crazy about Tyrone Power.....and Annabella was after him, so I wouldn't compete with her. I just went about....so she married him. But he or I would not have been any better off if I'd married him.....in the long run....

Ed: What about Allan Dwan?

Loretta: I think he's right. If that's his.....because he's an honest man. If that's what he says, I believe him, and I could see where he would think that. I did not want to play the part, that's true. I did think I knew better than Daryl Zanuck how she should dress because that's *all* I could do in the picture was dress. I remember....I was so mad at Daryl that he said, "Now, after you make the test, you cannot change one single thing." I wanted to carry a handkerchief in a ballroom scene, and we had not tested it with the handkerchief....so, I said to the script girl...."Send someone up to Mr. Zanuck's office and tell him that Miss Young wants to carry a handkerchief in the ballroom scene, and may I carry the handkerchief?"

Daryl was on the polo field at that time, and I said, "I want to carry the handkerchief in this scene.....I could do it better with the handkerchief." We sat and waited until he got back from the polo field. Well, that's enough to drive a director up the wall. And, if I were the director, I would have put my foot down, and said, I think, "All right, I'll take responsibility for it....you wear the handkerchief, and I will tell him I okayed it." You would think that would happen.

And I wouldn't cut my fingernails for that picture. Which was *stupid*! The only thing that I condescended to do was take the red polish off. If that didn't annoy him (Allan Dwan, the director), it should have....

Ed: .....that's not what he's saying, though.

Loretta: No. He's saying that I am ambitious and self-centered ...which I ....*was*.

Ed: ....and very aloof....

Loretta: Well......I don't know.....just think I'm better than others. I probably *did*. I probably *did*.

Ed: ....vastly superior to everyone?

Loretta: I don't know to *everyone*. I didn't think I was superior to Tyrone because I was crazy about him, and I didn't think I was superior to the director because he was the director, and the director has always been, to me, the King of the set.

Ed: Were you just behaving like stars behave....

Loretta: Well, one of the reasons you're a star is because you do think you're superior to everybody, and everybody tells you you're superior to everyone.....

There's probably a great deal of truth in that if that's what he saw.....he'd have no reason to be nasty. And yes, they're all unattractive traits, and I'm sure I *had*....I hope I've gotten rid of some of them.

I hated SUEZ because I was playing second lead to Annabella and I was furious.

Ed: Ah ha.....

Loretta: I only went ahead with it because we were in the Sunset house, and we needed the money. But I was so mad, and I had the long fingernails, and I thought, "I'll just spoil the picture".......crazy thinking.....it was just crazy.

Ed: Well, that's part of what made you a star, really....

Loretta: I guess. I don't know. It would have been better for me if I had refused the picture and taken another layoff, but I don't think I could.....

I remember something else on that picture. I insisted on leaving the set *promptly* at 6:00. None of this business of five minutes later. I guess to prove that I could.

Ed: ...... you had that power...

Loretta: ....that I had that power. I remember somebody saying one day......"Well, it's just a little shot.......you ask her. I don't want to go through the whole boring explanation again...." and I overheard him and burst out laughing, and I said..."That bad, huh?" He said, "Well, pretty boring...." I said, "Well, I got pushed around. I had good teachers. I *learned* to be like this." He said, "I know, Loretta. Don't worry about it. It's all part of the game."

KENTUCKY

Loretta: (laugh) (laugh) David Butler (the director) was darling. He loved horses. I was scared to death of horses ...... still am. Don't know how to ride, couldn't ride, but I looked gorgeous on the horse in that picture. I'm built to be able to ride, and I looked like it, and I had a wonderful instructress and she'd say, ..."Sit back Loretta....." I just looked marvelous on that horse. They'd say, "Cut," and I'd fall right off. These were long shots. I not only had to ride them, but I had to hug them and kiss them and born them and pet them.....and, oh, she was right there. She'd just tell me everything I had to do.

I got so many letters afterwards saying I was the most marvelous horse woman in the entire world. All these.....and I never had the nerve to tell anybody that I didn't know anything about them.

I think there was some organization, and I don't know what it was......because it was from Kentucky. I made some excuse. I declined to go. I said, "Oh, no, I'll just make a fool of myself down there."

Walter Brennan was very interesting on that picture because .....We took eight to ten weeks to shoot it....I was on the set every day, and he worked almost every day, too. And I was bringing him coffee and bringing chairs to him.......he looked like he was old enough to be my uncle.

I treated him just like that. I waited on him hand and foot, and at the wrap party at the end of the picture, everyone was on the stage. All of a sudden, a very nice-looking man comes up and even his voice wasn't the same. I had no idea who he was. Dark hair, standing properly....had a drink. Said, "Well, Loretta, I must say I enjoyed working with you." I kind of looked at him....Finally, I said, "Who is that?" (laugh) (laugh)...."Walter Brennan". I said, "I don't believe it! I've been waiting on you hand and foot for ten weeks. How dare.....that's terrible of you not to have told me......."

He said, "I just couldn't leave the set without saying hello to you and without all that make-up and everything......"

Ed: So you really thought he was this old man......

Loretta: Yes, I'd never seen him before. Never seen him in the movies. At least if I did, I didn't know many of the character actors....

Ed: He won an Oscar, you know, for that performance......

Loretta: Oh, I'm sure he did. He should. He was darling in it. He's a wonderful actor as a matter of fact.

Ed: It says, ... "In color, Loretta Young is a beauteous Kentucky belle. Her lensing in tints will be accepted as the best of any actress to date...."

Loretta: That's interesting. I didn't know I was so pretty in it.....

Ed: ....I do

Loretta: What I think. I've discovered something about myself. When I like myself best is when I don't look like me ..... it's when I look like somebody else..... or something I haven't seen in myself before, that I like.......they are either pure innocence or she knows something I don't know.....it's usually more an expression than anything else.

In KENTUCKY, I had a lot of blue ribbons in my hair because I wanted my eyes to go blue as they could.....Irene made a very pretty suit for the race: a jacket, a skirt, and a shirt, but it was very good looking, very slick looking....this was with different tones in my hair......

Ed: "Miss Young displays a wealth of personality in the lead and makes the most of a meaty role that gives her plenty of opportunity to display ability to deliver a top performance...."

Loretta: Well, this man or woman .....I would call "Pro-Loretta." I'm glad they feel that way, I'm complimented but KENTUCKY was.....

Ed: I think in your own personality there is this fire.....

Loretta: Y-yes.

Ed: ....and this character tapped into that. That's probably what people connected with there.....

Loretta: Probably, Well.......

Ed: You didn't think much of that movie, did you?

Loretta: KENTUCKY? No, really, no. It was pretty, and that's about it. I'm not a horse lover. I can't get too excited about horse racing, or horse breeding, or anything like that.

Ed: It was kind of contrived that they used an English actor (Richard Greene) for the male lead.

Loretta: He was under contract. He was so attractive, so good-looking. Someone signed him, and they put him in anything to make a co-star out of him. He was a darling man, but he really was not *strong* enough.

Ed: Was there location shooting in Kentucky?

Loretta: They went to Kentucky; I didn't. They built the stables and everything on the sound stage or on the back lot.

(Loretta referring to a fan who had come to her door the previous day)

Loretta: He said, "I have a big poster of you with Robert Young; it's gorgeous….I paid $400 for it. Oh they're very expensive but they're worth it. My whole collection is around that. I have to go now. Thank you." He was so uncontrolled that I just thought, "That poor man, twenty-seven years old, he looks sixteen." He was so flustered, and I just felt so sorry for him.

He had said, "Oh, they won't believe this. I have liked only old movies since I was twelve." I asked him, "Why do you suppose that is because there are some wonderful movies today?" "No, no, no. The stars today are not stars." He heard somebody say that; what does he know about it? "Of course, there are stars, big stars, what do you mean?" "There's no glamour….."

Ed: You always do look very nice…..

Loretta: Well, yes, if I'm around the house...I guess that's just habit.

Ed: .... A good habit...

Loretta: For me it is. I'm more comfortable looking presentable than I do looking ratty or worn out.

Ed: .....he (the fan from the day before) was born in 1963. Your television show....your whole career was basically over by then....

1939

WIFE, HUSBAND, FRIEND

Ed: Warner Baxter, Binnie Barnes, Caesar Romero. Gregory Ratoff directed.....

Loretta: Oh, yes. Caesar was a voice teacher. Her voice (the voice of Loretta's character) was just terrible no matter how many lessons she took. I think she gave a recital in her own house......It wasn't anything. I did an awful lot of pictures that weren't anything.

Ed: Nunnally Johnson......

Loretta: He was a good writer, yes. He was under contract to 20th Century-Fox.......he just wrote. Good or bad.....he just wrote.

Ed: good reviews on this.

Loretta: I thought I was just divine as a comedienne. You have to think people like you, or you just can't do it.

THE STORY OF ALEXANDER GRAHAM BELL

Ed: Don Ameche....his signature movie....Henry Fonda.....Charles Coburn, and Sally Blane, Polly Ann Young and Georgiana Young.

Loretta: They played the sisters. She (Loretta's character) was one of four sisters, that's why. I don't know whose idea it was, but anyway, it was a good idea. Polly Ann had worked with me on WHITE PARADE, and Irving Cummings directed that. ....I thought they were all just darling. If for no other reason in my career, I liked it because the four of us were in the picture together. They weren't anything......just a couple of scenes, but we all looked pretty, and we were young and fresh and real, and it was fun.

Peter (Loretta's son who had just walked into the room): Dad said, I think you were doing ALEXANDER GRAHAM BELL and Aunt Sally came into the room where mom was getting made up.....and Aunt Sally's hair was a certain way, and Mom said, "You can't do that. You have to have it like this.....that's why you'll never be a star, and I am because these things......."

Loretta: Did Dad tell you that? Do you want to know how it really happened?

Peter: Yeah, sure.

Loretta: We were doing ALEXANDER GRAHAM BELL, and all four of us were in it. I was the star, so I had my star dressing room, and they were just little "bit" people, so they put them in a little dressing room and they had to go to the make-up department to have their make-up and hair done. I got to the studio early and got dressed early so I could go over to see they got #1 treatment, and that they weren't pushed around or anything....

I walked into the hairdressing department and looked at Polly Ann, and she looked marvelous.....she had little curls hanging down, and she looked gorgeous. Georgiana looked adorable, and then all of a sudden I looked at Bet .....and this woman was doing her hair, and I said, "Oh Bet, that looks awful." The hairdresser stopped and I said, "Oh, no. that will never do. Bet has a beautiful forehead, show it."

Bet was looking at me.....she was so mad at me. I said, "Bet, I'm sorry..." She said, "She spent an hour doing this hair, and I think it's lovely." I said, "Well, I don't. You're beautiful and that hair...." I said, "Put her hair... do that...." and I told her how to do it. Bet was so mad that she didn't speak to me for two days on the set. She did finally say to me, "I just think it's terrible because the hairdresser worked one hour on my hair..." I said, "Did you like it?" She said, "Well, no, but she was working so hard." I said, "You can't do that, Bet. You're the one who's being photographed. She's not going to be photographed."

Now, I never said to her that's why you're not a star.

Peter: Well, maybe he just said that....

(Why Loretta didn't want to do THE STORY OF ALEXANDER GRAHAM BELL)

Loretta: I just thought it was not a big enough part for me. I didn't mind doing the picture; the character was fine. *Boring* I thought. And same old leading lady stuff I'd done forever, and I just didn't want to get pinned down to that ALEXANDER GRAHAM BELL bit...

Ed: Mrs. Alexander Graham Bell never spoke......

Loretta: Oh, she didn't?

Ed: You wanted to do the role without speaking anything.....

Loretta: If I did, I certainly didn't get my way. But it would have been wonderful......

Ed: What about Charles Coburn?

Loretta: He wasn't cold or anything, but he was too old to bother with all the nonsense that goes on on the set. A set can be fun, and it's a place to play as well as work if you have the right group of people.......it can be very, very, pleasant......

(Loretta's meeting with Zanuck and her refusal to sign a new contract)

We had this famous meeting with Myron (Selznick) and Joe Schenck (who partnered with Daryl Zanuck to create 20th Century Pictures and, a few years later, became Chairman of 20th Century-Fox) and Daryl Zanuck and me, just about six months before the time was up, my contract was up. At which Mr. Schenck said to me, "I just don't understand why you will not happily re-sign with us." That's what they wanted me to do was re-sign another seven year contract.

Ed: I thought it was two million dollars for five years. Maybe I'm ......

Loretta: I don't know. They wanted me to sign again, whatever it was. And, I said, "I just can't. I....I...I'm still doing leading lady parts here. I was a leading lady, and Tyrone Power comes along and he's a bit player, and the next I know, he's the star and I'm a little bit player in SUEZ. Not even the lead. I don't want that kind of career. I want to keep going up, and I know I can do that ......but not under Daryl Zanuck because he doesn't make women's pictures." Daryl's sitting right there.

Daryl said, "I don't know why you're so unhappy." I said, "First of all, you never sent me any roses. You never have given me a raise. You never......anything. And Tyrone tells me he's had four in the year and a half he's been here."

He said, "You've never asked for it." I said, "That's exactly what I'm talking about. I don't want to have to deal with something where I have to beg for everything. He should know he should send me flowers. He should know when a part is good for me or it isn't. That's no way to build a career...."

Anyway, the result of that meeting was that I said, "No, I'll work the time out, but I will not re-sign."

Myron hadn't said anything. Finally, he said, "All right, Loretta, that's enough......you can go now. Now we'll finish....." I got up and said, "Good-bye, good-bye, good-bye..." and left the office while they wrangled out the business deal of it.

I couldn't continue. I cannot continue an on-going battle. It wears me down and OUT. And whatever talent or energies I might have are wasted on fighting. I can't do that.

After that meeting, I remember one other meeting with both Myron and David Selznick ....David tried talking me into reconsidering....He said, "Loretta it *is* a good studio and if you can ......Zanuck can be awfully cruel when you leave the studio. He's really a hot-headed man, and you've really done him in on his pride."

My seven year contract was coming to an end. He had already tacked on probably another year, whatever it was, for the time that I had walked off and was taken off salary....... Daryl was not prepared to start ALEXANDER GRAHAM BELL so they shot three days and then closed it again for three or four weeks to finish his preproduction. But he had hooked me in, see.....

Ed: Was there some kind of stipulation that....

Loretta: Some clause....once you started something, you had to complete it ....something in the contract.

Part Eight: Freelance

(After leaving 20th Century-Fox)

Loretta: Before I left 20th Century-Fox, every producer I would see would say, "Oh, I have a script I'm dying to send you...." and I was waiting for all these scripts to come in, and after nine months I hadn't received one single script. Jimmy Townsend, who was one of the agents working for Myron, went to Myron and said, "Loretta's being blackballed."

So Myron came to me and said, "I know exactly what happened. In one of their Sunday night poker games, Daryl Zanuck says, 'Hey, nobody here is interested in Loretta Young, are they?' 'Oh, no, no.' That's it. That's all it takes." He asked me, "What do you want to do about it?" I said, "I want to work; that's what I want to do."

Myron said, "It only took one man to blackball you, but it also takes only one guy to break that, " and he said, "I think I know the man.....Harry Cohn. Harry's got a couple of scripts over there, and one of them I know he tried to get Irene Dunne for and she was tied up".....I think it was DOCTOR TAKES A WIFE..... "and he's looking around for a substitute, and if I give him a price on you, give him a bargain, I think he'll do it."

And within two days I was signed up and ready to do this picture. And it did. It broke the blackball. Myron knew the industry backwards, and he knew the men and their personalities backwards and forward.

(Loretta on how she has been perceived as "difficult")

I know I want things my way. I know in the studio, everyone used to say and they still do, that I'm not the easiest person in the world to work with...producers and writers...... I know I'm not.....I've had more experience than most of them, and I think I know a script better than they do, when it's good and bad and where it's weak and when it doesn't make any sense or when it's stupid. Because I won't just ......won't just do it ....then I'm difficult.

ETERNALLY YOURS

Ed: I'm not sure the order of things but ETERNALLY YOURS was released seven months before THE DOCTOR TAKES A WIFE. Do you think it's possible that you made your deal with Walter Wanger before Zanuck blackballed you?

Loretta: That's interesting.........maybe that's how it happened. I didn't make a good business deal with Walter Wanger. He offered a percentage of the net for a lower salary. What a fool.....Never take a percentage of the net. There is no possible way that you'll ever get five cents because you can't send a bookkeeper around every time they play the thing. If it's the gross.....this is what Jimmy Stewart did at Universal......that just put him on easy street forever......No, I'll take it on the gross...

The clothes, I think Irene did all of that. Everything was white. No one else noticed it except moi. I thought it was very clever because she was a wonderful designer.

I enjoyed the tricks (that Loretta learned in her role as a magician's assistant) because I could play them at all the parties I went to because I knew all of them.....how they work. You know I've forgotten those tricks already....

Ed....well, already......?

Loretta: ....the only one I remember is the one on the piece of glass. He puts her on a piece of glass, and there are four Nubian slaves in robes that would carry it off the stage. He put me on the glass, put a curtain down in front of me and this he did this......(?)...I was gone. You couldn't tell. It's very cleverly done......

Ed: Billie Burke, Zasu Pitts, Eve Arden.....

Loretta: Zasu Pitts and Eve Arden went into having their own television shows and everything else...

Ed: ...Broderick Crawford?

Loretta: Very pleasant to work with. Not a very attractive man physically....but big, good. Very warm personality and warm on the set.

Ed: ....I didn't read to you the review on ETERNALLY YOURS..."Miss Young and Niven are excellent and only through their ability are they able to remain untouched...." I liked the movie myself.....

Loretta: Apparently, a lot of other people do, too, because it goes on forever on television. David had a very refreshing kind of ummph effect on people.

1940

THE DOCTOR TAKES A WIFE

Loretta: I loved Bill Perlberg (Producer). A very interesting man. He and George Seaton (Screenwriter) worked beautifully together. They did many pictures together......producer, writer, director. Like Bob Riskin and Frank Capra.....

It's too bad that there are not more of those combinations. It's like the composer of the music and the lyricist.

Ed: ... we saw this movie. Gail Patrick.

Loretta: She was in almost everything....always the second lead in all those light comedies. She was the second lead with Cary Grant.......

Ray Milland was married to a very good friend of mine...Mal Milland. They always have been married. I think he had a fling or two with other people, but nothing serious. Mal, as a wise woman, just hung in there. Mal is a Christian Scientist and a good one.....and when they're good, they're wonderful people.....because they really do treat everybody else the way you'd like to be treated. They really do. God is *love* to them.....

Everyone who has ever known her feels the same way about her. Jack was not easy to live with. He was beefing all the time. He'd tell anybody....."Oh, I married an angel....."

Ed: Why did you call him Jack?

Loretta: Because that's his real name....Jack Milland. Ray is his professional name.....like Loretta is mine.

Ed: Was he complaining when you were making this movie?

Loretta: No, because he was having a ball. But he's a beefer......He did say to me......I said, "What's the matter?" He said, "I'm so afraid of the drunk scene. I don't know what to do. I don't know how to play a drunk scene. " I said, "Well, have you ever been drunk?" He said, "Yes. But I don't know how I am." I said, "Well, just laugh all the time......be one of those drunks....."

He did a marvelous, marvelous, performance in LOST WEEKEND.....and that was a serious drunk. That's what he'd naturally be......because he's Welsh and they're ......everything is way down there.......but the minute he hit on the happy drunk his worries were over, see, and he just had a ball with it.....

(Loretta on movies she tested for and those she did not)

There were many disappointments in my career. Such as not getting REBECCA when I made a test for it, and I disdained making tests.....but I presumed I already had it and that's why I said... "All right, I'll make the test." And I didn't get it, and I was terribly shocked and disappointed until I saw it and watched Joan Fontaine act in it. She was absolutely perfect casting. She looked it; she acted it. Her accent was.... She was perfect in it. And all that resentment just kind of faded away. I said, "She's better in it than you...that's why you didn't get it."

Ed: Did you do anything for David Selznick?

Loretta: Nothing. No. He offered me a picture. Ingrid Bergman had done it in Europe. And I said, "No."

Ed: INTERMEZZO?

Loretta: No.....Yes! Yes! And I said, "No, David. I'm sick of playing leading ladies (as opposed to the central character of the story).....The man's the lead in that..." I said, "No." He said, "Loretta, it would be wonderful for you." I said, "I don't want to do it. Why don't you get the girl who's in it.....teach her English, she'd be marvelous!" I didn't know that he already had her under contract and hadn't brought her over yet..... She was wonderful in it.

Ed: I've seen it....

Loretta: She was wonderful in anything.

Ed: Weren't you in contention for Scarlett O'Hara?

Loretta: I wouldn't test for it. I said, "No, I wouldn't be right for it, David; you'll end up wanting me to play Melanie, and I'm not going to play second part to anybody," and the other girl was better in it than I would have been, Olivia de Havilland.

Ed: You're sure you never tested for Scarlett...

Loretta: Yes. I was sure Bette Davis would get it. Bette Davis, I thought was perfect for it. Never heard of Vivien Leigh at that time. Bette Davis had made JEZEBEL and she was perfect in it, and she was simply the character JEZEBEL.,,,,

(Loretta's appeal to movie goers)

Ed: (Having just mentioned both Bette Davis and Joan Crawford) I'm thinking back over your film career. If you look at your films, say from 1940 on...there really isn't a Loretta Young persona....

Loretta: I think, between you and me, I was not as big a star as either one of these two (Bette Davis, Joan Crawford). I think that the reason was because there wasn't that......

Ed: ....larger than life (referring to Loretta's screen presence)?

Loretta: Yes. THE FARMER'S DAUGHTER got an award so there must have been something in that character. She was pretty, honest, flat-out but not aggressive....feminine....but there were a lot of people like that.

Ed: Would you say, looking at Loretta Young movie star, that you may not have been the star that Bette Davis or Joan Crawford was, but that you were more consistent? Didn't your movies generally make money? .....Not blockbusters.....

Loretta: Yes, but so did theirs.

Ed: Oh, Joan Crawford sure went through a slump.....

Loretta: Oh, within the last few years when she left Metro.

Ed: Before she did MILDRED PIERCE .....that was in the '40s.

Loretta: I don't know why. I was more..... believe it or not....more acceptable to the average. During my years, there were a lot of awfully nice, pretty, sweet, honest, average women. The average woman today is....I don't know what she is...But she's certainly not like they were in the '40s...(laugh)

I don't know. But I would guess.....not the intellectuals, not the neurotics......... not the shop girls or secretaries....that would be Joan Crawford's. If you have to find an answer to this question, the only thing I can think of is, there are an awful lot of women like me out there....

Ed: the kind of woman who generally played by the rules.....

Loretta: Yes. Honorable and didn't sleep around and wasn't very aggressive. Both of my marriages didn't last.....but they were based on the same kind of woman. A woman is the heart of the home, and the man is the head of the home......

Ed: Loretta Young movie: A happy ending......

Loretta: That's what I was geared to. A nice husband. A nice lover. No abuse of any kind. That's what the hero and heroine were in those days.....

Ed: .....and you were not ever bitter......

Loretta: On the screen? I don't think so. BORN TO BE BAD was as near I came to it. Even then......she wasn't. A happy ending.

(Another time, Loretta discussed her appeal to movie fans)

Loretta: I received a letter......long letter.......two pages.....and it was from a man, because he said, "One of the things that my wife and I had in common and one of the reasons I'm sure we got together was because both of us were enormous fans of yours and," he said, "I always looked at you and thought, 'Oh, that poor little thing, I'd like to take her out and buy her a big steak...'" he went on talking....then right in the middle he said, "Oh, I ought to tell you, I'm black and so is my wife," then he went on talking, see....

It was the first time that I had been conscious ....of what my appeal was. There was a certain vulnerability about me.....and they treat you that way. I've never had anybody grab me or hit me...

HE STAYED FOR BREAKFAST

Loretta: ....with Melvyn Douglas who is probably one of the best actors we ever had in the picture business. I thought when he got older, he got better and better and better and when he was very old, he was in HUD. I haven't seen a better performance, particularly for a motion picture actor to be that unconscious of the camera....that real......

He was a little uptight with me because at that time I think the hearings were going on about communist activity in the motion picture industry .....and he was down at these hearings......

Ed: They were having hearings in 1940?

Loretta: They certainly were. He wasn't at work because he was down at those hearings.....I don't know what hearings they were......we all knew he was down there ....but he never mentioned anything on the set. Never mentioned it. Never....absolute marvelous control.

He was known around town as one of these militants, if not a communist, certainly a fellow traveler. He was married to Helen Gahagan....who was *very, very* liberal. And they'd all turned into the heroes in history, and Bob Taylor and Adolph Menjou and a few others turned into the villains (because there testimony aided in the blacklisting.)

Ed: ....they took Robert Taylor's name off of a building at Metro-Goldwyn-Mayer....

Loretta: Oh, that's terrible.....just in the last six months.

Ed: Any more to add about Melvin Douglas.......

Loretta: He was funny. He was a marvelous comedian......ironically, the picture was kind of a spoof on communism. He was marvelous in that picture.

Ed: What about the director, Alexander Hall?

Loretta: He was kind of a .....I wasn't too comfortable with Al Hall. I don't know why....I don't think he was too comfortable with me. He was never sure what I was going to do or what I wasn't going to do because most of my fights....I'd spend most of my energy telling Harry Cohn what to do and how to do it......I didn't have any time left over for the director, see. Al Hall did another picture I did. He did the one with Freddie March and me.....

Ed: That's coming up.......Eugene Pallette...

Loretta: Yes, I did a lot with him. He was a darling big old fat man. He was charming. He always sounded like he had a frog in his throat.

Ed: What was the story about the dress......

Loretta: It was a black lace dress over nude. That was the first one I'd ever seen and Irene designed it. The whole body of the dress, right down to where your legs begin was black lace over nude and from then on, it was black, solid black right down to the floor. Long sleeves and high neck. When she showed me the sketch, I said, "Irene, that's gorgeous. How are you going to do that? She said, "It's nude underneath, but it just looks like there's nothing underneath it." I said, "Well, I think it's the prettiest dress I've ever seen." The lace had design in it so it looked like the body…..

We made tests and Harry Cohn called me at home and said, "Loretta, I've just seen the tests of the clothes." "Aren't they beautiful, Harry?" He said, "Well, yes, they're beautiful…..but you can't wear that black lace dress." I said, "I can't? Why?"

"Well, it's dirty looking; it's just lace. You can't wear that dress." I said, "Oh, no, Harry it's nude material underneath it." He said, "It doesn't look like it." I said, "Well, I know. It's not supposed to look like it." He said, "You can't wear it in the picture." So, I said, "I never thought of it that way, but all right, I'll get another one….and if you don't mind, I'll buy that dress from you." He asked, "Where would you wear it if you bought it?" I said, "I'd wear it at the Mocombo, I guess, or I'd wear it to a party at Jack Warner's house….. or your house if you gave a black tie party." He said, "You would?" I said, "Yes."

"Well, I guess if you'd wear it, I guess it's all right." Anyway, I wore it in the picture.

Well, there was so much to-do over this dress, and the reviews came out (laugh) (laugh) and they mentioned the black lace dress. That's what they talked about.....Never mind the performances or anything. I think I got one of them and just underlined like that and put it in an envelope and said, "Guess who?" and sent it to him.

He called back and said, "I know, I know.....everybody's talking about the black lace dress...."

Ed: (Review): "Miss Young displays her eyeful lines and curves in a series of gowns and negligees, and she carries the role of the captivating charmer in fabulous fashion...."

Loretta: It was a little story. It was in France and he was running away from....

Ed:.....he was a communist....

Loretta: She thinks he's attractive so she protects him. He hasn't got any clothes, so he puts on one of her negligees....."Oh, you smell....go take a shower....." and she hides him and when they come, she says, "Oh, no. Nobody here." Eventually, she leaves her husband, Gene Palette, who is fat and rich .... the bloated capitalist....... and runs off with the communist, see. And they said Hollywood was not full of them.....(laugh) (laugh).

THE LADY FROM CHEYENNE

Ed: Director Frank Lloyd…

Loretta: Really? Because he was a wonderful director. But I don't remember him on that. He did MUTINY ON THE BOUNTY, the first one………you're right, he did do LADY FROM CHEYENNE….. I wasn't cast properly for it. The story was about a girl so unattractive that the men just couldn't cotton up to her. She was just *uggggly* ….

Finally, she goes, at a certain part of the story, and she gets into what she thinks is a boarding house, but it's a house of ill-repute, and the Madame and the girls in the house get hold of her and dress her up so she's divine, and, of course, the leading man just falls all over his feet for her…..

I know the reason why I did LADY FROM CHEYENNE. Frank Lloyd came to my house and he told me the script and he was so charming. Everything he did was so cute. He said, "She's got a little hat on with one feather….it sticks out just like this…and every time she moves, the feather does this, see." I thought I was going to be just like he was. And, of course, I wasn't at all. I was just as attractive in the ugly outfit as I was in the beautiful outfit; therefore, the story just didn't hold up. It was just stupid. The man starts to kiss her, and he looks at her and he goes, "Oh, no, I can't…" and a big close-up of me without any make-up on, nothing…..was just beautiful….. "What's the matter with that nut!"

It was kind of cute, politically, but I don't think it did well….

Ed: the review wasn't positive... Was this the first movie you
made after marrying Tom Lewis?

Loretta: Yes, it was. I was supposed to have made BALLERINA,
but I was busy learning how to be a ballet dancer while I was
making this picture. I'd go home at night and practice two hours
in my garage. I had already hired the ballet dancer in New York,
the teacher, and I brought him out with me. I'm trying to think
whether I paid him or the studio paid him. I think the studio
did.....

I know what happened. We were living in New York, and that's
where I started with the American Ballet. George Schimmel
called. He was a dancer, and he was a teacher, also. He started
with me there......

THE MEN IN HER LIFE (new title for BALLERINA)

Ed: Gregory Ratoff directed....I read where he had a booming
voice....and the only way he could direct this child (who played
Loretta's daughter) was through you....

Loretta: Probably, because Gregory was very excitable, and
grownups could read him but I'm sure a child couldn't.

His wife, Eugenie Loentovich, was a big star in Europe. She
played TOVARICH all over the stage in Europe......she played my
maid in the picture, but she was with her (Loretta's character) all
the time. She was great. She was a little woman. She just looked
wonderful. Great discipline and he used to yell at her. I think he

did it because she was on his turf; she had always been the important one. He was an actor but not a big star, and I think she was doing him a favor....

One day she said something, and he said, "Eugenie! You are *not* the star in the picture. Loretta is. So will you, please, *butt out!*" He went on and on and I finally said, "Gregory, please!" I don't know what he thought he was doing, but he was embarrassing me. He was making everybody uptight.

Finally, I got him over in a corner and said, "Gregory, if you don't stop yelling at her, I'm going to walk off this set. I cannot stand it! No woman understands that kind of treatment, particularly your wife, and particularly Eugenie Leontovich. She is a *big* star."

I must say, in front of me, he didn't do it again. I don't know what he did when I wasn't around. I probably have a print of that; I'm sure I have it some place. Have you seen it?......

Ed: Yes, a couple weeks ago.......

Loretta: It was released through Columbia, but we made it at Pathe Studios which turned out to be David Selznick's studio.

Ed: It starred Loretta Young and Conrad Veidt...

Loretta: ...a wonderful actor. He played the dancing master.

Ed: Dean Jagger...

Loretta: He was excellent in it. He played the rich American whom she marries and has a child by......and Sheppard Strudwick.

Ed: ...John Sheppard....

Loretta: They changed his name. Sheppard Strudwick was his real name, and he was very good. They were all very good in it. It looked like a European picture.

Ed: Was he the love interest?

Loretta: Yes. He was the juvenile lead........but back to Conrad Veidt.......one time we had a scene....it was the only time I've ever really been knocked out......there was a scene where he was supposed to slap her, see, and boy, he hit me, and I went back like this and all I remember is falling forward on his chest and thinking, "I hope they don't stop the camera," and then I passed out and slid right down his body. And Gregory Ratoff was so scared and he said... "*Cut!*"

I could have killed him after that. When I came to, I said, "Did you get it? Did you get it?" He said, "You'll have to do it again...." he didn't get it. Then, of course, Conrad Veidt, poor man, was scared to death to come near me....(laugh)

Ed: ....an older man wasn't he?

Loretta: Yes

Ed: ...German?

Loretta: Yes. Good actor.

Ed: (Review): "....Woman's picture, a period piece about 1860....about the training of a ballet dancer and her love life along the way. Miss Young through a sterling performance does much to maintain interest....."

Loretta: That's good. The costumes were beautiful in that, too......and the look of it was beautiful but again ......there was no progression of growth in the appearance of her ....over ten or twelve years. I think the little girl was about five at the end of the picture and it starts out with my character at age 14.

She's a horseback rider, a bareback rider in a circus, and this dancing master is at the circus, someplace in Paris or Budapest or some place. He notices her hands, and he says to her, "Hands are as important to a ballet dancer as her feet, and you have beautiful hands. I think I can make your feet match them." Anyway, he takes her on.

Ed: You were twenty-eight playing a fourteen-year-old at that point?

Loretta: That was simple to do. Just take off the make-up and put braids in your hair and just...That's easy to do.

I remember one day on the set.....there was an emotional scene......the dancing master, Conrad Veidt was driving her a little too hard on the bar….and he'd say, "Faster…." he's right there telling her everything what to do……finally, she's supposed, at the end of the scene, to collapse and sob and cry, and he says, "Maybe I've been working you too hard…" As we were playing the scene…..we had rehearsed it a couple of times and I was tired….and I think there were plies ….. and then down, up, flat and up on the toe and then back and then down…..all with the bar. I had my hand on the bar…..As he would talk, I would get out of breath as it should have been ……finally, he said, "Faster, faster……." I went down on the floor, and I couldn't get up, and I couldn't talk.

And, my eyes wouldn't shut. Every muscle in my body froze…….paralyzed. I had been taking in too much oxygen as you do when you hyperventilate. The thing that scared me was that I couldn't undo my hand. I couldn't get my arm down from the bar, and I was on the floor sitting and …..my eyes wouldn't close……they started to burn…

The director, poor man, came running over to me…"Take your hand off!….Take your hand off!" I just looked at him ….. I couldn't move….I couldn't talk…..I couldn't do anything. Finally, Schimmel , very wisely said, "Get a doctor, *quickly*!"

Fortunately, they always have a doctor at the studio …..and he came running over and took one look at me and then ran back and got some….I don't know what they gave me….a muscle relaxer, Robaxin, or whatever it was, and he gave me a shot.

When I finally did collapse, I was so exhausted I went right to sleep. I didn't lose consciousness; I just went to sleep right there on the floor. They took me to the hospital on the lot and I slept for about three hours. This happened at about 10:00 in the morning. *For the first time in my life I had absolutely no desire to go to the set and act.* I was that sleepy.

I finally went home that day and went to bed and slept it off. The next morning I was all right. So we went ahead and did the scene again, but he had printed all the stuff from the day before and, really, that's what they used.

Ed: ...how did you do this picture? Is that something you sought?

Loretta: It was a book....Lady Elinor Smith wrote a book called *Ballerina* and Gregory Ratoff had taken an option on the book and sent it to me. Gregory knew me from 20th Century-Fox. He was going to direct it, and he had a very good cast

About the same time, Harry Cohn wanted me to do something.....that's where Elizabeth Blackwell comes into my life. She was the first woman doctor. There was a director......John Stahl was his name. He made wonderful movies, but he had a reputation.....Two or three of my friends had worked with him.....Claudette Colbert had made IMITATION OF LIFE, Irene (Dunne) had done MAGNIFICIENT OBSESSION, and I checked with them and each one of them said, "If you never work again, don't work for Stahl. He's a beast to work with." So, I had to tell Harry, "I'm sorry, I want to do this thing. I love the story; it would be a wonderful picture….but I simply don't want to work with John Stahl." I had had approval of the director written into my contracts. "His reputation is too rough, and I'm not willing to stand still for it. So I think you better get another actress. "

I presumed he was going to get another actress, and Gregory Ratoff had sent me this book and I loved it. It was about a ballerina, and I knew Gregory and liked him, and it was an independent but released through Columbia. So I agreed to do it with him. Then Harry calls back and says, "I fired John Stahl…..now what director…." I said, "Oh, I can't. I've already signed to do another picture."

He says, "You can't do that." I said, "Yes, I can. We already agreed that you had John Stahl and I couldn't work with him." Anyway, they never did make the picture. John Stahl didn't make it; I didn't make it; nobody made it. I think it's still on the shelf at Columbia…"

We had finished MEN IN HER LIFE, and Tom and I were going to Honolulu ….. so it was probably 1941….. We were all packed and ready to go, and I think there was a ship strike so I said to Tom and the manager, "Just put the trunks on a plane and we'll go over on another plane. By that time you could. Then the studio called and said, "*We have* to have some retakes for this picture." I said, "They're going to have to wait until I get back." They said, "No, you're going to be gone a month, and we have a release date,"…..whatever….

"Anyway, you have to come tomorrow to do retakes." I was so mad. It was going to postpone something; I don't remember what. We went to bed that night, and I couldn't get to sleep. I had to get up at 5:00 to be at the studio, and at 3:00, Tom said, "This is ridiculous. Here, take a sleeping pill." I took it, but it just started to work when I had to get up.

I think I was driving myself, too. I had a maid at home who went with me to the studio, but I think I did the driving. I got to the studio and I put make-up on......I just dragged myself onto the set. I was still out. I had all this Seconal in my system.

And I sat down on a little stool that they had for me.....I used to lift the hoop skirt and put it over and then sit on the stool. Well, if you'd try to get up without lifting the skirt, the suction would hold you right down on the ground. I couldn't get up. I was falling asleep, I guess.

The assistant director said, "We're ready for you, Miss Young." I said, "Fine," and I made an effort to get up and couldn't. So I did it again. Finally, I said, "I'm too tired." He repeated, "Miss Young, we're ready for you." I said, "I don't care, I'm just too tired." I couldn't get up, and I couldn't go to sleep. I couldn't lie down because I was sitting on this stool.

Anyway, he went to the telephone and called my agent, Jimmy Townsend who was representing me at the time, at Myron Selznick's office. He said, "Jimmy, you better get over here....there's something wrong with your girl."

When Jimmy walked on the set, he said, "Hi, Loretta. What's wrong?" I told him, "After I got nervous and mad, I couldn't go to sleep last night, so I took a sleeping pill at 3:00 and then got up at 5:00." He said, "Okay, I'll be right back."

He came back and said, "Here, take this little pill." I took Benzedrine, and in about ten minutes, I felt so *marvelous*! I had the energy of a bull. I just picked up the hoop skirt and I went into the scene and we shot and we shot and we shot.....

Ed: Bennies?

Loretta: Well, Benzedrine, (laugh) David Selznick used to take it all the time.

Ed: Like speed, today?

Loretta: Probably......speed, I think. It gives you all this energy, and you feel that everything you do is divine....(laugh) (laugh)

Anyway, I danced off to lunch, and we had two or three scenes to shoot afterwards and the minute I ate lunch, of course, any medication after four hours is gone out of your system, supposedly. I started to droop again, see.

I went back to the set, and they called Jimmy again, and he came over. And I said, "No, I'm not going to take any more of those pills. Otherwise, I'll never go to sleep." Anyway, I don't know how I got through the rest of the day....but the effect of Benzedrine was astonishing....it was so wonderful. I can well understand how people would become addicted to it. I had that one fling, and that was it. I've never even tried marijuana.....I'm afraid I'd like it, and I don't want to have to break a bad habit in order to start a good habit again......no.

I blame my terrible feet on the fact I did that ballet picture when I was twenty-eight, and I did it in nine months when I should have taken fifteen years to get on my toes and do it. I broke my metacarpal arches, lost every toenail on both feet, and the knuckle joints on both feet just popped.

Ed: Ooooooo

Loretta: That's what ballet dancing is. It's absolutely opposed to what nature made.....it's just turned right around.

BEDTIME STORY

Ed: December, 1941, BEDTIME STORY...

Loretta: It was one of those romantic comedies.....

Ed: ....Review: "Fredric March teams with Loretta Young for a pair of top-notch performances..."

Loretta: That's nice of them.....

BEDTIME STORY....that's when Harry Cohn and I had the terrible fight about a dress. I had been shopping for myself......Bernard Newman was a wonderful designer for Bergdorf Goodman in

New York and he came out here but didn't like the motion picture work ....because he couldn't design what he liked. He had to design what the producer and star liked, so he left the picture business and went to Magnins downtown, and he was their head couturier.

He called me one day before I started the picture, and he said, "We're having a marvelous sale down here. Why don't you come down and we'll play with some of these clothes?" So, I went down and we picked out, on the on-sale rack, a beautiful white net dress. Maybe it was $165.00......it had a few little spangles on it. He added a few more spangles and a scarf .....he gussied it up, and I paid extra for that. Anyway, we did this with four or five things down there.

We started the picture, BEDTIME STORY, and we needed an extra dress the next week or whatever. So, I said, "I have a beautiful dress that I have bought, and I haven't worn it yet, so I'll sell it to you for the picture." The wardrobe people said, "Fine." I called Magnins and said, "Send the white dress to Columbia Studios' wardrobe and send the rest of the stuff home."

The wardrobe guy asked me what the dress was going to cost. I asked, "What'd you pay for the other dress?" He said, "$750." I said, "Fine, $750." So the dress went to the studio.

My agent called me...."What's this about a dress that you sold Harry Cohn and he's madder than a hatter. He says you're charging him $750 for a dress you paid $165, and he thinks that's just disgraceful. You shouldn't be making money on it....."

I got so mad. I said, "It's none of his business what I paid for it. How does he know what I paid for it?" "Well, it seems the dress went to Columbia, and a lady in the wardrobe department saw the price tag on it, and she knew what you were charging, and she called Harry Cohn's office."

That made me madder. I said, "It was a sale's dress and Bernie Newman, because he's a friend of mine, we spent hours and he added a scarf and he did this and that......and besides, that's what Harry paid for the other dresses, and that's what he's going to pay for this one."

He called me back in a few minutes and said, "I just talked to Harry Cohn, and he says no way is he going to pay you $750.00. He won't buy the dress. He's sending it back to the house." I said, "Fine. Tell him to find a dress that I do like." He said, "He'd copy this one...."

That started us off. Overtime at the studio is very expensive, and I would not fit (be available for fittings) over the noon hour. I would fit after 6:00 when I finished work, and therefore, it put them, all the beaders and all the seamstresses and everyone into overtime. We'd get in there and I'd say, "Oh, this beading is lovely, but it should be down here about an inch, maybe." So, they'd take it all off and put it all back on again.

I don't know how much money I ran up on that dress. He must have paid $5,000 for that dress and he was so stubborn, he wouldn't give in. Finally, they finished and I said, "Well, I've leaned on this enough so I guess I just better okay it." So we used it.

Harry was so furious with me that he sent word to me, "Tell her she's not to take her stockings home anymore." So, I said, "Oh, okay." So I'd take my stockings off and put my fingernails all the way through them just so they'd rip and nobody else could wear them. They were new fresh stockings.....rip! For years at the studio, when I'd put on a pair of stockings, I'd just wear them home. Up to that point, I never bought a pair of stockings in my life, and nobody seemed to mind it because the star is not going to come in and say, "Whose stockings were those? Who wore them before?" ....you know. Now, they didn't supply your underwear, but anything that you could see was supplied ...... you see stockings.

Anyway, I was supposed to have first billing on that picture. Both Freddie March and I were under contract to the same agent at the time, I guess it was Myron Selznick, and we both had first billing, but Freddie said, "Well, she's a lady so fine, I'll give her first billing, and I'll take first billing next time." And Harry Cohn got so mad.....he said, "Tell Miss Young she's not going to get first billing. I'm putting her *below* Freddie March's name." There was nothing I could do about that either. Anyway, he had his way.

Well, we'd go to parties, and I'd see him and ......I had to be mad at Harry Cohn all night. Finally, this went on for two or three years. When I wouldn't see him, of course, I wouldn't think about him. But I'd see him and get mad again.

Finally one night, at Mervyn LeRoy's house, I walked in and Tom said, "There's Harry Cohn." Harry's back was to me, and I walked into the room and I thought, "Oh, this is stupid and it takes so much energy to carry on an argument like this." So, I walked up behind him and said, "Don't turn around, Harry. It's Loretta. I'm sick of this being-mad-at-you game. If it would make you feel any better......you were right and I was wrong. Let's just stop this nonsense. If you don't want to stop it, just walk away from me. But otherwise, let's just make up and forget this whole thing."

And he did a long pause, and I almost walked away from him, and then he turned around and smiled and said, "Yeah, I'm ready to make up." And from then on, he never mentioned it again, and we became very good friends until the day he died.

I liked Harry very much, and he told me later on that he had a terrible crush on me the first time I worked at his studio. I said, "Well, I never would have known it." He said, "You were picking up with Spencer Tracy at the time." He was not sure of himself either. I think that's why he yelled so much. But I liked him.

I was given the #1 dressing room at the studio for MAN'S CASTLE which I expected anyway, and I didn't know at that time that at the back of the closet of that dressing room there was a door that led right into his private office.

Everybody else seemed to know it. But I must say, nobody ever rattled the knob. Years later he told me this. I said, "I don't believe it." He said, "The next time you're at the studio, I'll show you," and sure enough, there it was.

He said, "Oh yes, we had it put in there just for fun. See what you can get and what you can't get." He also had a chair in his private dining room, and mostly it was for the producers and writers and very few actors. He invited me to come up and eat in his private dining room every day, which I did because I found him very interesting. He has a chair, usually to the right of him that was wired, electrically. It wouldn't hurt you, but it would scare you to death, see. Fortunately, I had heard about that chair, and I didn't know if he would try it on a woman or not. He asked me to sit in a specific chair, and I said, "I don't want to sit in it. I'll sit down here. Until you can convince me that that chair's safe, I'm going to sit at the other end of the table."

So he very quickly put in a decent chair. But he probably would have had me sit in the wired chair just to see my reaction.

Ed: How would you rank Harry Cohn as a producer?

Loretta: Frank Capra owes everything he has to Harry Cohn because Harry left him alone. There are some people who have that quality. That's their genius, to get the talented people and then leave them alone to be talented. Most people today, their egos are such, that if they have a good story they want to make it better and they ruin it. When they get a good director, they tell him how they want it directed. If they get some good actors, they tell them what they're doing is wrong and how they want them to look and feel and …..you know.

Ed: Wasn't Harry Cohn considered unprincipled?

Loretta: There were rumors. And he was crude. Very bad manners. Quick to be on the attack. But one of the reasons I liked him was he took a chance on me when the rest of the community had blackballed me at the request of Daryl Zanuck.

Ed: Any more about BEDTIME STORY

Loretta: The only thing Al Hall said to me.....in this picture (compared to HE STAYED FOR BREAKFAST), "Please don't wear your hair hanging down and in back of you....don't put so much hair on." I said, "That's my hair." He said, "Oh, not all that....." He was right; I had added some extra little things....that was his whole communication to me. And he was right. I look at those pictures now and I say, "My God, I've got five times as much hair.....all sorts of bangs and buns ...."

Ed: I have a question: It seems like you have an east coast accent in that picture. I think I've noticed it before ....where did that come from?

Loretta: Oh, that was something we all did in those days when we were playing sophisticated women.......

1943

A NIGHT TO REMEMBER

Ed: ......time off between BEDTIME STORY and A NIGHT TO REMEMBER......one was January '41, and then the next one was released in January of 1943. Nothing released in 1942......

Loretta: The release dates don't mean a thing. I never did less than two pictures a year.....ever. One year I did seven or eight, I think for Warner Brothers.......

Ed: A NIGHT TO REMEMBER........

Loretta: A dull little picture. Brian Aherne. A silly little picture.

Ed: Gale Sondergaard...

Loretta: Yes.

Ed: ....Lee Patrick.....and Jeff Donnell. Samuel Bischoff....

Loretta: ......Producer. Very nice man.

Ed: Richard Wallace? the director.....

Loretta: Nothing at all. Richard Wallace......

Ed: (Review) NIGHT TO REMEMBER ".....mysterious things start to happen...."

Loretta: Nothing happens. There's a turtle that walks along at night, and somebody puts a candle on it, and they think it's a ghost, and it's just dumb......it's a stupid thing....

Ed: (laugh) (laugh) (laugh) "Miss Young, looking better than she has for some time, manages to create wholesome interest and screams proficiently at stated intervals....."

Loretta: That's about right.

Ed: Brian Aherne.....

Loretta: Dull man.....I thought. I thought he was wonderful in costume pictures where he played second lead. A great big fellah....typically English but without Ronald Colman's charm.

CHINA

Loretta: ....with Alan Ladd. Yes, that was during the war. Buddy De Sylva was running the studio (Paramount) at the time. Before I started that picture, I explained to my agent that I wouldn't do the movie unless a scene that condones suicide was deleted. I don't believe that suicide is the answer to anything. I'm not going to say, "That's the thing to do." Anyway, I got the okay from Buddy De Sylva that the scene would be deleted.

They put the scene back in, and I went to see Buddy. He said, "It's only a movie." I said, "I'm sorry. It's not only a movie. If you read some of my fan mail ....they *do* know it's only a movie, but they take it very seriously."

He said, "God Damn it. This is not a church. This is a studio.....we're making pictures to entertain ......" I said,

"Perfectly all right with me.....you can recast......you can do anything you like. But I will not do that scene," and I walked out of his office. The scene was deleted.

Ed: The picture was a big hit....

Loretta: Alan Ladd was a *great big star*, and it was during the war, and it was a rah-rah thing.

Ed: You had top billing........but I think I read that his image was bigger than yours in the posters.

Loretta: I was freelancing. My agent said, "Sure, she'll do it, but she's got to get top billing."

Ed: Did you like Alan Ladd as a person?

Loretta: Not very much. I found him.....I mean any man who calls for his agent every time he doesn't get his own way.....I found him petulant. I also found him......I don't remember hearing him laugh, or ever seeing him laugh. Everything that concerned him was very serious.

He was married to Sue Carroll. She had been an actress; then she became a political activist and an agent. She was Alan's agent, and the least little thing that would happen, he'd get on the phone and say, "Sue, you better get over here and straighten this out..."

One time on CHINA, there was a rain sequence, and my dressing room was inside the stage, and his dressing room was outside the stage, and he didn't like that. He said, "I'm going to get just as wet as she is; I can get pneumonia just as quick as she can. You better get over here, Sue."

Sue came over, and there simply was not room on the stage for the set and the camera and two dressing rooms.

Ed: What was the set?

Loretta: Oh, it was an outdoor set with a bunch of kids and a truck we were taking across China.....and it was raining. But it was done inside, you see, not outside. So, anyway, he would not work until Sue got there. Everybody sat. When she finally came, she talked with the assistant director. Later he told me what he said to Alan, "When you get to be as big a star as Loretta Young is, *then* yours will be the one inside, and maybe your leading lady's will be on the outside, but at this point, there's no choice between Loretta Young and Alan Ladd, although this is your studio......"

Ed: Paramount....

Loretta: Anyway, he was disgruntled the whole time, and I think he was mad at me because of it. Sue really was his right hand.

Ed: Why do I think of her as a big woman? Am I right in that impression?

Loretta: She's round, but she wasn't big.

Ed: What did you think of Alan Ladd as an actor?

Loretta: He had a certain screen personality......but as an actor.....I never made any contact with him. He wouldn't look at me. He'd say, "I love you..." he'd be looking out there some place. Finally, I said, "Alan, I'm *he-ere!!*" I think he was very conscious of his looks. Alan would not look beyond a certain point in the camera because he didn't think he looked good. What difference does it make what a man looks like so long as he looks like a man? With a woman, it's very important.

 Ed: Was he self-conscious about his height?

Loretta: Oh, yes.

Ed: How short was he? Short as you, say?

Loretta: Shorter than I. He was about 5'6" in his shoes and I was 5'6" without my shoes. And, if my hair was the least bit high, I was taller than he, so quite often we played scenes where we weren't walking or standing together. That's perfectly acceptable for actors to do that; at least in those days it was, anyway.

But Jimmy Cagney was not tall but somehow Jimmy was at terms with himself, always. I don't think Alan Ladd ever came to terms with himself.

Ed: Did you have a sense that CHINA was going to be a big picture?

Loretta: Oh, I thought every picture I ever made was going to be a big picture....Oh sure. You have to......You don't go into a picture if you think it's going to be bad.

Ed: .... as you were in the process of making it? Did you continue to be optimistic?

Loretta: Yes, I thought it was going to be good. It was a war picture. It was full of action and a bit of vindictiveness....pretty little orphan girls...........

1944

LADIES COURAGEOUS

Loretta: I don't remember too much about it. Walter Wanger was the producer, and Myron Selznick invited me to a business lunch between him and Walter. They were arguing back and forth. I think it was between $200,000 and $150,000, whatever it was. I finally said to Walter, I'll agree if you agree to split the difference but you have to buy me lunch every day. He said, "Fine, it's a deal."

After we left the restaurant, Myron asked me, "Did you really mean that?" I said, "Yes. This is the way I do business." If they go on too long......I'll do anything to get out of a meeting... see. This is why I have to have an agent. So, Myron said, "I think you're foolish but if that's what you want to do…..okay, that's what you want to do."

So, we went to lunch every day and I ordered the best things on the menu. Walter seemed to go along with it……. because I think he was just as thrilled with movie stars as anybody I've ever met. He liked all that kind of glamour behavior.

Ed: (LADIES COURAGEOUS) ……it was released in March of 1944…..

Loretta: It was a story of women who ferried the planes back and forth…..a bunch of women aviatrixes……it wasn't very good.

Ed: Geraldine Fitzgerald…..

Loretta: A very, very good actress. I think she sat out her career. She was too picky about what she did, I think, because she didn't work enough. She did DARK VICTORY, but she ended up in the second leads all the time. She did some wonderful films but she didn't get credit for them. As I said, the better the actors are around you, the better you look. I always looked forward to doing scenes with her because I knew I was going to learn something.

Ed:…… Diana Barrymore?

Loretta: Well, I was crazy about her. She was a darling girl. She wasn't very pretty and that's too bad when you had a very handsome father like that.

Ed: John Barrymore's daughter?

Loretta: Yes, by......not Dolores Costello, but by a writer.....his
first wife (Blanche Oelrichs).
We went on location and I saw quite a bit of her (Diana
Barrymore). The other girl (Geraldine Fitzgerald) kind of stayed
to herself. There was a very pretty blonde girl (Ann Gwynne?
Evelyn Ankers?), too, in that picture. I thought she was going to
be a big star, but unless you had the studio behind you to push in
those days......

Ed: ......on location?

Loretta: To Long Beach. They had an airfield down there. We
used the Army airplane base and we were down there for two or
three weeks.

Ed: That's probably the most time you ever spent in Long Beach
(Ed lived in Long Beach at the time of these interviews).

Loretta: (laugh), (laugh). I think so.......it's a nice little place.

Ed: a half million people today. Largest Cambodian population
of any city in the United States.....

Loretta: No! That's interesting. I wondered why they landed
there?.....

Ed: Barrymore......wasn't she kind of a tragic person?

Loretta: Yes.

Ed: …..drinking problems….

Loretta: Yes. She didn't at that time because she was just
starting. They didn't know where she was going to go. I think
Walter Wanger had her under contract. She was a young girl,
younger than I was.

Ed: Was she a good actress?

Loretta: You couldn't tell. She wasn't bad. She knew her
dialogue. She said what she was supposed to say and did what
she was supposed to do….but….

Ed: Confidence…..?

Loretta: I think there was an awful lot of weight on her
shoulders. If she had changed her name, she might have had a
better chance.

Ed: LADIES COURAGEOUS……did you feel you were somehow
doing your…..?

Loretta: Oh, yes. That was the whole tenor of the times;
everybody was talking war. You were either in it or praying
about it or working in the factories. Everybody was doing
something. Even children were saving pennies.

Ed: ......you were only thirty or thirty-one when you made that movie but you had a lot of maturity.....top woman officer.....

Loretta: Well, you should at thirty. I met this woman. She was a real woman, the first ferry pilot. I don't think she was any older than I was. Maybe she was. She was charming.

(Loretta moving on from Myron Selznick as an agent)

Loretta: Myron was an alcoholic. One night Joan Bennett and I sat up all night at his house at Arrowhead, begging him to at least stop a little bit. But he'd get *stoned* every night, and he finally got to the point where one drink made him drunk.

I finally had to say to him, "Myron, I want someone who is aware of where I want to go in the business and what kind of parts I'm looking for, not just to make the deal after they're called. Because money will come anyway. Money is not the whole bit. It's what I need to live on, but I want parts, and I want someone out there looking them up for me. I want you to do that, but apparently you can't do that. You've told me you're not interested in that. So I want you to find me an agent who will do that."

He looked at me and said, "You want your agent to go out and find you another agent?" I said, "Yes, you know more about them than I do. I'd rather it be you. But, if it can't be you, then you find me somebody that it can be." He thought that was the strangest thing he ever heard of....but he called me in about a month's time and he said, I think he said three men..... "You have to see all of them, and then you decide which one you want to go with. Any one of the three would be all right for you." One was Bert Allenberg, one was Johnny Hyde, and who was the other one? Whoever he was, I didn't like him right away, so I've blocked him out of my mind. Between Johnny Hyde and Bert Allenberg, Bert Allenberg had more time to spend on me.

AND NOW TOMORROW

Loretta: I *loved* that movie. I loved the book.

Ed: ....Director Irving Pichel.....

Loretta: He was an actor, and he was very easy for me to work with. I thought he was wonderful. It was an interesting, well-written script.

I think I was three months pregnant with Christopher, and when I see myself in that picture, I've got the tiniest waist you've ever seen. I don't know where that child was hiding. I must have had a minimizer or something on. But all the clothes were this fashion in those days. We had to do some retakes a few months afterwards.......by then all they could do were close-ups.

Susan Hayward......She was marvelous in it......there was a crying scene, and when she finished the two-shot, I said, "Oh, Susie, you were just marvelous....." She cut me off with "ssssh—ssssh." I backed away and went into my dressing room and left her alone. What she meant was, "I'm in the mood; I don't want to get out of it.....so shut up until we finish." I understood as one actress to another. You understand that. She never apologized, but I just took it for what it was worth.

This town is very strange, uh. I guess you can't help it that Susan was not an easy person to work with. I don't know if she was a perfectionist or what it was. But who did a picture with her? Oh, Robert Wise was telling me the other day. I went to a dinner party and sat next to him at dinner. And he directed the thing that she did get the award for.....

Ed: I WANT TO LIVE?

Loretta: Yes. And we were talking about it, and I said I loved her as an actress and that I did a picture with her. I told him about how she didn't want to come out of the mood, see.

He said, "Oh, I know exactly what you mean because the picture I did with her, she'd finish a scene, and she'd walk right to her dressing room and close the door. I wasn't used to that. I'm used to talking with people and feeling them out. So after two or three weeks, I said, "What's with Susan Hayward? Is she mad at me?" I was told, "That's just the way she is."

(Loretta continues) I don't think anyone really understood it. I mean, I don't think she would have won a popularity vote.....but they finally had to give her an Academy Award because she was so good.

1945

ALONG CAME JONES

Loretta: I had a good time doing that. You don't hear much about it.....it was not one of Gary Cooper's best pictures. He was not very good in it.....not a very good role for him. His shyness in real life was charming .... as long as it went with his great good looks and his masculine charms .... because you felt that there was a big undercurrent, that he wasn't very shy at all......it was just part of his personality. But when he played it as a kind of dumb man who doesn't even know how to shoot a gun.......I don't know.

By this time, Gary was deaf, and I never realized it.....he never admitted it....but we'd be sitting and talking and the assistant director would come and say, "We're ready, Mr. Cooper," and he'd just go right on talking. Then, I'd say, "Gary, they've called you." ...."Oh!"

I had a feeling all through the picture that he was a beat behind......

Ed: What about your accent......your cowgirl talk.......

Loretta: There were a bunch of cowboys on the set. I probably picked it up from them. I didn't know how to shoot a gun either. Gary said to me one day, "Oh, I can show you....." so at noontime we'd go on the back lot, and he'd say, "Now, honey!" And he'd throw it at me and say, "Now grab it with this hand here, put it here, lean into it. Pull the trigger at the same time you lean into it." Well, I tell you, that poor shoulder of mine......Finally, I got it.

When we finished shooting, I said to Mom one day, "They're having the preview of ALONG CAME JONES in the Village (Westwood). How many tickets do you want? She said, "Oh, dear, I don't think I can go tomorrow night...." I said, "Gary Cooper's in it...."Oh, fine. I'd like about...." She was crazy about Gary Cooper.....She really didn't understand, nor did she like, motion picture people, but she liked him.

I didn't realize it at the time because I was driving a buckboard and everything else in that picture, but I was pregnant with my second son. When I finished the picture, I thought I was two weeks pregnant, but it turned out when I went to the doctor, I was, indeed, four months pregnant. That meant I had had a couple of periods right along but I still held the baby. Why hadn't I had a miscarriage........

I was under contract to International Pictures. Bill Goetz was head of that. It was a multi-million dollar seven-year contract, and I had already made ALONG CAME JONES. They wanted me to go immediately into Benedict Bogeaus's production of THERE GOES LONA JOHNSON. The costumes were kind of the bustle-type which meant that you had to have an hour glass figure, and they had sent me the script, and I thought that if I was only two weeks pregnant, that by the time I finished the picture, I'd still be all right. I had agreed to do it, but when I found out I was four months pregnant, I called the studio and said, "I'm terribly sorry, I can't do this picture because I'm already starting to straighten out on the sides. I'm four months pregnant, not two weeks."

So I expected them to postpone it until after the baby was born, and then I would do it. Not at all. I think it was twenty-four hours later that I got a call...... "Could I come......"

So, I did. We arrived at the studio and we went into the board meeting. It was the first time I had been invited to attend, and it was a little scary. Bill (Goetz) was not the Chairman of the Board; I think he ran the studio. Anyway, this Chairman of the Board proceeded to explain that I had only done one picture under this new contract and that the board felt that I was more interested in having a family than I was in my career because I was insisting on "going ahead with this pregnancy". They felt that in all fairness to the studio that they'd have to cancel the contract. It meant a lot of money, and that's what we lived on, the whole family, and so I really couldn't believe my ears. Because in those days, abortion was absolutely verboten. If a woman had an abortion, she was looked down upon, and the doctor, if he was caught, went to jail and lost his license.

I've forgotten who this Chairman was. Bill was sitting there He was a dear friend. We were friends since I was thirteen, I guess. He used to work for Corrine Griffith as a go-fer. Anyway, she liked him a lot, and this is how people became assistant directors, directors, and producers. They just stayed around the set and learned the business. He rescued me one day. I was under contract to First National, and I had to transfer on the bus three times. I missed a bus and I knew I was going to be late. I was scared to death because I had already been bawled out once before. I called Bill, and I was crying, and I said, "Bill, I'm at the corner of Sunset and ......I missed the bus." "All right, all right,

Gretch, calm down, I'll come and get you." He came and got me, and I got to the set just on time. He was sweet and good, and he treated me that way, and now he was the president of International Pictures.

He was always very kind. Till the day he died, I loved him. He was married to Edie Mayer (Louis B. Mayer's daughter). Anyway, he couldn't look at me. I looked at him a couple of times, and he was looking somewhere else or going over some papers or something. He was too embarrassed. Anyway, the Chairman got all the way through, and I just looked at my agent, Bert Allenberg, and I said, "Is that it?" So, I got up and left the room and Bert followed me. We got outside and I said, "Did he say what I think he said?" He said, "Yes, I'm afraid he did." I said, "Do you want me to tell them or do you want to tell them?" He said, "Oh, no, no. I would be delighted to tell them." So I left. I went home.

He called me about six that night and said, "They're not only going to cancel the contract if you go ahead with this pregnancy," mind you, I was four months along, and they knew it. "They want you to pay back $22,000 which they have paid you since the last picture, not knowing that they would be canceling your contract." I said, "Tell them to *drop dead*!"....and I got off the phone I was so angry. To make a long story short, they did cancel.

A few years later, I was in the Brown Derby. I had taken Peter who was about four. We had gone to the doctor, and he had gotten a shot. I had promised him if he didn't cry, we would go to the Brown Derby to lunch, just the two of us. He didn't know what the Brown Derby was, but he knew it must have been something special. So we did.

We were sitting there .....and of course, the head waiter and everyone was making a big fuss. As I had walked in, I saw Bill Goetz over at one of the other booths, sitting with some other men. He saw me, too, so we nodded. I hadn't seen much of him, socially or otherwise. Not too much.

He came over on his way out and stopped by the table. I said, "Bill, sit down for a minute." So he did. And he kept looking at Peter. I said, "Well, do you think he's worth five million dollars?" or whatever the contract was supposedly for. He said, "Oh, Loretta, don't even talk about that. There was not a thing in the world I could do. I was just out-voted on it." I said, "I know that, Bill."

Peter, strangely enough ...... well, maybe we've gone through more together. But Peter has always been, in problems and out of problems, always a great joy to me. I couldn't have been paid off any better with any other child, as far as I'm concerned.

1946

THE STRANGER

Ed: This film was for International. Was it negotiated as a way to settle your contract with that studio?

Loretta: Must have been. I know I did two pictures under that contract.

Oh, THE STRANGER. I was just crazy about Orson Welles. A big fat crush on him. He was perfectly charming. He had humor; he had talent........ he was good-looking at that time. He was fighting weight; he was always fighting weight. He was sensitive......

Ed: ....when you say sensitive...

Loretta: Yes...... as I said, I had a big crush on him.....his cherub face .....I couldn't help but laugh. Finally, he said, "All right, Loretta. I know I'm putting on weight, but you don't have to make fun of me in front of the whole set." I said, "Oh, no, Orson. I wasn't making fun of you. It's just when you get so serious, your face is so cute that it makes me laugh. Russell Metty (the cameraman) tells me that if I laugh too much, I'll have to go and change my make-up at noontime. I'm getting all these laugh lines around my mouth, and he doesn't want to photograph them."

He said, "Oh, that makes me feel a little better." From then on, when he wanted to give me direction, he'd come and stand behind me and he'd say, "Loretta, no, don't turn around. In the next scene, I want you to be so uptight that a pin dropping on the floor would make you scream." That's the way he directed me.

Toward everyone. In fact, he was so sensitive, I often wondered why that man didn't just throw up his hands and scream at everybody and just walk off the set. Because, I felt, Sam Spiegel, the producer, was jealous of him......the whole front office was jealous of him because he was so talented, you know. And he could juggle all these balls in mid-air. A lot of people have told me that THE STRANGER was the best picture I ever made. Well, I don't think so, but they do, and Orson directed and acted in it. One of those jobs is enough. All these people tested him all the time.....all the time......the men. They were so jealous.

Ed: Didn't he have a reputation for going over budget?

Loretta: Well, he didn't on this. They can give you any reputation they want in this business. Maybe he did go over budget in CITIZEN KANE ...... but it was worth it. If Louella Parsons had not been alive, those pictures would have been classics that made millions and millions of dollars but she was out to kill him because the picture was against Mr. Hearst, and Mr. Hearst had saved her life, literally, and she just adored the ground that he walked on......

Ed: ....her life or her career?

Loretta: Her life. She had tuberculosis, and she was young with a young daughter, Harriet. Mr. Hearst found out and said, "You're going to take as long of a rest as you want....you'll get your salary every week," and he sent her to Palm Springs......and, I don't know how many, four or five years she was there. She got well. And he said, "Your job is always here.....don't even think about it....."Saved her life.....and her career. You only hear the bad things about these people because they were successful. Both of them.

One of the most dangerous and stupid things I did, I guess,.........there's a scene where he's up in the clock tower which was at the top of the set, and those stages are three or four stories high.....there's this long ladder going up there .....he has filed a rung on the ladder so that she'll fall, but then he catches her with one hand. Anyway, I'm hanging there and this stunt man is holding my hand. They had a stunt woman, but they were getting a close-up. I think she did the long shot if I'm not mistaken. But I still had to get on the thing to do the close-up.

They put a little harness around my waist and then way back there, they put a wire through the sleeve of the coat, all the way down here and then way through his sleeve, and then it was attached to somebody else who was holding the wire in case the first stunt man dropped me. So I wouldn't drop, see. But every time we'd start to shoot, I'd take my feet off the thing, I'd swing and you'd see it (the wire)......"Cut..Cut" .... Finally, after the third or fourth time, I said, "What are the chances of your dropping me if they cut that wire?"

He said, "If I had a heart attack at that particular moment, I'd drop you. Otherwise, there's not a chance in the world. You only weigh 100 pounds, and I've got you by the wrist and you've got me......"

I said, "Cut that wire because we're going to be here all day. We're never going to get this shot." So he did. Of course, the next shot was fine, no wire pulling out at all, and he pulled me right out of the shot and everything was fine.

I knew better than to discuss this with Orson. He would have said, "I don't want you hanging up there from the roof of that stage....." You didn't say no to him because he was also an actor in the picture, and there's a certain vulnerability that you know, you just don't flat out argue with someone who is acting and directing in the picture.....I don't know whether I sensed this or thought it out.....but I would never have talked as bluntly to Orson as I did to, say, Bill Wellman.

Ed: Because he's part of the ......

Loretta: Of the make-believe that everybody kind of cooperates. None of us go too far with each other. The director is outside of that. So, with Orson, I simply defied him by not telling him. I just told the stuntman to cut the wire, see. Afterwards, he got mad. But he didn't get too mad because he got the shot, and he didn't have to take the responsibility for it. I understood that.

Before we started this picture, I said to Bill Goetz who ran the studio, "There's one scene in it .... there's dialogue that I'm not going to say." He asked why. I said, "Because it's diametrically opposed to everything I believe in, and I'm not going to propagandize something that is wrong." The lines were something like, "Did you ditch church, too?" "Yes". "Good, I'm glad." Bill knew me well enough. He knew me since I was thirteen-years-old. He said, "It's not that important, so do whatever you like with it."

We were on the set, and I noticed that the scene was back in the script. I said, "I'm sorry, that was cut out a long time ago as far as

I'm concerned." "Oh, but it makes them kind of co-conspirators....." I said, "That's right, it sure does -- on the wrong side of the fence as far as I'm concerned. "

Anyway, Sam Spiegel who was producing the picture came down to the set. He said, "Oh, now Loretta, after all, you're an actress....." I said, "That's right. I'm an actress who influences an *awful lot* of people, I'm sure. Every actor does......whatever they do. I'm the one who wants to get them into church, Sam, not out of church. So, I'm not going to say it."

"Oh, is there nothing I can do to convince you?" I said, "No, not a thing. I hope you're not mad at me, but I already told this to Bill before we started the picture." Then I said, "If she makes it a bad thing to do, I'll do it that way." "Oh, no, no. ......I want them to...... We'll pick something else other than not going to church....."

Ed: What about Edward G. Robinson?

Loretta: We didn't work together on *that* picture....

Ed: He browbeat you with those films of the Holocaust....

Loretta: We didn't work together the way we did in THE HATCHET MAN.....

I remember him as always fun and always professional. Between you and me, he was a *big* liberal, and I was a *big* conservative. I didn't know him socially...he went with a little older group than I did, I guess.....and more....you know.....liberal.

Ed: How about Richard Long?

Loretta: He was just a kid, I think eighteen, and here he was working with Orson Welles, Edward G. Robinson and Loretta Young. He had the most beautiful eyelashes. They were longer and thicker than the false ones I was wearing, and I used to kid him about it, saying, "Richard, why don't you put some mascara on those gorgeous lashes?" He was horrified of course.

I came back from lunch one day. We had done Richard's close-ups before we went to lunch, and now we were going to do mine. Orson said, "Come on, Loretta, we're ready." I got in place, and Orson said, "Roll 'em." I started my dialogue and Richard turned around. He had on these fake eyelashes; they were horse eyelashes. I got one line out before I burst out laughing. The trick, of course, is not to laugh, to just ride over it if you can.

Oh........ about the dog. There was a trainer on the set; the dog Red played an important role, and Judy wanted a dog, so I asked him about it. He asked, "What kind," and I said, 'Well, she's ten. I think any kind will do. See if you can find something by Christmas. Two months later, he called me. "The only thing I could find was a little mutt. He's only five dollars. If you don't want him, I'll give him to my son." I said, "Oh, I want it, but I can't have it until Christmas....so you keep it and train it and everything you're supposed to do with it." He said, "Fine."

I was so impressed with his generosity that I went out and bought a full outfit for his son, hat, dress coat, everything, and gave it to him as a gift when he brought the puppy. Then I got a $600 bill for training the dog......and then it went all over the carpet. I was so mad!

Ed: A lot of people today don't want to watch black and white pictures...THE STRANGER....would it have improved it if it were shot in color?

Loretta: No, it wouldn't. We're used to color now. But in two minutes you're used to black and white. If I look at any of these old movies of mine, which I don't do very often, but if I do....when it first comes on it seems very boring, very dull.....then in five minutes if the story is any good....you've forgotten that it's not in color.

1947

THE PERFECT MARRIAGE:

Ed: You did a cover for *LIFE* magazine......did that impress you?

Loretta: Oh no. That was just part of the routine. Most leading ladies were on the *LIFE* magazine cover.....because no matter how you slice it, good, bad, or indifferent, we were all of interest to a lot of people.

Ed: More like a model.....

Loretta: I was making THE PERFECT MARRIAGE. Their idea for the layout was, the first year of marriage, a very sexy nightgown, to the tenth year and the one they used on the cover.......sleeper feet and everything. ...It was *LIFE*'s idea. It was shot at Paramount. I don't know whether they used a Paramount photographer ....Hal Wallis was producing that film.

Edith Head designed ten different night gowns and so they showed me in these ten different nightgowns inside, and this one on the cover.

Maybe we were all spoiled back then, but it was just another photo sitting for me. Because when I'd go to New York I'd do *Vogue* or *Harpers*. *Saturday Evening Post* did only one important story on me, and as I said, I didn't like it at all when I first read it. Then when I got talking and thinking about it, at least it was more interesting than the blah story which it usually was. Beautiful pictures they used...Johnny Engstead did those.

Ed: Virginia Field. Here's what she said about you: "She was sickenly sweet. A pure phony. Her two faces sent me home angry and crying several times." ("Village Voice, December, 1986)

Loretta: I didn't feel any animosity toward any of the women I worked with. Even those who didn't like me....I didn't know they didn't like me... I had no idea that Virginia Field felt one thing about me or the other.....much less send her home in tears. *And not to know it*.....see...that's what bothers me. It does bother me ....that you can hurt someone that badly and not know it..... Call her and find out what it was all about. I'm sure you can get her number from Norman (Norman Brokaw, Loretta's agent).

Ed: (After calling Virginia Field): I have my own theory on how you affected Virginia Field, and that is.....she said you were 'sickening sweet', so you were probably very nice to her, yet you were focused on getting exactly what you wanted. Some people.....they'd rather...

Loretta: They'd rather you'd be honest with them....

Ed: You probably were being honest...but with a smile......somebody who is so me, me, me usually isn't going to be that nice. I mean, I just talked to her for a minute. She was very crisp; she probably didn't relate to sweet......

Loretta: I'm sure I was not as understanding or compassionate or even as interested in anybody else as much as I am today......

Ed: Now, Leonard Spiegelglass had something good to say about you. He said that he'd rewrite a certain scene and bring it to you, and you'd say, "Oh, that's beautiful, but I'm not a good enough actress to do it..." His point was that when you didn't want to do something.....you had such a charming way of not doing it.

Loretta: Well, maybe....Maybe I did, I don't know. I've used all sorts of ruses in my career.....(laugh). I loved Lenny. He used to live right across the street over here. He was with his mother. He was amusing, and he was on the set all the time...writing and rewriting.

Ed: .....but what made me wonder, did you really *think*....

Loretta: .....that I wasn't that good...No...... of course, not. I wouldn't have lasted if I had thought I was not a good enough actress. It must have been something that I didn't *want* to do.

Ed: Did you usually have a good relationship with the writers?

Loretta: Yes, if they were flexible enough. I would usually read a script ten or twelve times and get sooo accustomed to the character and the ideas of the character...I wouldn't memorize every single solitary word, but you have to know the *intent* behind everything.....I never stuck too closely to the script because I found it sometimes quite stilted...

I'm sure there must have been writers who could have torn their hair out with me....but it wouldn't bother me at all to re-write a whole scene and say, "This is the way I want to play it." Sometimes I was right, and sometimes I was wrong.

(Back to THE PERFECT MARRIAGE)

During the making of PERFECT MARRIAGE....I had a big fat fight with Hal Wallis. I was a fashion designer in the story, and there was a scene set at The Stork Club on a Sunday night. I wanted to wear a long white draped, jersey, jeweled dress with a jeweled hat that went with it and a white broad-tail coat over it.....the most expensive fur you can buy....Russian broadtail.

I had it made, and I tested it, and I thought it was gorgeous. I'm not a New Yorker; I'm a Californian. If I had been a little smarter,

I would have listened to the producer, Hal Wallis, who did know New York very well.

Edith Head was right with me. She said, "I think the dress is beautiful," but she, too, is not a New Yorker. Hal Wallis called me and said, "The white outfit is gorgeous. It was my favorite outfit...but you can't wear it in that scene." I asked, "Why?" He said, "Because it just isn't done in New York on a Sunday night. They don't dress that way. You should have a simple little black dress and maybe a mink coat over it, short....."

I said, "I'm sorry, Hal, but I like the white dress, and that's what I'm going to wear." He said, "But, Loretta, you can't. It's not proper. They don't do that." I said, "I don't care what they do. This woman is a designer; she can wear anything she likes and that's what I want her to wear..."

Ed: ...um huh....

Loretta: I said, "I'm sorry. That's the one I can best act in...." (laugh) so what's the poor man going to do.

Ed: ...um...huh....

Loretta: My agent called me. He said, "Loretta, are you sure you're right?" I said, "Yes, I'm right. I'm a movie star......." I think it was Bert Allenberg because Myron had either died by then or had already turned me over to Allenberg. Really, I wanted to wear it because I knew I shouldn't have spent that much money on that one outfit, and I was really kind of caught. Nobody mentioned it to me except deep down inside I knew that. I just wasn't smart enough to listen to the wiser man at the moment.

Anyway, I wore this outfit, and Virginia Field was in the same scene with me, and she may have heard this whole, dumb fight that went on between this idiot actress and this very good producer, which Hal Wallis was.....until the day he died....

Anyway, there wasn't anything he could do about it, and I'd go on the set, and I was just showing off like mad, and everybody said, "It's gorgeous." Sure, it was gorgeous, but it wasn't right for the scene, that's all.....and particularly for a designer, she would have *known* better.

Now, Virginia Field came in looking absolutely marvelous in a very plain little black dress and a black mink coat over it and her blonde hair and her little pearl earrings....anyway, she looked perfect, and I looked, I don't know, Mae West at the carnival....or something. But I didn't know it then.

I think it was about eighteen years later that I saw this picture on television. I had forgotten about the fight that we had over the clothes, and I looked at it and thought, "Oh, you jerk! What have you got that on for?" Really, I talked right out loud to the film. Then I remembered the whole fight....

Ed: ....ah...hmmmm

Loretta: and I sat right down and wrote a letter to Hal Wallis...(laugh)... what does he care now...twenty years later...

"Dear Hal, I have just seen THE PERFECT MARRIGE, and you are a wonderful producer, and I only wish I had been better in it than I was, and I must tell you ....this is an abject *apology* for that *ridiculous* white outfit that I wore on a Sunday night to the Stork Club in New York City. I apologize.... Loretta"

Well, I got the biggest bunch of roses you've ever seen in the entire world the next day. His note read, "It doesn't make any difference. You're still one of my favorites...." It was only because he was a charming man.

Ed: What about Director Lewis Allen.....

Loretta: He was an Englishman, very good.

Ed: How about working with Eddie Albert?

Loretta: Eddie Albert became a *wonderful* actor when he got older. He was always good, but he ripened up, beautifully. He did one of the television shows with me. We couldn't afford him to do another. I just remember that one show in which I played a floozy blonde.

Part Nine: Peak of Movie Stardom Years

THE FARMER'S DAUGHTER

Loretta: THE FARMER'S DAUGHTER had been written for Ingrid Bergman, the script, and she turned it down. Rightfully so, because it was no trick for her to do it. She was a brilliant actress, and I just loved her. Anyway, why Dore Schary thought of me I'll never know. He came over to visit me on the set of THE PERFECT MARRIAGE.....I think he sent me the script the week before .... and I read it and thought, "Well, she's very nice."

Anyway, he came over to have lunch with me on the set, and he said, "How do you like the script?" I said, "It's a charming script, but you know, I don't have a Swedish accent." He said, "I know that, Miss Young; I've seen you on the screen. But would you like to learn one?" I said, "I don't know whether I could or not." He said, "Would you like to try?" I said, "Well, I could do a southern accent if you like...." He said, "No, the point of the story is that the woman is foreign born. Why don't you let me find a coach for you and try it." And most producers, at least the producers nowadays, they are not interested in what you think or what you feel or anything. All they're interested in is making a deal, and they try to squeeze everything they can out of you. They really don't know whether you can give a good performance or not. I don't think they recognize a good performance, most of them, anyway.

Anyway, Dore to work for, I thought.....he and Frank Capra were my favorites to work for because they treated me as an artist, not as the star.....but as an artist. They were more interested in that.

Ed: So what does a producer do....?

Loretta: They choose the story. They choose the director and the writer and the stars and the cast.......Howard Koch is a producer and a very good one...

A lot of people had trouble finding what a producer does. Unless they're exceptionally good producers, it's kind of a waste of money, I think. Except, you have somebody to go to and crab and see if they say, "yes" or "no."

Ed: Someone beyond the director.....

Loretta: Yes. Because the director is fighting for his directorial rights. If he's a camera oriented man, then the scene will be pretty, but the performance will be nothing. You should sacrifice the technical for the creative end of it because that's what touches the people. Dore Scary was a very good producer, and a good writer, by the way, and he knew how to arbitrate my impasse with the director on THE FARMER'S DAUGHTER....otherwise, who knows how that would have turned out.

(Back to THE FARMER'S DAUGHTER)

Ed: Alex Kale (sp?)

Loretta: Oh, he was German. The camera work is always very important to me, always, and I wanted my own cinematographer and still man. I wanted Milton Krasner as the cinematographer. Dore wanted me to use Alex Kale (as still photographer) but I wanted someone else who I had worked with before. Dore said, "Alex Kale is under contract to the studio. Would you use him for two days, and if you don't like his work, I'll dismiss him and you can get your cameraman?" I agreed. This man came, and I really waltzed through the still pictures the first day, and he brought the proofs to me the next morning on the set.....they were absolutely gorgeous! Gorgeous! He shot all day again, and they were all gorgeous. I have some. I'll get them for you.

Ed: (looking at a photograph): Where is this wheat field you're sitting in?

Loretta: Petaluma, right outside San Francisco. We were there for three weeks.

Ed: Wasn't Judy with you on that location?

Loretta: She was there for three days. She came for the weekend after school, and then I sent her back Sunday night. She came up on the train alone, and I met her. The governess met her when she went back. She had a ball; she loved it.

Ed: .....on location....

Loretta: Yes, on a real farm .... Petaluma. I stayed at the
Fairmont Hotel in San Francisco...

Ed: Anna Q. Nilsson.....

Loretta: Yes, she played my mother. She was a star in the silent
days, and she told me a very interesting story. Herbert Brennon
hosted a dinner party at which she was a guest, and he showed
them tests of eight or ten girls........... they had started with
fifty....... for the part in LAUGH, CLOWN, LAUGH. She said, "I like
the one with the buck teeth and the big eyes. That's the one," and
that was me. He said, "Oh, no, we don't want her....her legs aren't
good." She said, "I can't help it. That's the one I like." I had never
seen her (Anna Q. Nilsson) before or since.......(the making of
THE FARMER'S DAUGTHER during which this conversation took
place).

Ed: You were blonde.....

Loretta: Every Sunday, I spent the whole day bleaching my hair
because you could see the least little thing....when I finished the
picture, it was like cotton candy. I couldn't even get a comb
through it when it was the least bit damp. I wanted to dye it back
to my own color but my hairdresser said, "Let it grow back." I
said, "I can't walk around town for a month......" she said, "You
have to...." After a month, I couldn't stand it so I had it dyed
brown and of course it looked just like I had a hat on; it was all
one color. I was walking down the street in Beverly Hills one day
and in a window I saw myself......that terrible looking woman
with that terrible looking hair, and I thought, "My God! That's

me!" I decided that I'd have to do something about it, and if I saw a beauty shop, I'd just go in and tell them to give me a permanent and get it up and cut it off, get it shorter…

I found one in about a block, and I had to walk upstairs to get there. Of course it had been so mistreated, this poor hair of mine, that when the woman got it all up in these little tiny permanent things and turned the heat on, all of a sudden I saw her …….this man came tearing over to me and switched off the heat and grabbed these two things on the back and they came right out at the roots. Burned my hair right off at the roots! He said, "We'll have to let it cool first." I asked, "Is that hair in there?" (laugh) (laugh)….Finally, the poor man …….. I said, "Just take all this stuff off…."

Ed: ….they knew you were Loretta Young?

Loretta: Oh, sure, I said, "Take them off carefully, please. I had a big hole back here (Loretta pointing to back of head). I thought, "Well, we'll see…." I had already decided that I'd have a bathing cap designed that was just gorgeous and I'd wear it all the time because I knew I'd lost all my hair.

Anyway, the man was shaking so; he was scared I was going to sue him and make a fuss. I said, "Look, it's not your fault, my hair has been bleached until they couldn't bleach it anymore, and then I had it dyed back so all that dye is on it …….don't worry about it. Just pray that *all* of it isn't going to come out." Well, it didn't. I lost two or three holes around here, but there was just enough…… "Now, just wash this stuff out very carefully, and I'll just wrap it in a towel, and I'll go home that way…"

Sure enough, I walked around with a kind of turban on for two or three weeks and little by little, it just fell out. I lost a lot of it. Then it started to grow back in. It grows a half an inch a month anyway, so in two months the holes were gone and then I let it grow back in…

Ed: Somewhere I read that your hair never grew again after THE FARMER'S DAUGHTER…

Loretta: That's not true. It grew beautifully. I can show you pictures with it, so……

Ed: …..Joseph Cotten…

Loretta: He was never temperamental. He had a lot of temperament but he was never temperamental. He was always able……if I would fly up and say, "Well, I don't think I want to …..!!!!!" He'd say, "Why don't we go and have a soda instead of all this arguing, come on….."and he'd woo me out of it.

Ed: Wasn't that the job of the director (Henry Potter)?

Loretta: Yes, but this director and I were the ones who were arguing. He'd say about something I'd want to do, "I think it might be a little annoying," so that's hardly the way to direct anybody.

One day Henry wanted me to walk across the lawn the first time she's going into the house to get the job. I said, "She's a farmer. She wouldn't walk across the lawn." He said, "It makes the shot better." I said, "I don't care. Have the camera follow me. I'm going down there and up there on the concrete." And we got in a snit about it, both of us. He was just as petulant as I was. That was one day Joseph Cotten came in and said, "Henry, I think it's just about lunchtime." He looked at me and said, "Don't you? Come on, let's you and me go out and get a hamburger.....to hell with these box lunches."

By the time I got back I was all calmed down, but I said, "I'm still walking on the concrete." Henry said, "All right!" But I was right because she just wouldn't. Too much respect for the earth.

(A still of where Katie is stacking the dishes)

Ed: ...so your boarding house days came in handy?

Loretta: As long as the plates aren't too large, you can do that......

Henry and I ....this was another argument.....in the script, it says she goes over to sharpen a pencil, just for something to do while they're trying to get together, these two, and the pencil breaks and as she gives it to him, he touches her hand and she kind of does this.......Henry didn't like the scene and I asked, "Why? It's a perfectly natural thing to do...." This is what you call having a story conference on the set....Finally, I got to the point where I wouldn't argue. I said, "Why don't you send for Dore;

he's the producer. Let him decide." I said, "I like this script the way it is, and this is why I accepted to do it, so I don't see.....unless you can find a better way of saying it......."

Ed: Once you had misgivings about a director, was it downhill from there?

Loretta: If a director was not good, I didn't mean to, but I'd say, "Where did you get that idea? Why wouldn't she do that?" If he couldn't give me a good reason for it......

Ed: you were always rational about.....

Loretta: Yes! Yes!

(more on Joseph Cotten)

I was never in love with Joe, but I liked him so much that I felt no embarrassment with him at all. If you're a little bit in love with somebody, you just keep a little bit attentive, to hope everything you do is perfect, and everything you do they'll think is divine. I was much more at ease with Joe because he was just solid and warm and kind, and I knew he wasn't going to criticize me, but I also knew he wasn't going to go along with me if he didn't think so....

At that time Joe was very secure in his acting and in his behavior on the set. The director would say, "Oh, do something else, do it a different way... do anything." "Fine, okay," and he'd do it ten different ways, and finally the director would come back to the way he did it in the first place. I'd look at Joe, and he'd say, "He's the director." He was a very reasonable man. Most actors who are that reasonable aren't very good. But Joe was. He always had a spark in him, and he looked like he knew something I didn't know. He always had that kind of little look about him.

Ed: He wouldn't patronize you…..

Loretta: Oh no……oh no. He just rode above all that kind of stuff. But there was nothing petty about him, and he would not indulge in the little things on the set. "Who gets their close-up taken first…….?" …….none of that kind of nonsense…..and I knew he liked me.

Ed: ….it comes back to that….

Loretta: …and he did.

(Another still photograph where Katie is arriving at the House of Congress)

Loretta: I guess Edith Head did that…..that was my necklace and my earrings. Later, they were stolen from me. That belt is marvelous; that was my belt. Edith just made the hat and dress coat. Very pretty.

Ed: Ethel Barrymore….

Loretta: She played Joe Cotten's mother. Oh, she was a fabulous personality. Everyone was scared of her, including me.

I found myself running to get her a cup of ...... "Would you like a cup of coffee?" "Oh, yes, I would, Loretta..." "Do you take cream and sugar?" "No, black is fine." So I ran over and got .....The prop boy said, "I'll take care of it, Miss Young." "No, that's all right. I'll take care of it."

She didn't demand any of this but she was elderly.....she wasn't excitable at all.....she would come in and sit down and drink her coffee. When we were ready for rehearsal she would run through the scene....we all tried to do what we were going to do....and we'd discuss it, "I like this, and I like this...." She'd do it the way she liked and she'd ask, "Is that all right?" Henry (the director) replied, "That's fine," and she'd say, "I'll go to my dressing room, and the stand-in can rehearse anymore because that's what I'll do, and you call me when you're ready to shoot." And nothing budged her.

Our director used to change a lot of things, and he couldn't do it, of course, with her, and I was glad he couldn't because he just liked to fuss on the set. I don't think he knew when he had it. But anyway, I was crazy about her.

I had a miscarriage on that picture, and they had to close the picture for ten days because I was in everything...When we came back, we were at the Ebell Club down on Wilshire Boulevard, and we had our dressing rooms outside in an alley next to the theatre......those little portable dressing rooms. Mine was the first in line.....they do it by caste system....the star and then the leading man and then the character people and on down.

When I got out of the car she (Ethel Barrymore) was standing in front of her dressing room, and as I walked from the car to my dressing room she walked over to me, very slowly and she said, "My dear child, you've been through a great deal ....you must rest as much as possible. I think you've come back to work too soon. Nevertheless, that's your business, not mine, but you must rest. So I'm going to put my chair right here in front of your dressing room door, and nobody will get by me unless it's vitally important." I said, "Oh, wouldn't that be marvelous."

Boy, for three days, we were down there, and nobody........when I'd finish on the set, and I'd go to my dressing room.....and if I sat in the chair she said, "No, you lie down." She never talked while I was lying down, never waited on me or anything. She was a sentinel sitting there. "Oh, don't disturb her......she's working so hard, and she needs her rest."

Ed: Charles Bickford.....

Loretta: Charles Bickford, a perfectly *fascinating* man! Loved to gamble. He was very quiet on the set all through THE FARMER'S DAUGHTER. He and Ethel Barrymore were two of a kind. Never missed a line or a cue or an eyebrow or a comma or a period on anything. But both of them were very self-contained. They did not need anybody else around. All they would do .....they would do it perfectly.

Loretta: Another argument I had with the director was about the accent. I was feeling really proud of it, and one day he said, "You know, I've been thinking about this thing, and I think it's time now that you drop the accent. After all, you've (Katie) been to night school." I replied, "Yes, for six months. Why, if I had always gone to American schools, and I hadn't lost my accent by the time I hit twenty-five, which was the youngest I could be and still run for Congress, why would I lose it with six months at night school?" Henry said to me, "Well, I feel you should lose it." I said, "All people will say, 'Oh, Loretta forgot her accent.'"

We went back and forth, and finally I said, "You'd better get Dore down here to settle this; it seems we can't." Henry and I continued our argument, and Dore finally said, "Loretta, I think your accent is charming, but if it bothers Henry that much, do you think you could just lighten it a little?" I looked at him, and I said, "No. If you want to, Dore, you can recast." It was about 4:00 in the afternoon by this time. Dore said, "Well, it's late, why don't you go on home?" I said, "I'm going home, but I'll see you in the morning with the accent, so prepare yourself." We went back to the set the next day, and I must say, Henry never mentioned it. Dore used to come on the set every day after viewing the rushes from the day before. About four or five days after the 'drop the accent' incident, he said, "Come here. I want to tell you something. You just keep going the way you are, and you're going to get an Academy nomination. You may not get the award, but you will get a nomination. Don't let anything rock your boat." I said, "Fine, I won't." I thought it was just a little pep talk to make me feel better.

When I did get the nomination I didn't think at all that I would win, but it was an excuse for getting a new dress. I said to Adrian,

"I've been nominated for an Academy Award, and I want a beautiful dress." He said, "Look at my line." I hemmed and hawed and finally, I said, "Look in there". He always kept a chest. All designers do. They keep a chest full of materials that they just love and don't want to give up. He came out with some green taffeta.....it was like shocking pink only it was shocking green. He said, "I love this." I said, "Fine, fine." He made a great big dress, ruffles all over it, up and down and big red and pink roses all down one side and long green taffeta gloves. I was really quite happy with my nomination and my new dress.

(the night of Loretta winning the Academy Award is covered in detail in "Behind the Door: the Real Story of Loretta Young")

The reason I think I won an award for THE FARMER'S DAUGHTER was because the girl absolutely made sense right down the line. Every attitude, every look, everything about her. She was true to herself. And she was a charming character because she came out with things but not in a bossy way. She just came out with facts and truths, and out it came.....that made sense, the whole character. And the other people around her were charmed by her. It is very important how the other people in the story react to that person. All you had to do was have one person.....say, "Umm, what's that," and you would have wondered..... "Oh, they want us not to like her...."

I dressed out of the studio wardrobe because I needed a brown suit, and it didn't make any difference what kind. And a hat that turned up in front. The shoes I had to buy. Also, the well-fitted maid's uniforms. Edith Head did design the last thing I wore in the picture.

Ed: I noticed the way you walked…..particularly in the early scenes….not like you walk in real life……

Loretta: It was the way that Katie would have walked……for roles in other pictures, it would have been different. For certain parts, high heels are absolutely necessary because it gives you a certain walk. If you're willing to put one foot across the other, it gives you a wonderful walk…..(Loretta demonstrating) …just like a cat, see…and it makes your body move. It's marvelous to do that. There's a trick to it.

Ed: Various walks…..does the director…?

Loretta: Oh, no. The director doesn't know anything about that. These are women's tricks. It's a model's walk. It allows you to swing your body without swinging your hips because the whole body goes with it. It's movement, and it's very graceful looking….and if they take a picture of you, and your legs are just crossing like this, it makes a wonderful line.

Ed: It depends on what you're playing. Are you conscious that that's what you're doing?

Loretta: You don't say, "I'm going to walk this way in this scene. That isn't the way it works. There are certain things that you just do. It depends on the character…..she moves in a certain way, she hesitates, she talks, she dresses in a certain way....she lights her cigarette a certain way or drinks her wine a certain way.

It's playacting all the time. Little girls always like to dress up and look like mama. That's really what a "look at me" does.

Ed: So you're saying, "Look at me and look at me for all the things I can do...."

Loretta: I don't know. I know it's showing off. Otherwise it would not please me most when the camera is going because everybody is going to look at me big, blown-up. Now if it's something bad........on my TV show, if I saw a terrible shot I'd say, "*Kill that*; I don't ever want to see that again," and I didn't have to look at things that weren't attractive or appealing.......

THE BISHOP'S WIFE

Ed: Any memories of Sam Goldwyn during THE BISHOP'S WIFE?

Loretta: Lots of them. He came to the set one day when we first started shooting. I had been dismissed, but he didn't know that. It was about 2:00 in the afternoon.

Ed: ......dismissed just meaning.....

Loretta: I finished my work for the day, and I had sent my maid out to bring the car around from my dressing room to the stage. I'd just get in it there, and she'd drive me back to my dressing room, and then I'd go home.

The stage door was open. The big stage door. I was, I don't know, talking to Cary or David or somebody, waiting for the car. All of sudden, Sam walks on the stage right through the big doors and he says, "Loretta! Loretta!" I said, "Yes, Sam." Just the way he was talking I knew that something was upsetting him. He walks right up to me and shakes his finger right in my face and says, "*You are ruining my picture!*" I said, "What do you mean I'm ruining your picture?" He said, "I've just seen the rushes." I said, "Yes?" He said, "And your lips are too thick!" I looked at him and said. "Well, I'm sorry! There's not much I can do about that." He said, "Well, yes there is! They are too thick!" I said, "No, Sam, I'm sorry, Theresa Wright," she was supposed to do the part originally, " you're quite right, she has a charming little, thinner mouth than I have….but I was born this way."

Finally I said, "You mean the make-up." He said, "They're too thick." I said, "Sam, we did a scale of about 7 or 9 different kinds of makeup, starting with nothing. By the time I got to 7 or 8, I had all the false eyelashes and everything else on. We agreed on #3."

Ed: We?

Loretta: He and I and the director……everyone agreed #3 was the right makeup. It was just enough, but it was not too much. And I said, "That's what I have on now. That's what I had on yesterday. So I'm sorry if my lips look too dark; it's the same color lipstick I've always worn…" Well, he started……..

Just then, I saw my car drive up. I thought, "I'll fix you." He started arguing, and I said, "Sam! To tell you the truth, I'm very offended that you would walk on the set and say a thing like this to me in front of all these people. That's embarrassing....and if you don't mind.....I'm going home! I've had it!" And I said, "Goodbye!" I walked off the set and got in my car and drove off!

Ed: ah ha......

Loretta: Henry Koster (the director) told me later that Sam watched me the whole way.....and that there was dead silence, and nobody said anything. Sam never spoke to me throughout the entire production. Never. And he never knew that I had been dismissed (by the director). I never told him.

On the last day of the picture, they have what they call a wrap party. Of course Sam was on the set with his publicity department, and there were a lot of press. They'd invite the press to the wrap parties, and they'd get a lot of interviews. Anyway, this man who ran the publicity department came over to me and said, "Miss Young, would you mind coming over and having your picture taken with Mr. Goldwyn because the press wants the picture?" I said, "I would be delighted to have my picture taken with Mr. Goldwyn, but he's the gentleman and I'm the lady, so you ask him to come over here." He just looked at me. I said, "That's it." And I watched out of the corner of my eye and nothing happened. Finally, all of a sudden, Sam sidled up to me and had his picture taken. Then, I finally turned around, and he said, "I think it's going to be a good picture, Loretta." I said, "Yes, I hope so." That was all.......

Oh, we did have another …….big discussion on this picture….The original story as it is written in the book, Robert Nathan I believe wrote the book…and in the original script that I read, the woman goes to the angel and says, "I'm going to leave Henry because I feel I'm in love with you and wherever you go, I'm going to follow you. I'm in love with you." He said, "No, you can't do that. You really can't." She said, "Yes I can." He said, "It's not love for me that you feel in your heart." She said, "Now you're telling me how I feel. That's what I'm going to do." He said, "Julia, you can't. I'm an angel." Anyway, she doesn't believe him. He said, "I am. What you're feeling in your heart is the love being reborn for your husband and when I go, and I will go, you won't even remember, nor will Henry, that I've been here, but your marriage will be back on track again and everything will be fine." She looks at him and says, "I don't believe you." He says, "You will one day," and he walks away.

There was a young man named Leonardo Bercovici who was a writer and a friend of Cary Grant's, and Cary used to love to play with scripts *all through* the shooting of them. Leonardo Bercovici was a very attractive man, wonderful looking. He and Cary got together and they went up and talked Sam Goldwyn into switching these parts so that the angel says to the woman……and they based it on the assumption, well, there aren't really angels, but a lot of people have good enough traits, so they seem like angels.

They switched the parts so that the angel says to the woman, "I'm sick of being neither hot nor cold, fish nor fowl; I'm going to stay here with you." And she says, "No, no, you can't," and she runs upstairs.......which is nothing. It doesn't mean a thing. Then he takes the other part of the scene and says it to Henry in a different scene.

When I got the pink pages on this thing I burst out laughing......I thought somebody was kidding me. Finally, he said, "No, we're going to shoot it tomorrow." I said, "Oh, wait a minute, wait a minute." So I tore up to Sam Goldwyn's office, and I argued with him and argued and argued, and they did postpone a couple days of shooting it while we argued. Finally, Sam said, "No, Loretta, I think he's right. No, we're going to do it......."

Anyway, they did it this way, and THE BISHOP'S WIFE is charming, but it missed its point.....because it told you, well, yes, he's an angel and then finally that he's not an angel. And angels only wish they could be human beings, and the whole thing falls apart.

Bercovici was so seldom wrong that people went along with his ideas. But it's only when you're looking at it from a purely human point of view. That is what you want to come up with because you want human beings to be the end of all, and we're not. Neither he nor Cary believed in angels. I kept saying, "Listen, if he isn't an angel, then how does he make the wine go up in the bottle and get the typewriter typing itself? Or keep the bishop glued to the chair?" They didn't have any answers.

Ed: How did you view your character of Julia?

Loretta: With her, I felt the simpler and the more uncomplicated the better. Because it wasn't her. It was because of the bishop's greed that the marriage was falling apart. She wasn't. She was just a limited, simple, straightforward, uncluttered woman. Married to a man, doing naturally what she should have been doing, taking care of him and her household and the child and being kind to people. Everybody loved her....What was ruining their marriage was his (ego)....... he wanted this huge edifice of a church and was willing to take money from a woman who wanted it as a memorial to her husband instead of a house of God. He had lost sight of the real priorities in life. With her, I made her as sensitive as I could make her.

Ed: Ah ha.......

Loretta.....to everybody and everything. And that's another reason why it was right that she should have fallen in love with an angel. She didn't know he was an angel. She didn't want to fall in love with him.

Ed: She just knew that her marriage wasn't very satisfying.....

Loretta: ....she knows that, and he knows it, too. Well, he didn't even notice her hat. He said he wasn't too crazy about it.

Ed: You didn't actually do any ice skating yourself, did you...?

Loretta: A little, but just to stay on. But none of the fancy work....No, they had three wonderful......they did a very wise thing. The took masks of all three of us...Cary Grant, James Gleason and me....

Ed: oh, yes...

Loretta: and they put them on the doubles so when they came very close to the camera, you didn't know. Cary.....the man wasn't as tall as Cary, that was the only thing. But I thought the skating sequences were so charming.....

After the picture was completed, Claire Luce was in town visiting with Sam and Frances Goldwyn, and the first night she was here, Sam showed her THE BISHOP'S WIFE. I saw her a couple of days later, and she told me, "I saw your picture, Loretta, at Sam's house, THE BISHOP'S WIFE." I asked, "How did you like it?" She said, "It's fine. It's all right, it's good." I said, "That's all?" She said, "Well, it doesn't really.....it's not true to itself.....is he or isn't he an angel? They can't make up their minds." I asked, "Did you say that to Sam?" She said, "Yes." I asked, "What did he say?" He said, "Oh, you just don't understand....."

Ed: David Niven.....

Loretta: The only thing I remember about David is that Koster (director) told him, "Be cold to her. You don't like her......you're bored with her, David......don't laugh at anything she does........no contact...." He said, "Gretch, I just can't be mean to you." I said, "You better! ......Or he's going to jump down your throat." David was more of a personality than an actor. It would take nothing at all for Spencer Tracy......which he proved in EDWARD MY SON. My God, he was ruthless! Some actors just can't.

Ed: Command Performance.....

Loretta: I had been invited by the English government, I guess that's who paid for it. My husband and I, Bob and Delores Hope, Robert Montgomery and his wife, Craig Stevens and Alexis Smith, the eight of us were the American contingent. I was invited because it was my picture they were showing. They had a big charity affair and they had chosen THE BISHOP'S WIFE. There was a big dinner before, and then everyone came to the theater, including the royal family, and then afterwards there was a reception upstairs in the theater. I met Princess Margaret at that time but not the present queen, because she was on her honeymoon, Queen Elizabeth.

Ed: It would have been right before her father died....

Loretta: Yes, a ha. He was charming. So was the Queen.

Ed: Any butterflies meeting these people....

Loretta: Oh, no. It was my picture they were looking at. Why would I have butterflies? And it was their charity I went over there for. You'd be surprised how important a movie star feels at times. Reigning kings and queens don't mean very much unless they come into your life in the way this did. But just to meet a king or queen, I don't know, I'd never go out of my way to do it.

There's another story….The suit I was wearing when we were getting ready to disembark *The Queen Mary* was called the "new look", "the "Dior look." We came into the harbor and apparently the zipper ….. I hadn't hooked it properly, and apparently the skirt had slipped down so that it hit me almost at the ankle. The waist must have been riding on my hip someplace. Anyway, they had a close-up in a London paper, "This is the *newest* length in styles, the newest thing to come out of Paris!" They accepted this because I had been on best dressed lists and had a reputation for wearing good clothes.

1948

RACHEL AND THE STRANGER

Ed: Have you ever hated to have a movie production come to an end?

Loretta: MAN'S CASTLE. I enjoyed RACHEL AND THE STRANGER a lot. Almost every picture you finish you don't like to see it end because you're going to miss all the people, and you might not get back with them again.

RAMONA, RACHEL AND THE STRANGER. They are what I call star roles. RACHEL AND THE STRANGER was a kind of three-way thing, but because she's the only woman and it was about Rachel.

Ed: …right

Loretta: We were shooting on a ranch near Eugene, Oregon. The little farmhouse, or whatever we had, was built on a little hill. The house was supposed to burn down at the end of the picture but someone made a mistake and shot a flaming arrow, and they couldn't put the fire out. Norman Foster, my brother-in-law, was directing it. Everybody started to panic and he said, "Never mind. Set up three cameras, right away, as quick as possible. Shoot the whole thing from every angle you can get it." It burned to the ground. That's what a good director does.....and he'd run an Indian in and out every once in a while.

There was a shot of Rachel riding side-saddle on a horse and an Indian just grabs her off the horse.....their little house is burning, and the two men are inside, and she comes back to the house...

The double did it once, and I said, "Norman, I think I can do that." He said, "Over my dead body you'll do that." I said, "I can do it." He said, "We're in the middle of the picture.
Suppose you sprain an ankle or break a leg? Then where are we with the picture?" They did it two or three times, and I watched. I said, "Oh, thank you, Norman, for not letting me try it." He said, "That girl is a stunt rider, and the Indian is a stunt man, and their timing has to be perfect .... he can't be worried about taking the leading lady off at the right moment."

Ed: Did you like that movie?

Loretta: Yes, I loved it. I liked doing it, and I like seeing it. There were a lot of good things about that movie. And the men were just darling, both of them.

Ed: ....and the little boy was good, too...

Loretta: Very good...

Loretta: A very interesting thing. Dore Schary called me. When I accepted the role, it was called RACHEL, that's all. When we finished the picture I was in Princeton, New Jersey, visiting the Gallups (George and Mrs.) and he had taken a Gallup poll that Semitic names were not very popular, and Rachel was a biblical name....

Dore called me and said that they wanted to rename the picture to A TALL DARK STRANGER ....that that would bring more people to see the picture. He said, "I'm telling you this because I want to know if you have any objections." I said, "Yes, I do. One of the reasons I accepted this role was because it was the title role and focused attention on me. And now you're changing the title to A TALL DARK STRANGER which is Robert Mitchum, and it's Mitchum's studio, so it could very well be his picture, and Bill Holden and I are down at the bottom someplace...."

Ed: .....Posters?

Loretta: Yes.......Now ordinarily, I can't imagine any other producer even calling me and asking me that. It would be none of my business, really, because I'm just an actress, but Dore was most respectful of me, and I was of him. So he said, "Let me call you back."

Ed: I can see why you would feel uncomfortable with this…

Loretta: He called me back in a couple of days, and he said, How does RACHEL AND THE STRANGER feel to you?" I said, "That's acceptable, but I don't think it's acceptable to Bill Holden." He said, "I'm not asking Bill Holden; I'm asking you." I said, "To me, it's acceptable." That was the kind of attention Dore gave me both on THE FARMER'S DAUGHTER and RACHEL AND THE STRANGER.

Ed: Who requested the poll on the title?

Loretta: Gallup had a service that he sold to studios to poll actors, their clout at the box office, also titles…..all sorts of things. RKO would pay for them to do a poll on what's the best title for this picture.

Ed: What was the story about Robert Mitchum and William Holden coming to your trailer for a drink?

Loretta: No. no. It was a Saturday night, and I had a little house up there. I didn't stay in a hotel. The studio had rented a house for me, and I took my own maid, and we hired a cook up there. It was a nice little house. It had a backyard with a swing in it. Very pleasant. All the rest of them were in a hotel. I don't like hotel living that much, and I think we were up there eight or nine weeks.   On Saturday nights I used to invite Norman, my brother-in-law, for dinner and the Holdens and the Mitchums.

Ed: Was Sally (Loretta's sister) up there, too?

Loretta: No. She didn't come on location. Anyway, I think it was the second or third Saturday that we had dinner at my house....Bob and Bill drank a bottle and a half between them of Scotch, or maybe it was Bourbon. The next day I called them both over, and I said, "Listen you two, you're going to be big stars, both of you, but not if you continue to drink the way you do. I can afford it, but you drank a bottle and a half between you last night. "Bill said, "You're right, I should cut down. You're right. Next Saturday night, just limit us." And Bob just kind of looked at me and said, "Are you through, Reverend Mother?" I burst out laughing and said, "Yes, I'm through." Bob said, "Don't let it bother you too much.....I've been smoking marijuana since I was fourteen." I thought he was showing off.....I said, "Oh, come off it..." and it wasn't too long after that they picked him up for marijuana....

But Bob was one of the finest I've ever worked with.....and one of the nicest, too.

Ed: Finest actor?

Loretta: One of the finest, yes. And professional and charming.....he doesn't make a false move as far as I'm concerned....

Ed: …. You admired him…

Loretta: I liked everything about him. He was honest. Bill Holden was honest, too, and he had misgivings about his drinking. This one (Mitchum) didn't feel he was drinking too much. He still doesn't feel it. Maybe he isn't. He's still working.

Ed: the point is that he's a strong man….

Loretta: Yes. I guess so. Also, he's a man's man.

When he got picked up (for possession of marijuana) he didn't whine about it. He didn't blame anybody else about it. "So what?" He went to jail and swept the jail out, and he…..he was true to himself, in every way, shape, and form. He came out before he went to trial and he called me. "My lawyers want some character witnesses. The men are fine but they asked me, 'Don't you know some responsible lady?' I told them that I just finished a picture with Loretta Young." They said, 'That will do if you can get her.'"

I said, "I'd be delighted. What does it entail?" "Well, they'll send you a questionnaire." I said, "Fine, tell them to send it over. I'll be delighted to fill it in." And it wasn't anything that I couldn't answer honestly, so I did.

Someone once was quoting Bob as he was giving one word descriptions about people and the one he had for me….it's something about…..it's gone…..but it was very complimentary, and spiritual, strangely enough. Bob seems to be such a worldly he-man, but he has got such standards that he's true to.....people today don't have them anymore...

Ed: What were your reflections on William Holden?

Loretta: I found him charming, and his wife was beautiful...Brenda Marshall.

Ed: ...... and he was with a French actress for a long time, Capucine...

Loretta: Yes....beautiful......

Ed: .....you heard what happened to her....

Loretta: No.

Ed: She jumped out of a window yesterday....

Loretta: When?

Ed: Yesterday. That's what I heard on the radio. Eighth floor window.

Loretta: Jean (Louis) will die. He made some clothes for her in a movie that were gorgeous ...where? Paris?

Ed: I don't know. Somewhere in France. It said that she had suffered from depression.

Loretta: Oh, sickening.....

Ed: I read a biography of William Holden about a year ago. That's how I knew about Capucine....

What was it like working with two leading men?

Loretta: Bill and I worked for about a week or ten days before Bob came to the location, and I noticed......Bill was the cock of the walk. He was the leading man, and I was the leading lady, and Norman was the director, and everything was fine. All of a sudden, Bob Mitchum walked on the site quietly but firmly. He didn't do anything or say anything, but Bill's feathers were ruffled and for two or three days, he didn't like it.

Finally, I said to him, "Don't let this kid get under your skin like that." He asked, "What do you mean?" I said, "You were fine until Bob Mitchum walked on the set." "Oh, Loretta, it's just your imagination." But I must say he seemed to pull it together, and they started to laugh and kid. They were supposed to have a serious fight over Rachel, and Norman said, "I can't see you two actually fighting seriously, so let's make it a funny fight about your egos." So when they hit each other, one guy would end up in a barrel, and he'd hit the other guy and he'd go into a haystack....that kind of fight. Well, it was like two kids fighting, not like two grown men fighting for their lives.

.....The whole picture....Norman kept saying to me, "Make it simple, Gretch, just say it, just do it. Don't dramatize it." He was a very good director ..... but Norman was moody .... I think the reason he didn't go further in the business as a director, if he thought something was right, he fought for it......whether it was important or not. He was tough to get along with. I don't know why he was, but he was. He directed an awful lot of my television shows in the last couple of years. He didn't do any playing around on the set, and he got the picture in on time, usually on budget and on schedule, and he'd cut on the set, too.....

One day Norman asked me, "To work with Dore Schary, does he mind if you change dialogue?" I said, "Oh, no, all he wants is as good of a picture as he can get." And so we were changing dialogue, and I thought it was much better, and I was in the projection room with Dore one day, and a scene came up where we had changed dialogue. He said, "Who the hell changed the dialogue" I said, Forgive me, Dore, but I think I did." "What did you do that for?" I said, "Well, because I think it is better." And he said, "And Norman allowed it?" "Yes, he agreed with it, too." He let it go, but he never hired Norman again, and he should have.....because one of the reasons I think RACHEL AND THE STRANGER stood up was because of Norman's attitude toward the movie.

1949

THE ACCUSED

Loretta: I loved THE ACCUSED. I loved the script.....she (Ketti Frings) was a wonderful writer........ she knew and liked women....she also knew their stupid little frailties. So simple, that woman (her character). Had she not been an uptight spinster lady and embarrassed to tell the police that it was an attempted rape.......... instead she shoved the body over......when she killed him.....she didn't mean to kill him....it was a mistake.....it was a very good story.

Ed: She was pretty sexually suppressed...when he was kissing her.....

Loretta: He was on his way to rape....and she knew it...

Ed: Didn't she submit?

Loretta: If she did, I didn't intend it....

Ed: Okay.

Loretta: It wasn't my intention, and I don't think it was the writer's intention. He was kinky, always taunting....teasing her, and she was leery of him always.....Trying to be "with it," she never should have gotten in the car with him.......knowing that he was..... he'd come to her office, and she'd back out, see.

Ed: They stopped at a little drive-in on the way, and she had a martini at the drive-in.....

Loretta: Yes, it was a drive-in. There's a place on the beach here, and you can either go inside or you can have it in your car....

.......Before we went into production......cast was set and William Dieterle was directing and everything was fine. Hal Wallis was producing.....he was wonderful to work for....I hadn't apologized (about the white dress in THE PERFECT MARIAGE) ......I don't know why he ever hired me again... He did hire me again and just before we went into production, Hal called and said to me, "Now, Robert Cummings is supposed to play the lead and Wendell Corey is playing the detective....However, I think the parts would be better switched." I knew he wanted to switch because he had just put Wendell Corey under contract, and Robert Cummings was being eased out. I said, "It's up to you, Hal, but I don't think so. I don't think Wendell Corey is a leading man" ....and indeed, he wasn't. He was a very attractive second lead. Bob Cummings at one time was a leading man.

Hal said, "Well, the reason I'm mentioning this to you is because you agreed to do this thing; this is the way it was set up. Think about it. It's not vital. They're equally good parts." I knew they weren't. There's a leading part, and then there's a second lead. Anyway, ...these little nuances ....you have to have been bought up in the business, otherwise, you believe anything that the producer wants you to believe, and there's always a little secret motive behind everything they do....

He hadn't hung up the phone for ten minutes, and Bob Cummings was on the phone to me. He was *livid*! He said, "Loretta! Do you know what they want?" I said, "Yes. Just talked to Hal Wallis." I said, "Don't worry, I don't think I'm going to agree to it anyway....Don't worry, Bob, I think you're better in the leading part."

The second lead was really a longer part than his, but anyway, I don't know why, but Hal didn't hold this against me either, but I think, really in a way......he knew he was right.

Ed: Douglas Dick?

Loretta: I don't know. I didn't know him personally. He looked like he was kinky. On the set I wasn't conscious of him one way or the other except that he was very professional, knew exactly what he was doing. Dieterle was very pleased with him. But then I was used to good actors, and I only noticed somebody when they weren't good. Because if they're not good, you're not good.

Ed: ....the attempted rape scene, was that on a set?

Loretta: No. I think we were on location. We went on location at night because we had to have the car, and we did all that driving.....I think we were on location for the drive-in sequence.

Ed: The boxing sequence looks like it was on location....

Loretta: It may have been at the arena, I don't know. I've forgotten. The outside scenes, I know, were on location.

Ed: Were you making this film when you got the nomination for THE FARMER'S DAUGHTER?

Loretta: No, we had not started the picture yet. That's the last picture I did for Hal Wallis, THE ACCUSED. He called my agent after I won the award and said, "We made a deal for," I don't remember what we made the deal for, let's say it was $150,000, "but now she won the award, and usually that doubles somebody's salary. But we've already signed the contract, but I want to do whatever she feels is fair." My agent asked me, "What do you think?" I said, "There's no reason why, if I won the Academy Award, this man should have to pay double. We signed the deal before so that's perfectly all right with me to do it for what I agreed." My agent didn't say, "You shouldn't do that. You should get the money." He should have. I guess it spread some good will, but now I realize that $150,000 on a picture like that doesn't mean a thing. It's all studio money anyway....what's the difference. And it would have set my salary......my salary would have been way up there for future deals.......

Hal Wallis bent over backwards trying to do everything nice all during the picture....but there wasn't anything he could do to make it a good picture as far as I was concerned. And, there were no clothes in it, so he couldn't say, "Take all the clothes ....."there weren't any that I wanted....

You know, it's funny: we're going over these movies, I'm amazed how really few *good* ones there are. I saw a picture (photograph)of Deborah Kerr and Irene (Dunne), and I don't think either of them ever did a bad picture. They were just marvelous all the time and had marvelous parts.

Most of this stuff I say (of her old movies),"Oh, my God! I don't know how I got another job. Thank God I was pretty......in those days....when I started.....all you had to be was pretty, really, then we grew into learning....

Ed: Here's a review about THE ACCUSED: "Well above par in all departments. Miss Young's portrayal of the distraught professor plays strongly for sympathy. It's an intelligent delineation, gifting the role with life. She gets under the shine in bringing out the mental processes of an intelligent woman who knows she has done wrong but believes that her trail is so well covered that murder will never out...."

Loretta: That's good.

Ed: Where was the classroom?

Loretta: UCLA? Must have been.

Ed: Why did they have the French girl in there?

Loretta: I don't know. Maybe she was supposed to be an exchange student....or maybe she was a young actress, and somebody thought she was going to be a big smash success....

......Kitti Frings was not a sloppy writer. She tied up every little thing and she didn't just throw things in as they do nowadays.

......I remember while I was making THE ACCUSED, I went off the stage one day and went walking to my dressing room or to the commissary, it doesn't make any difference which, and there were some men constructing a set on the other side of the street. I was absolutely unconscious of anybody, and I had gotten over the thrill of having won the Academy Award. And, way up, one of these construction guys said, "Hi, Champ!" And I heard it, but I didn't know he was talking to me.....so I went on walking.

He says, "Loretta! You are the champ!" I looked up and said, "Oh, thanks, thanks!" But it is all so fleeting. For a year you are, and then the next year somebody else is a champ. But many pleasant memories. Some people actually say it's a problem to get an Academy Award because you usually set yourself out of a job because nothing is good enough for you. Well, thank God, I couldn't afford that because I was a breadwinner. I had to work, regardless, so the Academy Award was just pleasure.

Jerry Wald, who did some wonderful pictures, called me and said, "I have a wonderful script. I think you'd be marvelous in it. Would you like to read it?" I'm not sure when this was ....sometime after THE FARMER'S DAUGHER.

So I read it. It was called THE BLUE VEIL. Jane Wyman finally did it. It was about a governess. At that time, I was having a rough time to find a governess for the kids. I found them all ......possessive.....at least at that time.....maybe I was jealous of them having too much time with my children ....but I found something wrong with all of them, four or five in a row, until Miss Coney.....she fit right into my household perfectly. There were horror stories about governesses; that in order to have a child take a nap, they'd just put their head in one of the little ovens, give them a little gas and put them to sleep. Well, you know, a three-year-old kid doesn't know the difference.

Never happened to my children but....I mean... you hear all sorts of things. And, the governess in the script was kind of sentimental....Jerry said, "You'd be marvelous in it." I said, "I can't help it. I don't want to do a picture about a governess right now." He said, "Loretta, I don't know that you'd get it, but I *know* you'd get a nomination.....this is the kind you'd get a nomination for."

I said, "Maybe another time. Something else. Anything. I don't want to play a governess," and I shouldn't have because you would have seen it all the way through the picture. And, of course, Jane Wyman did get a nomination for it.

Daryl Zanuck hired Claire Booth Luce to adapt *Screwtape Letters* for 20th Century Fox, and they paid her $125,000. She had agreed to do it if they did not alter a particular theologically sound line of dialogue from the book, something like, "In the end, He (God) always wins." They attempted to change that line, and Claire held them to her contract so the picture wasn't made.

She was staying up in Ojai, and we had a house up there, and she said her conscience was bothering her. "These poor fellas, I really did take advantage of them; they didn't know what I was talking about when I put the clause in the contract." They thought, "Yeah, yeah, anything to get a story by Claire Luce," see... She had written THE WOMEN and a few other things and they were very good. So she said, "I called Daryl Zanuck and said, 'Listen, I'm a little bit embarrassed about taking your money and you get nothing out of it. So if you give me $25,000 as a donation to this group of nuns I know in Bethlehem, New York, I'll write you another story that will be charming, and you'll like it.'" Daryl said, "Fine, fair enough." So she went up to the Ojai Valley Inn, and she wrote it in two weeks, wrote COME TO THE STABLE.

Ed: It was well written. I just watched it last night.

Loretta: Oh, yes, she was a beautiful writer.

Ed: I mean so clever, so well connected all the way through.

Loretta: That's the way she does it. See, Claire never tells a story and rambles. You may think she's going off, and then she always comes back and ties it in a neat little package.

Anyway, she wrote it for Irene Dunne and me, and she took it over to the studio, and they all read it, and Daryl called her and said, "Claire, this is another religious story. We don't want a religious story...."

That was it. So it went on the shelf. She had let me read it, and I knew that Daryl was never going to touch it.

Claire Luce, I think of all the women I have met, the so called sophisticated, well-known, including actresses, was one of the most fascinating because she could be all things to all people at all times. She wanted to be an actress. Thank God she didn't waste her time, because a lot of people can act, but people do not have her quickness, her wit, her sharp......
She told me one time, "Loretta, the most terrible thing I had to contend with after I converted to Catholicism was this vicious tongue of mine. These little quips come into my mind..."

And she writes that right off the top of her head. She said, "They come to my mind so quickly that if I don't bite my tongue, it's already out. And usually, it's only funny because it's vicious....I know ....and I can see how it can stop people....and I wouldn't know that when I was doing it."

Ed: Did you have any conversation with her regarding your performance?

Loretta: No, she wasn't involved in it. But when she saw it, oh, she sent me a beautiful letter. "Oh, just perfect...."

Ed: You were nominated for an Academy Award for COME TO THE STABLE....
The other nominees were....Olivia de Havilland for THE HEIRESS, Jeanne Crain for PINKY, Deborah Kerr for EDWARD MY SON, and Susan Hayward for MY FOOLISH HEART......who did you vote for?

Loretta: THE HEIRESS......I knew I wasn't going to win it.

Ed: You did?

Loretta: Oh, sure. I looked at all the pictures. They were all marvelous, and mine was not. I got it the year before, you know.....

Ed: ...but you had a speech prepared...

Loretta: No, I knew I wasn't going to win it. Lightning doesn't strike twice that way or that quickly, unless you deserve it, and I didn't, compared to the others.

I would say the play is the thing. The story, the part......THE HEIRESS let's say. Anybody who played that part, who was good, should have won an Academy Award because it's a brilliant, brilliant part. I wish I had had a crack at it. Everything was there: the man, Richardson, who played the father, and Montgomery Cliff and William Wyler........You can't go wrong on a set-up like that. That does not take anything away from Olivia De Havilland who was brilliant in it. Ingrid Bergman could have done it magnificently. Deborah Kerr would have been marvelous in it.

The one that I wanted the most was THE SNAKE PIT. I didn't get it. In fact, I wasn't even considered for it. See, the industry....they had wonderful dramatic actresses, and they had wonderful comedians. They also had, a lot of, what I call my talent which is .....I hate to say it...."Jack of all Trades" because it minimizes me too much, even in my own mind, but I was ...could do and get away with it both, but see, not the *great* comedian that Lucille Ball....let's say....was, or the tragedian that Bette Davis was. Lucille Ball could never play heavy, serious drama. Bette Davis, I don't think, was any good at comedy.

When 20th Century-Fox wanted me to do MOTHER IS A FRESHMAN, I read the script and said, "Oh, it's nothing. I don't want to do this It's boring. Same old thing ...... silly woman goes off to college and pretends to be a college student....."oh, it was so dumb. I told my agent to tell Daryl, "No. I don't want to do that, but I do want to do COME TO THE STABLE. Daryl said, "NO, no, no. You're still trying to tell me how to run my studio. I'm not going to do COME TO THE STABLE."

Then he came back and said, "If you will do MOTHER IS A FRESHMAN, all right, then you can do COME TO THE STABLE" I don't know why; I got *furious*, and I said to my agent, "There he is, trying to boss everybody around, trying to get his own way." My agent said to me, "Loretta, you realize he's just offered you two pictures instead of one....and they're both good.....so I don't see why you're so upset with him." I listened and said, "Oh, all right....Only one thing. When he makes COME TO THE STABLE, I have script approval because it was a Jewish man producing it, a charming man and a very good producer, Sam Engel, but he didn't know a thing about nuns.

MOTHER IS A FRESHMAN

Loretta: Van Johnson was a big star in the business at that time, and because I didn't want to do the picture, I gave Daryl what I thought were impossible demands, but they met them all including doing it in Technicolor and getting Van Johnson. They borrowed him from Metro to do it. I didn't think they'd be able to do it.

We were doing poster art, and we were doing everything that was suggested from the publicity department, and finally in the end we got to kidding, and he sat down, and I sat down on his lap and I was making faces. And that's what they used....this great big thing and I'm going like this to the camera......

Now, I loved love scenes, all the touching and petting because I liked men. I liked them then, and I still like them and all the affection........but I remember poor Van Johnson one day. We came to a love scene in the picture, and he was ...nervous. I said, "Van, do me a favor," I said, 'Don't hurt my teeth and don't hurt my neck." He said, "What do you mean?" I said, "Kiss me very gently. Don't grab me! That's only for the young kids. Young kids grab each other."

You have to get to the point because a lot of actors on the set, they are afraid that they won't come across as masculine, and they'll hit your teeth......

Walter Morosco produced it. I think he was married to Corrine Griffith. I liked him. I had done some other things for him....

Ed: Lloyd Bacon....

Loretta: Director. I've worked two or three times with him, I think. Very sweet. Very nice. Nothing. But good fellow......I could do good work with anybody I thought was okay.....

Ed: MOTHER IS A FRESHMAN was a pretty successful film.....

Loretta: Oh, yes. Oh, yes, I'm sure. It was successful, but it was just a little nothing film, frothy little thing. I looked pretty in it, so ....

Ed: Rudy Vallee was in that movie (Laugh) (laugh) (laugh)

Loretta: That man had absolutely no sense of humor. I don't think I ever saw that man spontaneously smile unless it was for the camera. He took himself very seriously.

Ed: In what way was he charming?

Loretta: He wasn't as far as (laugh) I was concerned.

Ed: I had the impression that he was kind of an eccentric man.

Loretta: He was a silly man. He wasn't a man, I don't think. He was an egomaniacal trip, the whole thing.

Ed: Really...I remember reading when he died....he had kept every possible piece of memorabilia about himself....

Loretta: Oh, I'm sure.....

(About the swear box)

Loretta: I don't remember which picture it started on.....I didn't mind four-letter words but blasphemy disturbed me, and I think it upset other women as well. I remember on MOTHER IS A FRESHMAN I said to these two big strong guys, one was an electrician and one was a gaffer, "Please, if anybody gets away with it and won't pay up, before they leave the set you hold them and get in their pocket and put it in the box."

The crew didn't seem to mind, and we used to send the couple hundred dollars a week for St. Anne's. The guys would joke, "We probably have a little stake in this, anyway, in that it's for unwed mothers." But, we had a terrible time with Rudy Vallee and the swear box. I think his reputation was that he was not too easy with money. He said, "I'm not going to do it." I said, "I'm sorry; it's a rule of the set." One of the big electricians put his hand in Rudy's pocket and got out his roll and peeled off maybe four dollars while another big guy would hold him. He never laughed about it. He'd just storm off the set and the next day he'd say, "You haven't any right to do this."

I just heard a story the other day from Tom (a friend of Loretta's). Supposedly Ethel Merman was working on my television show. I stopped him right there. I said, "I couldn't afford Ethel Merman but go ahead with the story." "The story is that she came walking in on the set waving a $20 bill, 'Here, Loretta, take a good.......'"

I said, "That's not true." Tom said, "But it was an awfully funny story." I said, "It's funny that bawdy actress Ethel Merman, who did use these four letter words, suddenly comes to holy Loretta's set and say that kind of thing. It's funny but at my expense, but it's funny. But it isn't true. Ethel Merman was much too nice a person. I never heard her use a four letter word."

Ed: She would not have offended you....

Loretta: No. She had much better taste than to do that with anybody and much less if it were my show she was working on.

Ed: People want to reduce people, including yourself, to caricatures....

Loretta: Yes, exactly...

Ed: Did anyone really do anything like that: come on the set, put money in the swear box and really let go?

Loretta: A lot of people have claimed to have. I saw Mike Connors on "The Tonight Show" making such a boast, but he wouldn't have had the nerve ......

Someone did. I think it was Henry Hathaway who was notorious for his bad language. Henry walked on the set and said, "Loretta, bla-bla-bla-bla," and waved a $20 bill and put it in the box. I said, "Thank you for the donation, Henry, but all those words are free!"

COME TO THE STABLE

Loretta: Sam Engel, the producer for COME TO THE STABLE came to see me on the set of MOTHER IS A FRESHMAN. He had hired Dorothy Parker to do a rewrite, and he said, "Well, you were right. It just didn't work out. So now we have Sally Benson." I said, "Is that the Sally Benson who writes the sexy teenage stories printed in *The New Yorker*? He said, "Ah ha." I said, "She's the one with long green finger nails..." He said, "Oh, what's the matter with you?" I said, "She's not going to do any better on it. She doesn't know anything about nuns. Besides, I've already accepted the script I wanted. ......Just remember Sam, I have okay of script." "I know, I know.....you're going to love it...."

I had a few weeks' vacation after MOTHER IS A FRESHMAN, and then I made the tests in the nun's outfit; they okayed everything and everything was fine. It was the weekend, and we were to start on Monday. He sent me the script on Friday and said, "I've held this off this long because I don't want you to worry too much about it. It's so funny, so amusing, everything." Sally Benson had rewritten it.

I read this thing, and I just got sick to my stomach. It was just awful. They were two stingy old maids. When they crossed the toll bridge and got into a conversation with a man who had 12 children, even though they had a fifty dollar bill in their pocket, they talked him into paying the twenty-five-cent toll. They didn't want to break their fifty dollar bill.

Ed: But they were nuns, though......

Loretta: Yes, they were nuns, but this script had them as two dried up old maids, stingy at that. I read the script; then I asked Tom (Loretta's husband) to go into another room and read this thing and see if I'm wrong. So he came back, and he said, "You can't touch this thing with a ten foot pole." I said, "No, I don't intend to, but can you imagine anything going this far wrong...?"

The next morning, Saturday morning......in those days, all the executives met in the steam room at 20th Century-Fox....and they spent the whole day there, gabbing and talking. It was kind of a club, and they had their steam and their showers and their rubs and played poker....whatever they did.

I called and asked for the steam room, and I said, "Is Mr. Sam Engel there for Miss Loretta Young?" Anyway, he came to the phone, and I said, "Sam, don't say one word because I know everybody's around including Daryl........I've read your script. I can't touch it. I don't like it. I think it's awful. Gene Tierney just got back from New York, and she doesn't know beans about this. Give it to her. She'll be marvelous. She can fit right in to my nun's habit....."

Ed: I always thought that Gene Tierney kind of filled the void after you left 20th Century-Fox...

Loretta: Yes. And he said, "What are you saying?" I said, "Just that." He said, "Could you meet me in my office in about a half hour?" I said, "Yes, I'll be there."

In the meantime, I called my agent and said, "I'm on my way over to 20th Century-Fox to tell Sam Engel in person that I can't do it. I want you to go to Daryl Zanuck's office at the same time to tell *him* that I'm not going to do this picture because of my approval of the script, and I don't approve of this script."

So he did, and I did. When I walked in, Sam looked green in the face. He said, "What am I going to tell Daryl? I spent another, I don't know, $150,000 on this thing...." I said, "I don't know, that's your fault; that's your problem; it's not mine..."

Ed: He spent another $150,000, did you say...?

Loretta: Uh huh.

Ed: ...for the rewrite?

Loretta: Uh huh.

Ed: Okay.

Loretta: Maybe they didn't. Maybe it wasn't $150,000; I don't know. Whatever he spent, Daryl Zanuck was going to kill him. I told him that the script was offensive to me, and then said, "I'm going home now." Then I said, "Sam, this has nothing to do with your coming to my house for dinner tonight." He said, "Oh, I couldn't....." I said, "You have to..." He came. He didn't drink much ordinarily but had two martinis quickly. And he looked at my husband and said, "Your wife can be such an albatross around my neck; she makes me so angry." He said, "Well, she can be that way."

We got to dinner and he kept .....and I said, "This is not going to be a business meeting; this is dinner. I don't even want to talk about it." So, after dinner, he said to me, "Listen, what would make you do this script? I know you're wrong .....on the other hand I know you're not wrong because if it weren't for you, we wouldn't even be making this picture. I've seen the tests, and I looked at them all over again this afternoon. What would make you do it?"

I said, "The original script, and you've got it." He said, "No, we can't do that. It's much too long." I said, "No it isn't. You don't have to cut one *thing* out of that picture. Everything ties up, everything meshes....."

He said, 'Well, how can I go to Zanuck?" I said, "Sam, I don't know. That's your problem..."

He said, "I can't make it without you; I just can't." I said, "I hope not." He asked, "Would you be willing to postpone a week?" I said, "To do what?" He said, "To smooth the waters." I said, "Yes, I'll give you an extra week."

Ed: What about Henry Koster?

Loretta: Henry Koster was wonderful. Very sensitive but he just didn't understand a lot of the things. For instance, there is one scene...Henry said, "Loretta, you sit down in a chair, and Celeste (Celeste Holm), you sit on the arm of the chair..." I said, "No. We're not Siamese twins .....we haven't got the same mind. We're not connected in any way. We just wear the same habits, but she's a French woman, and I'm an American woman.....that's ....different. She'll sit there, and I'll sit here."

He said, "Oh, Loretta!" I said, "I don't care how pretty it is; it doesn't make any sense. They wouldn't do it..."

Another time we were doing a scene (laugh)...(laugh)... we were talking a gangster out of some money...

Ed: Luigi….

Loretta: …uh huh…. We were coming out of his office, and I came first and Celeste came after me. There are three or four gangster guys standing around, and she takes a little metal out of her pocket and puts it …..(into a slot machine)

And as she does ….. she would give them a little bump. She's French, you see, a little bump with this and a little bump with that one. And I saw this out of the corner of my eye, the first take. So I looked at it and said, "*Stop!!!!!!*" The camera, everybody stopped. I said, "Oh, I'm sorry, may I have another one?"

So we got back…I was thinking she wouldn't do it again, see. Sure enough, I walked out and deliberately looked at her, and here she is doing it …..her little bump….Finally, I said, "Stop. H-H-Henry…..Celeste, you can't give a bump. You can't do that. You're a nun."

Ed: Now, what is the bump again?

Loretta: Well, it's a little burlesque dance step, sort of. But you do it with your hips, see?

Ed: A little grind…

Loretta: It's very Frenchy ……a little grind…..just a little one…..see? Celeste said, "That's my French personality coming out…" I said, "Not with a bump, not in a nun's habit, sorry."

Henry said, "Oh, Loretta, you're just driving me crazy." I said, "I know it. And it's driving me crazy, too, but you can't do that."

I knew I was going to get beaten to a pulp........I was the only Catholic associated with COME TO THE STABLE. Then I got the idea to enlist Sister Winifred as a consultant. So ......every time we had an argument, I'd say, "Look, I can't argue this and then go and play in it. So send the car to St. Anne's for Sister Winifred and bring her out and let her decide. She's a nun; I'm not."

So they'd send a car down for Sister Winifred who was on Occidental, almost half way downtown, bring her all the way up to the studio, and she'd come and settle the argument, whatever it was....

Sister Winifred arrived, so Henry says, "When she comes in, Celeste, do that..." So Celeste did it for her, and she asked, "Why is she...why is she making that movement? What is that?" So, we got over that one.

Another time we were on a hill. They were planting a metal......

Ed: Was this all done in the studio, by the way?

Loretta: Uh, huh. This was a big hillside on a set. During rehearsal, I was on my knees and I looked back and Celeste, rather than kneeling, was leaning back, resting on her legs. Never did get on her knees. I said, "Don't do that, Celeste. We don't do that." She was Lutheran, by the way.

Ed: Ah, ha.

Loretta: ...so during the take, he said, "Oh, that's beautiful. Print it.." and I turned around quick and looked, and she's back, leaning on her legs. And I said, "Henry, I'm sorry, we have to do another take. He says,   *"Now what?"* "Well, instead of kneeling, she's leaning back. Certainly nuns would never do it." He said, "I told her to do it that way because it's lovely with you kneeling straight, and then she is behind you..." I said, "Yes, like a frog, crouching. You have to take another....."

"All right! .....Set up another one." So, we set up for another one, and she was straight up like this, and he said, "Now, does that suit you, Loretta?" I said, "Yes, that's much better. Thank you, Henry."

We finished the picture, and I'm someplace else doing another picture, and I get a call one day from my agent, "They need one line of dialogue at 20th Century-Fox. If they send a car for you, could you run over there on your lunch break and give them that one line of dialogue?" I said, "Yes, I can do that. Just tell them to have it all set up; I don't want to have to sit around and wait because I want to get my lunch, too. "So I tore over to the studio and it was the scene on the hill. There she is, leaning back on her legs. He had used the wrong take ...... on purpose, of course.

Ed: This is Henry?

Loretta: This is Henry.....AND the producer, I don't know. But anyway, the scene where they needed the one line of dialogue was that one...

I didn't laugh. I didn't think it was funny. I asked Sam Engel to come down. I said, "Sam, there's another print someplace, another take." "Maybe it wasn't printed." "Look it up and have it printed because I'm not going to give you the line of dialogue for that thing. That nun wouldn't do that, and I explained this to Henry while we were doing it, and he took another take, both of us are kneeling upright."

Ed: Oh, was this at the beginning when the dog comes up...?

Loretta: Yes. And he said, "Loretta, you ought to know better." I said, "I do know better, and you should have an authentic picture. It should be right. " He said, "I can't get it right now." I said, "When you find that thing, and you get it into the picture, you call me and I'll come over to the studio, any time, day or night that I'm not working and give you the line when you get the right shot in," and he did. He called me in about two days and said, "We found it, and it was printed." So I came over.

Ruth Roberts was with me on COME TO THE STABLE. She had taught me the Swedish accent for THE FARMER'S DAUGHTER; then I did one picture without her, and then I said I'd rather have her with me all the time.

Ed: She served as what ...?

Loretta: Kind of a sixth sense for me. For instance, one day she said to me when we started shooting COME TO THE STABLE, and the director said, "Print," she said, "Henry, wait a minute." Then she came over to me and said, "I don't know what you are doing. In the rehearsals you're fine, and all of a sudden in the take, you look like you're smelling something bad. You're Mother Superior, and it's not attractive." I asked, ".....The way I'm talking?" "No, it's your attitude." So I went over to Henry and said, "Ruth feels I look kind of snooty." "Well, you are Mother Superior." I said, "No, that's the last thing I want to be. I want to be a nun who happens to be the Mother Superior." So he said, "All right, take it again." You see, he has to watch the whole scene and can't be focused on me. Ruth could. So we started again, and she stopped it. He cut, and he looked at her, and he looked at me, and I asked what was happening, and she said that I suddenly looked like I had a rod down my back. I had this wimple. You put this thing on first, this white thing, then you put a thing under here and tied it up there and tied it behind, and then you put the veil on. Now, when I was trying this on, I had my head up and when I relaxed like this my face was tight .....I had this thing on too tight. So I loosened it so that I wouldn't feel it doing that to my face. I might have gone through the whole picture with that rigid sort of .....and it would have destroyed the whole....I never would have gotten the nomination for it, which I did, because one of the things I've always loved about the nuns that I knew in school and still know – I have many friends who are nuns – is their absolute lack of rigidity. They are so at home with their life and their love of God that you can hardly shock them.

My character in COME TO THE STABLE was perfectly at home. Now, there's the difference between ignorance and innocence. That woman, Sister Margaret, was an American and was in this convent in France. I'm sure she knew everything. She knew that this man and this woman were sleeping together in this house. She didn't make a big deal of it, no sense in going in and embarrassing them. But, in innocence, she doesn't judge them and he becomes so annoyed with her innocence.

Ed: COME TO THE STABLE might have been your biggest money maker.

Loretta: I don't know but…..she was a pleasure to play because they were good. They were not sweet, per se. They were not goodie-goodies. They were sharp…..but had blind faith. That's always fascinating, particularly when it works.

In COME TO THE STABLE I didn't wear any makeup…..but as I look at it now….it looks like I had on eye shadow and lipstick, but I had nothing on. Neither did Celeste. None of the nuns did.

Ed: What about Hugh Marlowe?

Loretta: Yes. He said to me one day….I was pushing the hair out in front of the mirror, and he looked at me and said, "You know, you are such a beautiful woman. I can't stand to see you in that outfit." And my makeup man was standing near, and he said, "Oh, don't say that. She looks gorgeous in this habit." He said, "Not for me. I can hardly stand it." He picked on me that whole time. It didn't bother me because it was part of his character that he was playing.

Ed: Review for COME TO THE STABLE: "It's a drama of considerable charm in its devotion to the tenets of the Catholic Church. It has moments of poignancy, but often it skirts the bounds of entertainment in telling too pointedly its story of godliness and faith."

Loretta: This person obviously has no faith. So what do you expect........

I was having lunch in the commissary with a whole table of extras whom were playing nuns, and a writer, whom I've never liked, walked by and said, "Is this where you get none?" The extras thought he was hilarious, but I found him disgusting.

There was a scene at a tennis court that was shot at Henry Fonda's home. He wasn't in town. In fact, we didn't see anyone, but I think Jane was a little girl at the time...

Ed: ......well, 1949....twelve...

Loretta: Anyway, a little girl. I don't remember seeing her, but Celeste said something one day that the kids were peeking out the window. I don't remember seeing her.

Part Ten: Movie Career Wind Down

<u>1950</u>

KEY TO THE CITY

Ed: with Clark Gable and between COME TO THE STABLE and CAUSE FOR ALARM.

Loretta: A little nothing picture. It was a shame to waste him or me in it, I thought. But it was a program picture.

Ed: How did it come about?

Loretta: Dore......You never really know how or why, when you're working in a business but there are just certain working actors.....you never really know...

Ed: It was kind of cute...KEY TO THE CITY....

Loretta: It was all right. I was fine. It certainly wasn't good enough for Clark Gable...

Ed: ...or Loretta Young....

Loretta: ....not at that time...

Ed: You were coming off your most recognized work.....

Loretta: I like many of my television shows better than anything I did in the movies.....

I had a miscarriage on that picture, my second one....and it just nearly killed me. I didn't get babies easily. We were doing a scene, and I was in that baby dress, and Clark was in the little boy outfit, or whatever he had on, and we were supposed to be coming down from a long shot into a close-up, and I didn't feel too well that day. I was kind of nauseated and a little bit of discomfort.....I kept taking....the doctor gave me some pills for cramps....I think it was aspirin and codeine....It stops the pain, but it leaves you groggy too. Not enough that it impaired anything I was doing, but.....I was three-and-a-half-months, at the same time I lost the other one (during THE FARMERS DAUGHTER).

We were standing there, and I got awfully dizzy. I said, "Oh, I'm sick." Clark asked, "What did you say?" I said, "I feel terrible," and that's the last thing I remember. Apparently, I passed out because of the cramping. Clark had caught me and carried me to my dressing room on the set, and Beatrice (Loretta's maid) was there. I said, "Don't tell Mr. Lewis about this." She said, "You'll have to tell him; you're having a miscarriage." I said, "No, no, no."

Anyway, they had called the ambulance and took me home, and that's where I lost the baby, when I got home. I had been in bed for an hour and a half, and I lost it, and then the doctor took me right to the hospital, and I was in the hospital for ten days. Why? I don't know.

I had asked the doctor if the baby had been baptized, and he said, "Yes, I did, Loretta, don't worry about it." I always think of those two miscarriages as two of my children. They are children. At three-and-a-half-months….they've got everything. Nothing more is added….they're just more developed.

They had closed the movie, and they sent me flowers every day while I was in the hospital. George Sidney was directing the picture, and he was a marvelous amateur photographer. He had Clark and the cameraman and everybody all hanging over this sign that said, "COME BACK, ALL IS FORGIVEN," and it was tied to this big bunch of flowers. They all signed little pictures, and they sent little notes. Very sweet and very considerate. Dore sent me some flowers and said, "The last time this happened, you got an Academy Award for it…..so here's hoping. "

Ed: Z. Wayne Griffin…..

Loretta: He was the producer. He used to be my agent. He's a darling man….just crazy about him. Just died a year or so ago. He was my agent with Myron Selznick's office….

1951

CAUSE FOR ALARM

Ed: You had had a big hit with COME TO THE STABLE. Why did you do CAUSE FOR ALARM at that time?

Loretta: Because Tom produced it.

Ed: Surely, there were other offers.....

Loretta: Oh, yes. But I liked the story. It had been a little radio story with a wonderful actress named Lurene Tuttle. She was wonderful on radio. I think this was an hour show.
Dore asked me, "Is there anything you would like to do?" I ran into Mel Dinelli who had something to do with THE NEXT VOICE YOU HEAR, and I said, "Didn't you write CAUSE FOR ALARM (on radio). He said, "Yes, I did." I said, "It would make a marvelous movie. You write it and I'll act in it." This is how it came about.

Ed: How were you talking with Mel Dinelli?

Loretta: A lot of writers were often at our house. Friends of mine. We went out a lot and we saw an awfully lot of different people. Radio was hot stuff in those days, and whenever I knew that Lurene Tuttle was going to be on, I would listen because she was so good. And if you hear something that is good and it rings a bell, then it sticks in the back of your mind.

Tom had listened to it as well, and he said, "Shall I see if I can get it?" I said, "Yes. Dore wants me to make something else for him, and if we bring it in that way, maybe he'll do that." So he did.

Tom, I thought, very wastefully.... all he needed was to present the script to Dore....because I had already told Dore that I wanted to do it. But, oh, no. Tom went out, and he recorded it....hired the actors....my money....hired the studio.....made a half hour presentation of it. I said, "You don't do things like that in the picture business ....you just give them the script...."

Ed: That was his (Tom's) first......

Loretta: ...and only.

Ed: It kind of came out of the blue that he was.....

Loretta: ......that he was a motion picture producer? Yes. Well, I'm sure he wouldn't have had the opportunity if he hadn't been married to me. See, I had already done THE FARMER'S DAUGHTER and RACHEL AND THE STRANGER with Dore....

Ed: Give me a little more clarity on this...... you were one of the biggest of the movie stars....

Loretta: No one ever knows that when they're there......

Ed: So what was going on in the business in those days that you'd make such a little picture?

Loretta: I think that it was a labor of love because I hoped that it would launch Tom, and it didn't, because he didn't know the ins-and-outs of the industry. He didn't get any attention because it was small, and he brought it in under budget, and it didn't make any kind of splash....

I thought I was very good in it; of course, I wasn't Lurene Tuttle. We had Barry Sullivan who was very good and another young man (Bruce Cowling) who didn't go very far, but he was excellent in this. Tay Garnett was a fine director, and Dore felt, that, well, he couldn't go wrong. Why not take the chance? And it was a very small budget. It was $700,000 which was nothing for Metro.

You see, I knew the business well enough to know that unless you spend over four million dollars on a picture, you don't get any advertising budget. Tom didn't know that, and he wasn't listening to me, and I wasn't thinking in that area anyway. I was thinking of what to do and how to do it and act it. And we rehearsed, which was new for the studios, four or five days before we shot, which was excellent. We shot this little picture in 16 days and Tom felt that because he brought it in under budget, that he was going to get complimented for it.

No way. They just thought, "That dope. That isn't the way we do it." They'd string it out......He brought it in so under that there was no advertising, maybe a $100,000 which was nothing, because it wasn't worth spending more than that on that kind of investment.

But he wouldn't listen to me, and at Metro.....if he wanted to work at Monogram, then that's the way they worked but not Metro. But, he wouldn't listen. It didn't launch his career because he wanted to do it *his* way instead of their way, and the studios were still running the business in those days.

Ed: It's a good movie...

Loretta: Yes, very good, very good. Much better than a lot of them that I've done. *But* ...the game in each industry is different.

Ed: He was going to show them.....

Loretta: He was going to show them........and he never got another job.

Ed: ....the bathing suit shot...Surely that wasn't part of the original radio....?

Loretta: It was added after the preview. I guess they wanted to add a little more credence as to why he was jealous ....

I was playing a little housewife. It wasn't anything glamorous like Mata Hari. Joe Ruttenberg was considered the best cameraman at Metro at the time...the first thing any actress did was ask for the best cameraman....

I had already agreed to have Tay Garnett direct. When I asked for Joe Ruttenberg, Dore called me and said, "Everything else is fine, but Joe Ruttenberg is scheduled to do another picture, and I don't think it's important what you look like. You're supposed to be an ordinary housewife...."

I said, "Wait a minute, Dore. I want Joe Ruttenberg. I know that I'm playing a housewife, but I want to be the prettiest housewife you can find because it's very pleasant to look at on the screen. That's the only thing in this picture....there are a lot of heavy moments and unless it's well photographed, it's not very appealing." He said, "Let me think about it." So he called back in a little while, and he said, "You've got Joe Ruttenberg," but to say it doesn't make any difference.....it always makes a difference how you look.

Ed: What did you tell me during dinner the other night about the lighting tests.....?

Loretta: If you're working with a new cameraman who doesn't know your face, it's foolish to work with him without making tests so he can find out how to photograph you, unless he just washes you out completely and then everybody looks fine. If you snap a bulb and hold it with light over it, and do this with a light, and then you photograph it with light all over it, it's just beautiful. But it looks like a drawing of a face because there are no shadows or planes or anything like that.

So, I would stay there while he's lighting me. I didn't put the stand-in in because her face is different than mine. It's harder work because you have a half hour standing there like a dodo, but if he gets a good look at you, he can try to light different places to see where the circles come on or where they go out.

(Back to CAUSE FOR ALARM)

We had a preview of this picture. There's a scene, after she tries everything to get the letter back, and her dead husband is upstairs in bed......and she comes into the house which is a dark bungalow, and she starts upstairs then she decides to go back downstairs, then thinking, "No, I'd better do something about it..." so I went up again, and during this hesitation there's a man in the audience yelling, "Lady, time's a wasting." It didn't bother me because that's what previews are for, to find the problems. However, on the way home, Tom was very upset about it. When I tried to explain to him that this was constructive criticism, he took anything I said as an aspersion on him as a producer. Eventually, they did go back and cut it so there wasn't so much time there.

I did a lot of running down the street in that picture....One day I was talking and didn't hear "Roll em" and all of a sudden, Tay said, "Loretta, action!" I said, "Oh," and I took off too quickly and both of the calves in my legs must have spasmed because I fell down. They hurt so badly, I couldn't move and for the whole day I couldn't do anything. They had a physical therapist at Metro-Goldwyn-Mayer studios, and he was brilliant, and he worked me out of it.

Ed: Would this have been an A movie or a B movie?

Loretta: It would have been a B movie at that budget no matter who was in it.

Ed: Okay, so THE ACCUSED.....was that an A movie?

Loretta: Yes, that was an A movie.

Ed: I loved that movie.

Loretta: I did, too. That was Hal Wallis.

Ed: So, I guess my question ......if you had done B movies up to that point?

Loretta: No, never.

I had a letter from a fan, "I was so thrilled with Loretta Young in a Metro-Goldwyn-Mayer picture, CAUSE FOR ALARM. I thought it was going to be very good with lots of clothes and a very "up" picture and," he said, "this little tiny picture arrived. I was so disappointed."

 I don't think it did bad business, but it certainly wasn't a word-of-mouth, "Oh, you've got to see this picture," because there really wasn't anything to it except the day in a woman's life.

Ed: Here's another little clip about CAUSE FOR ALARM....
"Loretta's long hair is cut to give her the streamlined look of the modern housewife....." I didn't' think your hair was short for that movie....

Loretta: No, but it was down to here originally.......

Ed: Does that mean that in THE ACCUSED, that really was your hair......all that long hair?

Loretta: I think I cut it there. I cut it in THE ACCUSED.....part way through. They made a big thing about it......

HALF ANGEL

Ed: Milton Krasner was the cameraman

Loretta: Milton was with me a lot. In fact, I had asked for Artie Arling who did MOTHER IS A FRESHMAN, but he was busy, and Milton was under contract to 20th Century-Fox at the time. Milton came to me and said, "I'd very much like to do this picture." I said, "Milt, you're not a color man; you're black and white." He said, "I can learn to be a color man. Why don't we make some tests?" Of course, he was marvelous.....beautifully photographed......

Loretta: Norman (brother-in-law Norman Foster) brought me the script. I didn't know there was such a thing as a "package deal." I didn't know what that meant yet. Norman assumed that I did, I guess. He's a director, and he found a script, and he brought it to me, and I was crazy about it. I thought he brought it to me because he said, "I think you'd be marvelous in this." I didn't go a step further thinking that he, of course, wanted to direct it. I don't know why I was connected with 20th Century-Fox at that time. Maybe I just gave it to my agent and told him I'd like to do it. Somehow, 20th Century-Fox picked it up and called me. I called Norman and told him that 20th Century-Fox was going to do it, and I thanked him for sending the script to me. He didn't say anything. 20th Century-Fox put Jules Dassin in it to direct. I asked, "What's Jules Dassin done? I don't know his work." They said, "He has done some very good directing." I said, "This is a little comedy." They said, "Come over and we'll show you some of his work." They were all kind of really heavy black and white....

Ed: Political?

Loretta: "Sure. He had been a Communist. Everyone kept saying, "He's a pleasant little fella." It never dawned on me that Norman Foster should be directing it, and he would have directed it perfectly. Jules was a little guy, and he kept talking about how terrible the game Monopoly was. I said, "I don't play Monopoly. What's so terrible about it?" He said, "Well, it teaches kids to be pigs about everything, monopolize everything." I said, "I can't get too upset about that. It doesn't bother me too much. There are other things that take priority over that."

I didn't know at the time, politically, we were opposite ends of the pole. And as far as my being a practicing Roman Catholic, I'm sure it made him want to throw up.

Anyway, I was to play two characters (in the same person) in this part. The one was a prude when she was awake, and when she was asleep, she was kind of a tart, a slut who would climb in bed with this guy. She was crazy about him. In the daytime, she wouldn't even talk to him, but she had a secret crush on him.

In the original story, they had beautiful sets where it was supposed to be inside her mind, and at night the prude goes to sleep, and the tart gets up and goes out. The idea is that when she gets married, then these two mesh and make the perfect wife.....

We were doing the prudish stuff first, and I was very uptight with Jules Dassin, and I couldn't understand why. I kept telling myself that he was a good director. I was becoming more uneasy and was worried that when we started doing the tarty stuff, that I wouldn't be able to deal with this man......that he'd embarrass me. I said to myself, "He better not yell at me."

Sure enough, we were ten days into it and were downtown on location at some carpet store ..... and all these people were standing around. Joe Cotten was there; nothing ruffles him. Jules called me, and I said, "Yes, I'll be right there." I was doing something....my face or something.....probably with a mirror. See, all this kind of stuff he hated. Jules Dassin hated all that rich stuff ....all the pampering. He called me again, and I said, "I'll be right there, Jules. I'm just finishing my make-up." He said, *Loretta!* Get yourself over here!" I remember just stopping cold. I said to myself, "This is the time. That's it. I'll never be able to take direction from this man again. Ever!"

So I walked over, and I said, "Mr. Dassin, I'm going to my dressing room, and I'm going to call the producer, and when he gets here, come in." I walked to my dressing room and closed the door.

It took Julian Blaustein, I think forty-five minutes to get the message and get downtown. He knocked on the door of my dressing room, "Loretta, it's Julian." I said, "Come in." He said, "I'd like to talk to you alone first. I said, "All right."

I said, "Julian, I'm not going to finish this picture. You can get another director or you can get another leading lady....but I'm not going to finish this picture. I cannot work with this man. I cannot take direction from this man. I haven't been yelled at since Herbert Brenon yelled at me and nearly killed me.....and I'm not going to start with Jules for this....I'm not going to tolerate this, and he's not the right director for this picture. He's heavy-handed. Much too serious. This is light comedy. There's nothing in this that is anything but just charm......So it's up to you. I don't care what you do. I'm going home."

Anyway, I started out (to go home).....He said, "I really think you should talk to Jules." I said, "All right, send him in." Jules came in and asked, 'What's this about?" I said, I'll tell you what it's about. I can't continue. I don't think you're any happier with me than I am with you. One of us is going to go, and I think, unfortunately for you, at this point, I'm a bigger star than you're a director, and I think you're the one who's going to go. But that's up to Mr. Blaustein. He's the producer. I'm going home now, and I will be told what to do tomorrow morning."

Ed: Did you say that in the same tone you're talking to me right now?

Loretta: Yes. Yes. I tried to be very quiet so that no one outside could hear.

Ed: Were you angry with him when you saw him?

Loretta: I was sick to my stomach.....absolutely sick to my stomach because I had never done anything like this before, and if you're of the personality that you like people to like you.....I'm more comfortable when people like me than when they don't like me....I could smell it in this man. He didn't like anything about me. I don't think he liked my work, particularly....

He was married to a brilliant actress, Melina Mercouri ....a brilliant actress.....hard, tough, wonderful in her work....politically speaking, we, too, were at opposite ends of the pole. She was very strong.....mine was a passive sort of thing.....

I was sick to my stomach, and I kept getting hot and cold, how you do at times, because I never walked off the set before, but I knew at this time I had no alternative. Because at ten days, I had been struggling .....I could feel his animosity toward me....a director and a star....in a strange way, it's kind of a silent love affair .... a respect for each other and you play on that, and you build on that, and you draw from that.

Ed: Would you use the word "intimacy" in these situations, too?

Loretta: There is.....there is... but it's a silent one. You don't even talk about it. If you do something, and you look at the director and he does that.....then it opens valves and you go on. Now, there are no words spoken...no nothing. Nobody else knows that you've even done it.

(Back to HALF ANGEL and the meeting in the dressing room)

Loretta: He just looked at me, and then he said, "What annoys you so much about me?" I said, "Frankly, everything. I can't work with you. I haven't the time to figure it out. It will either be you or me, Jules, and whatever it is, I don't care. Good-bye and I wish you good luck," and I just went to my car and went home. That was about two in the afternoon.

I was sick when I got home. Frankly, I thought they might call and say, "We're getting Joan Crawford," or somebody to do the part. Because they could have, and it would have been a very difficult thing for me to swallow because I've never walked off the set. My deportment on the set...you may not like my acting, you may not like my work, you may not like *me*, but you have to agree that my deportment was always beyond reproach.

Julian Blaustein called about 7:30 that night and all he said was, "Loretta, this is Julien." I said, "Yes." He said, "Would Richard Sale be acceptable to you as a director?" Indeed, I liked him very much. He was married to Mary Anita Loos, a very nice woman, a good writer. I had seen them in the commissary throughout the ten days because they were writing something else. I said, "Yes, he would. Yes." "All right. Be ready at nine tomorrow morning and we'll just continue." I said, "Fine," so that's what we did.

Later on the set, Julian told me, "I could see it in the rushes, but I didn't know what to do about it." I said, "You're the producer, Julian, you should have."

Ed: What did he see?

Loretta: He saw a kind of a ...but I was playing that part anyway, the frigid woman...but there was an insecurity about it.....and I didn't want her to be that way. I wanted that girl to be just as secure in what she was doing.....she was a nurse, see, as the other one in what she was doing.....but I don't think we reshot anything.

Ed: Did this film make money?

Loretta: Oh, I'm sure it did.

What they did, which I thought was a shame, because the only innovative thing about it was this sequence every time she'd come in from the night's prowl, they'd go into her brain again, and it was a beautiful set. Zanuck just cut the thing right out. Daryl didn't get fantasy at all. He didn't get that. He was LITTLE CAESAR and WILSON. That's his cup of tea. But it would have been charming because it would have given it another dimension.....this is just a little idea.....therefore, when the two of them meet, together.............

When I was requesting that Jules Dassin be replaced, I should have requested Norman to direct it. After Norman died, I said to Bet, "You know, I realize now that Norman intended to direct that picture, and that's why he brought it to me. But I was just concerned with ME. I never even thought of Norman." She said, "I know, Gretch. I cried myself to sleep many a night on that account. We needed the money at the time."

I think between you and me, that's probably why I used Norman so much on the television show. First of all, he brought the things in on time. He did not overspend. He didn't overdo anything.....and also, I owed him.

Ed: Review: Miss Young ,within the limits of the role required, does a competent job. "
Overall, reviews are that the film fails as whimsy but succeeds as farce.

Loretta: I don't know what whimsy means...

Ed: ......it's what Daryl Zanuck......

Loretta: That's what I mean. If he had left that scene in, it would have been a nice little fairy tale...

1952

BECAUSE OF YOU

Ed: Joseph Pevney

Loretta: I did two pictures with him. I thoroughly enjoyed working with him both times...

Ed: towards the end of your movie career....

Loretta: Yes. I don't know where he came from.....anyway, he was easy to work with, and he knew just when to calm you down.

And if you were doing too much in a scene, he'd make you do it over and over again because you got tired of doing what you were doing, and then he'd get just what he wanted and just enough, see....

In BECAUSE OF YOU there's a scene with Jeff Chandler. She was in an automobile accident, and he comes in......he made us do that master scene at least five or six times because Jeff and I were over-acting like mad. Because the higher he'd go, the higher I'd try to go.

Finally, I said, "What's the matter?" He said, "I'm trying to wear you two out so you're not so active. He's in shock, and you've been in an automobile accident, and both of you are like you're running a marathon." He was very wise the way he did it.

He said to me one day in rehearsal......we'd finished the first day's rehearsal......he said, "May I walk you to your dressing room?" I said, "Sure, I'd be delighted." He said, "I've looked at five or six of your films, just all in a row, because I wanted to see if there were any little things that I had to be careful of or watch out for. What to build up and what to pull down." He said, "I've noticed you have a habit, and I want you to never do it in this picture." I asked, "What is it?"

He said, "When you're thinking....somebody's talking and you're thinking ......you bite your under lip ......like that. I never want to see you do that in this picture." I burst out laughing, and I said, "Fine! That was my biggest trick, I thought." He said, "That's right. It's a trick and I don't want to see it." But he did it so nicely and so quietly that he forewarned me, and every time I'd start to do it.....I'd say, "I need another take." He'd say, "I know, and I'd know why." He didn't take away any of my sort of aggressiveness as an actor, but he just cut out....and he was right. It had been a mannerism that had gone from one picture into another.

Ed: Do you have that mannerism in real life?

Loretta: I don't know whether I do or not....

Ed: I haven't noticed it.....

Ed: Did you know Jeff Chandler before you made this movie with him?

Loretta: We worked together in radio. We did three or four things for Father Peyton, one was an Easter show......I played Mary Magdalene, and he played Christ. He was very good in that, but he was more of a personality than an actor.

Ed: .....a big guy....

Loretta: ....sensitive too. A charming man.

Ed: Was he married?

Loretta: Oh, yes. He was too attractive not to have been. A good thing for me that he was married.

Ed: That's an interesting comment. Don't you think attractive men can be faithful husbands?

Loretta: I don't think it's easy. It isn't easy for a beautiful woman to be a faithful wife. If she's happily married, yes. Very easy for her to be. But if she's unhappily married and she's attractive, it's *very* difficult. *Very*.

Ed: .....you've always......

Loretta: Well, I was. But believe me, it was no picnic; no indeed. It's just by the skin of your teeth that you don't slip into extramarital relations. I learned very quickly that you don't even hold hands. You don't even smile too long at each other, and you certainly don't kiss each other.....because the next thing you know, ...boom, boom, boom! And that's that.

I had a crush .... deep crush on Jeff Chandler. He never so much as held my hand off camera, but I think until the day he died, we both were......If I'd see him on the street, I'd walk the other way because I didn't want to spark anything.....and he would too.

I said to him, "Jeff, we're just bad news for each other, so wave at me from across the room but don't come near me." During the picture.....during the rehearsal, we'd been rehearsing three or four days, I guess....I started to go to my dressing room, and he asked, "May I walk you out to the bungalow?" I said, "Yes. Delighted." So we were walking out, and he said, "I have to tell you something.....I've been thinking......I've been thinking I'm falling in love with you." I got very flustered. I said, "That's not necessarily bad…" The minute that came out of my mouth he looked at me, and I said, "No, I didn't mean that exactly." He said, "Well, what did you mean?" I didn't know how to put it. I said, "It's all right.….I'm married, and you're married, and nothing could ever come of it anyway; so it's not too terrible, but keep it that way." Anyway, once you admit anything like that.….it's just very difficult, but it makes for very nice love scenes.

Jeff was at our house a couple of times.….at big parties…. and I think I invited him because I didn't want to penalize him in any way. His wife was charming. She worked on my television show after he died.

Ed: .…as an actress?

Loretta: Yes

I don't think she ever knew there was a crush…… but nothing had happened. I think my husband was convinced that something had happened. He didn't say anything, but the way he was acting.….I don't know.….something came out one time. He said something about Jeff Chandler, and I looked at him and said, "Whatever you're thinking, it's not true. Nothing ever happened between Jeff Chandler and me that wasn't written into the script, on the set, in front of the camera with the camera rolling ……"and I don't think he was ever convinced that it didn't.

Ed: .….was that the only actor he ever.…?

Loretta: It was not his habit to....if he was jealous of them, he covered it up well. This is the only one. And maybe he did because I *did* have a special feeling for Jeff Chandler, and maybe Tom was sensitive enough to sense that, because .....he was not an insensitive man. He was just insensitive to what I wanted.

Ed: Here is a review of BECAUSE OF YOU: "Jeff Candler and Loretta Young make a fine romantic team. Sex angle is introduced with unusual prominence and played for all it's worth.."

Loretta: What's "played for it's worth"?

Ed: ...."the sex angle"

Loretta: Oh, well.....(laugh) (laugh) (laugh) (laugh) (laugh) (laugh)

Ed: It also says that, "Miss Young was an expert in the clinches..."

Loretta: It's the only chance you got, that's why.....you get paid for it....then you do it... (laugh) (laugh).

But you know, it's very interesting .....kissing in these days, they dive down each other's throats. There was none of that (laugh) (laugh). It was still the purest of kisses....

Ed: Still, you had to feel the reverberations .....even if it was a pure kiss...(laugh) (laugh)

Loretta: (laugh) (laugh) Reverberations is the word for it! (laugh) (laugh)

Jerry Lewis used to come on that set....he was a friend of Jeff Chandler's. One day he was standing behind the camera making faces at me. I didn't know him too well, so I just blocked it out and just concentrated on Jeff ....or whatever it was. I finished the scene and the director thought it was okay. He said, "Fine. Print it." I thought, "Oh gosh, he's not going to print, because I was just trying not to laugh." The director said, "It's very good."

After he (Jerry Lewis) left the set, then I said, "You better take that close-up again." He said, "By all means, but I didn't want him to think that my star looked like a fool..."

Ed: Didn't you say that you had made your own dress...?

Loretta: Yes

Ed: .....like a housedress? Something you made particularly for this movie?

Loretta: No. I just made it. We needed an extra dress, and I said, "I've got a perfect housedress...."

I tried doing something in that picture, but it didn't really work .....when I went to prison, you saw my hair grow out.....different wigs....and finally I had dark hair, see, but my face didn't change....because I had the same amount of make-up on.....

Ed: BECAUSE OF YOU got some good reviews....

Loretta: BECAUSE OF YOU was a good movie. I think it stayed a couple of weeks at the Roxy Theater in New York. It was a sleeper....they didn't expect the success it met....

PAULA

Loretta: I don't remember much about PAULA except Jean (Jean Louis) and the clothes ......and that I spent a week before shooting at the Veterans Hospital in the motor aphasia ward. That is where people stay who have had strokes, and they know what they want to say but they can't say it. This is what the boy was supposed to have had in the film after I hit him with the car. I watched the nurses work with a Captain from the Navy, I think. I remember they asked him to say, "Put the lap board on the floor." It took him about three minutes but he did it.

Of course, you can't take that much time in a film. But we should have. We should have condensed it into one scene.

Ed: This was on your own initiative that you went to the VA?

Loretta: Whatever you have to do. Yes. You have to do research on whatever you're doing. The director doesn't know what to tell you how to do it. You have to see it. For all practical purposes, I was playing the part of a nurse, and the boy was the Captain. The VA had a whole ward of these motor aphasia.....

Ed: ....the little actor....

Loretta: Charming. Beautiful child. Tommy Rettig.

Ed: Kent Smith ......

Loretta: Nice. Did his part well. Between you and me, very uninspiring actor....

Ed: Rudolph Mate ...... Good director?

Loretta: Ah, very gentle director. You better know what you were doing because he didn't direct you much.......he just kind of suggested here and there. But he really was a superb cameraman. Rudy Mate, Hungarian.....or maybe he was French. There was a French film, PASSION OF JOAN OF ARC, the actress had a shaved head and .... big close-ups. The first time anyone had ever done big close-ups, and Rudy did that.

Ed: Was it a silent?

Loretta: I think so ...

He also photographed LOVE AFFAIR with Irene Dunne and Charles Boyer, and he thought up that scene where...the Empire State Building was reflected in the window pane.....Rudy was very imaginative.

The best scene in PAULA is in the beginning where she has the baby and loses it. Rudy said, "No make-up, just put a little oil on your skin." And he was right. It was absolutely beautiful and real-looking. The bone structure and everything was marvelous.

Ed: Review: "Miss Young's efforts to teach a young boy to talk again after he's mute from injuries suffered in a supposedly hit-and-run accident. Miss Young, the unknown driver in the car and unable to have children, is moved to the task out of guilt and maternal instinct. As to be expected, Miss Young gives the principal role a lot of substance and doesn't let it go overboard….."

1953

IT HAPPENS EVERY THURSDAY

Loretta: It was not a bad picture, but it certainly wasn't a good picture. There was nothing I remember…..It was work. It was my bread and butter money.

It was shot at Universal. I had the Deanna Durbin bungalow, and it was beautiful. It had a living room and a dining room and a dressing room and a patio in the back. It was a regular bungalow. We were living at the beach then, and the commute was an hour and forty-five minutes both ways. I decided that I didn't want to waste those three hours in the car so I just stayed in the bungalow. Tom would stay with me, and on weekends I would go home. And it worked out.

The story…..a little comedy about a couple ….. based on a real couple who ran a newspaper. Nothing important, just a nice little family story. John Forsythe was in it, and the man who produced it (Anton Leader) had produced the radio show "Suspense," so he was a dramatic producer, see.

He'd come down on the set, and he'd say, "Oh, it's not dramatic," and one day I said, "You know, this is not a drama. This is a kind of very light little, charming, family show. And John Forsythe, he was very serious about the whole thing too, and I kept trying to lift it up. Joe Pevney was a wonderful director and agreed, saying, "I think we're taking ourselves too seriously."

One day I was sitting on John Forsythe's lap. I was laughing about something. He said, "You know, I think I'm the only person who doesn't know this picture's a comedy." I said, "That's right. You and the producer."

Finally, we came to one scene.....and I said, "I'm sorry, fellas, I'm sorry." Bill Goetz was running the studio at this time, so I went to his office at noontime and said, "Bill, you make fifty pictures a year so you can afford a few stinkers. I only make two pictures a year. I really can't afford a dud." This picture is a nice little, sweet, family film if anything, not a drama. Tony (producer), he's too serious. This is not a suspense film; there is nothing suspenseful about it. You're going to have to get a comedy writer around here who knows what they're doing......because the direction we're heading now won't work.

Or, you can stop and get somebody else to do the picture because I can't go ahead with it like this because it's going to be a stinker." He said, "Give me some time." I said, "Yeah, I'll go to lunch and then let me know after lunch whether I'm going to go back on the set and struggle with these guys or if you're going to do something about it."

Anyway, he called me in my dressing room and said, "There's a young man (Richard Morris) we've got on the lot. He's quite a good writer. He'll be over in your dressing room in about twenty minutes; we had to call him from home." I said, "You better send the director and the producer over here, too. They can't sit and wait on the set." We were sitting in the bungalow having coffee in the living room, and all of a sudden, this kid in white bucks and a tee shirt comes in.....blonde hair. He looked about twenty-five. I thought, "Oh, boy.....one of these."

I said, "He's not going to know anything; he's too young." He sat down and got out his little pad of paper and we all talked, and he wrote his notes. The director would say something; he'd write that down. I'd say something; he'd write that down. We talked about two hours and he hadn't opened his mouth. I said, "It has to be this, that, or the other." He said, "Yes, let me get off by myself and think about it. I can't bring anything back today." I said, "Well, that's fine." I then asked the producer, "Can we go home, now?" He said, "You might as well."

The next day, I don't know, 7:30 in the morning, I'm in my dressing room, and they come in with some pink sheets, and there were a couple of scenes we were supposed to shoot that day, and they were very good. They were not hilarious but at least they were reasonable and had a light touch, and he had some humor.......

Ed: You mentioned pink pages...

Loretta: that means rewrites...

Ed: ...final?

Loretta: No. If you get blue pages after that, that's the second rewrite. Then if you get yellow pages, it's the third rewrite. I don't know what they do with the fourth rewrite. I suppose they give you a new script. But the original script comes out in white pages.

Anyway, I got a call from Bill Goetz's secretary, "Mr. Goetz wants to know if the re-writes are acceptable to you?" I said, "Yes, they're not perfect prose, but they're good. At least I can do them." She said, "Call him this afternoon when you finish."

They put Dick (Morris) on it, and he just re-wrote all the scenes. So I thanked him afterwards and said, "You're talented; I'm sure you're going to go someplace." The movie went out and didn't do anything but didn't break anybody's heart, and I wasn't embarrassed by it in the least.

Then when I went into television, and we were looking for writers, I said to Ruth Roberts (who had been with Loretta since THE FARMER'S DAUGHTER), "Whatever became of the kid who came and rewrote IT HAPPENS EVERY THURSDAY?" Two days later she came back and said, "Universal let him go, and he's back in New York." I said, "Find his number and call him and ask if he wants to write for television, and if so, we'll pay his way out here."

She came back and said, "He's thrilled to death, and he'll be on the plane tonight." The next morning, he walked into the studio. We burst out laughing. He was just a natural. He knew how to get to the point."

(Summarizing her movie career)

Loretta: I was not fortunate enough in my career to be in really what I think are FINE motion pictures. There was no MRS. MINIVER.....there was no JEZEBEL.... there was no GONE WITH THE WIND. But that wasn't my lot, and it doesn't bother me....

Ed: the durability....all the more impressive...

Loretta: The durability.....I don't know why that is....

Ed: .....are you being coy? Don't you really?

Loretta: No. .....because I know a lot of other leading ladies at the same time I started out.....they worked just as hard and wanted to be movie stars too...

Ed: You know what I'm thinking? .... It might be that you were stronger than a lot of people to just hang in there.....and it could be your faith and the secure family you came from....

Loretta: It could be that I didn't put all my eggs in that basket of work.....and all the ups and downs didn't seem more than I could handle....

Loretta's movie career as star or leading lady lasted twenty-five years from LAUGH, CLOWN, LAUGH through IT HAPPENS EVERY THURSDAY. Her biggest triumph still lay ahead with the one-hundred-forty-nine television episodes of THE LORETTA YOUNG SHOW (1953 – 1961). It was an anthology series, a format that had been popular in radio, which allowed Loretta a wide spectrum of characters to play. One week could be drama, the following, light comedy, and suspense the next. What held it together was Loretta's iconic entrance at the beginning of each episode, beautifully gowned and bejeweled, introducing that night's show.

It proved most satisfying to her as an artist; she finally had the kind of roles that eluded her, by and large, in films. This wasn't an accident. She was in a position to make it happen and she did. Her belief that if you get the right roles, money will follow, proved true. Her shows continued in syndication, nationally and internationally, for more than a decade after the last episode wrapped. Her fame grew exponentially.

Loretta walked away from her career at age fifty-two. With the exception of two made for television movies in the '80s, she lived a life out of the lime light for the next thirty-five years. Loretta treasured those years as a time of personal growth, but she also continued to manage the Loretta Young brand carefully. She made few public appearances. When she did, they mattered.

I remember discussing an elderly Mary Pickford television appearance. It had taken place at her home, Pickfair, and aired in 1976, at which time she was presented an Honorary Oscar. Loretta's reaction, "Why did they let her do that? Somebody said part of genius is knowing when to quit. It was shocking. She didn't make any sense. Oh, it was just awful…..it just shocked people. I've never forgotten. I pray, '*Please God*, don't ever let that happen to me. *Ever*! Hit me on the head with a hammer, but don't let me do that.'"

God was kind.

Acknowledgement:

First and foremost, I want to thank Loretta Young for her willingness to discuss ninety-one of her ninety-eight films which opened a broad context of discussion. I would also like to thank Larry Wilson who, in transcribing over 100 tapes, captured such nuances as Loretta's raised voice for emphasis, her pauses when searching for the right word, and her throaty laughter, often expressed. I also wish to thank Jill Wright, Edward Russo, Theresa Schoen, and Malcolm Woodhouse, and Carolyn Benner who edited this book at various stages of its development.

LORETTA'S MOVIES BY YEAR

1917
THE PRIMROSE RING
SIRENS OF THE SEA

1919
THE ONLY WAY

1921
THE SHEIK

1927
NAUGHTY BUT NICE
HER WILD OAT
ROSE OF THE GOLDEN WEST (aka ROSE OF MONTEREY

1928
LAUGH, CLOWN, LAUGH
THE MAGNIFICIENT FLIRT
SCARLETT SEAS

1929
THE SQUALL
THE GIRL IN THE GLASS CAGE
FAST LIFE
FORWARD PASS
THE SHOW OF SHOWS

1930
THE TRUTH ABOUT YOUTH
LOOSE ANKLES
THE MAN FROM BLANKLEYS
SECOND FLOOR MYSTERY
ROAD TO PARADISE
KISMET
DEVIL TO PAY

1931
BEAU IDEAL

THE RIGHT OF WAY
THREE GIRLS LOST
TOO YOUNG TO MARRY
BIG BUSINESS GIRL
THE RULING VOICE
PLATINUM BLONDE

1932

TAXI
THE HATCHET MAN
PLAYGIRL
WEEKEND MARRIGE
LIFE BEGINS
THEY CALL IT SIN

1933

EMPLOYEE'S ENTRANCE
GRAND SLAM
ZOO IN BUDAPEST
THE LIFE OF JIMMY DOLAN
HEROES FOR SALE
MIDNIGHT MARY
SHE HAD TO SAY YES
THE DEVIL'S IN LOVE
MAN'S CASTLE

1934

HOUSE OF ROTHCHILD
BORN TO BE BAD
CARAVAN
THE WHITE PARADE

1935

CLIVE OF INDIA
SHANGHAI
CALL OF THE WILD
THE CRUSADES

1936

THE UNGUARDED HOUR
PRIVATE NUMBER

RAMONA
LADIES IN LOVE

1937

LOVE IS NEWS
CAFÉ METROPOLE
LOVE UNDER FIRE
WIFE, DOCTOR, NURSE
SECOND HONEYMOON

1938

FOUR MEN AND A PRAYER
THREE BLIND MICE
SUEZ
KENTUCKY

1939

WIFE, HUSBAND, FRIEND
THE STORY OF ALEXANDER GRAHAM BELL
ETERNALLY YOURS

1940

THE DOCTOR TAKES A WIFE
HE STAYED FOR BREAKFAST

1941

THE LADY FROM CHEYENNE
MEN IN HER LIFE

1942

BEDTIME STORY

1943

A NIGHT TO REMEMBER
CHINA

1944

LADIES COURAGEOUS
AND NOW TOMORROW

1945

ALONG CAME JONES

1946

THE STRANGER

1947
THE PERFECT MARRIAGE
THE FARMER'S DAUGHTER
THE BISHOP'S WIFE

1948
RACHEL AND THE STANGER

1949
THE ACCUSED
MOTHER IS A FRESHMAN
COME TO THE STABLE

1950
KEY TO THE CITY

1951
CAUSE FOR ALARM
HALF ANGEL

1952
BECAUSE OF YOU
PAULA

1953
IT HAPPENS EVERY THURSDAY

About the Author

Edward J. Funk had been a ghost writer for business moguls who wanted to write their life stories to help promote their enterprises. The opportunity to work with Miss Young was quite different. It escorted him inside the golden age of film and the early days of television, both eras that had long held his fascination. His relationship with Miss Young has produced a trilogy of books about her; this is the third. Mr. Funk now lives in Indianapolis, Indiana.

Photo by Paul Robinson

Cover photo: permission to use from the Loretta Young estate

Cover design by The National Group

CPSIA information can be obtained
at www.ICGtesting.com
Printed in the USA
LVOW12s0116230316

480337LV00003B/221/P